PENGUI

MAKING A DIFFERENCE

Alok Ranjan got his BA (Hons) degree in Economics from St. Stephen's College, Delhi and MBA from Indian Institute of Management, Ahmedabad (IIM-A). He subsequently joined the IAS in 1978 after securing the fourth rank in the country. He was allotted to the Uttar Pradesh cadre and served with distinction in various assignments in the State Government as well as Government of India before superannuating as Chief Secretary to the Government of UP in 2016. Throughout his career, he served with dedication and integrity.

He has previously published two books: *The Collector Today* and *Towards Adult Literacy in India*. He writes a fortnightly column for the *Millennium Post* and regularly contributes articles on issues of public policy and governance to *The Economic Times*, *Business Standard* and *Hindustan Times*. He is an acclaimed public speaker and thought leader. The Lucknow Management Association recently presented him with the 'lifetime achievement award' for his contribution to public service.

PRAISE

'This former UP Chief Secretary's book provides an insider's unique perspective on the IAS, its vital role in public administration and development, and how he personally made a difference. A truly enlightening read'

—Parameswaran Iyer, IAS retired, Ex-Secretary,
Drinking Water and Sanitation, Government of India

'The IAS can still make a difference. There couldn't have been a better person to write on the subject because Alok Ranjan made a big difference in his career, rising to become the Chief Secretary in UP. Brilliantly articulated'

—Anil Swarup, IAS retired; Ex-Secretary, Education,
Government of India

MAKING A
DIFFERENCE

THE IAS AS
A CAREER

ALOK RANJAN

PENGUIN BOOKS

An imprint of Penguin Random House

PENGUIN BOOKS

USA | Canada | UK | Ireland | Australia
New Zealand | India | South Africa | China

Penguin Books is part of the Penguin Random House group of companies
whose addresses can be found at global.penguinrandomhouse.com

Published by Penguin Random House India Pvt. Ltd
4th Floor, Capital Tower 1, MG Road,
Gurugram 122 002, Haryana, India

Penguin
Random House
India

First published in Penguin Books by Penguin Random House India 2021

Copyright © Alok Ranjan 2021

10 9 8 7 6 5 4 3 2 1

ISBN 9780143454700

Typeset in Adobe Garamond Pro by Manipal Technologies Limited, Manipal
Printed at Thomson Press India Ltd, New Delhi

www.penguin.co.in

This book is for all those members of the Indian Administrative Service who have worked with dedication and integrity to make a difference to society.

Contents

Contents

Preface

My dear friend and colleague of many years, Alok Ranjan, decided to pen his thoughts and his ideas delineating the role of the Indian Administrative Service, which came into existence post Independence, as a successor service to the British Indian Civil Service. The result is this book that he has aptly titled *Making a Difference: The IAS as a Career*.

The title itself gives an indication of his motivation behind writing this book. He wants the members of the service to dedicate themselves to 'making a difference' to the lives of the people whom they are serving. This was unlike the aim the British had creating the Indian Civil Service (ICS). The officers of the ICS were mandated primarily to maintain law and order, and to ensure continuation of the British rule. The Indian Administrative Service, on the other hand, was created not only to maintain law and order but also to promote development, and ensure welfare of all sections of society in a democratic environment. And this is what the author of the book emphasizes. The IAS officers should not behave like rulers but act in the spirit of being of service to the citizens.

Alok has given examples from his own career, of how development schemes were framed in consultation with the stakeholders, and not arbitrarily imposed from the top. He would go to the villages himself, discuss the problems faced by them and then come up with solutions. This is what we call participatory administration.

Alok, while reviewing the present environment in which the Civil Servants are working, has brought out how decision-making has been stymied because of the four C's, namely the Comptroller and Auditor General (CAG), the Central Bureau of Investigation (CBI), the Courts, and the Central Vigilance Commission (CVC). People are afraid to make decisions and prefer to be rule bound rather than take initiative even in emergencies like natural calamities, floods, earthquakes, etc. The civil servant would prefer to write notes on files, not based on what he thinks is right, but anticipating what the boss wants.

Alok has narrated his experiences both as a field officer, as well as working with the State Government and the Central Government. As a District Magistrate (DM), he is the eyes and ears of the government. All the various departments of the government working in the field look to the DM for help, whenever there is a problem. The police also work in close coordination with the DM. The DM is a protective shield for all the field agencies. But his leadership depends on the initiatives he takes in effective implementation of government policies and ensuring coordination amongst them. In the days of the British rule, the post of the District Magistrate was supposed to be the most powerful position in the entire Empire.

But as Alok rightly points out, the IAS of today should not try to compare itself with the ICS. The world at that time was different from what it is today.

The IAS, however, remains the most coveted post for the young people of today. In the initial years after Independence, the glamour of the erstwhile ICS attracted youngsters to join the service. After finishing university, as graduates or postgraduates, they would try their luck not once, not twice but three times to get into the IAS or the other Central Services. As the upper age limit for taking the IAS exams was increased, the applicants would try their luck repeatedly till the upper age limit was crossed. The author has rightly pointed out that increasing the age limit is neither good for the applicants nor for the government. With upper age limits, the years of service are reduced and it becomes difficult to mould the officers.

Working with politicians is not easy. They expect you to implement the orders they issue, irrespective of whether it is within the law or the relevant rules. However, as the author correctly points out, it is the duty of the Secretary to point this out to the minister and persuade him to withdraw such wrong orders. As Alok states, more often than not, the minister or the Chief Minister, as the case may be, if properly persuaded, will withdraw those orders.

The author has worked as Secretary to three Chief Ministers of UP. The fact that he was not labelled as any party's man speaks volumes about how he worked impartially and within the rules. Every minister or Chief Minister prefers those officers who can give him the right advice. They realize that if the department functions well, it is they who get a good reputation.

The author has highlighted three cases in which, because of his initiative, the projects were executed within the timeframe and without cost overruns. The most talked about is the Agra–Lucknow expressway, where due to his constant monitoring and advice, land acquisition for the entire stretch was completed in record time without any major legal hassles. This was because of a mutually workable partnership between him as Chief Secretary and Sri Akhilesh Yadav as Chief Minister. Similarly, the project of Dial-100 took off most effectively.

Alok Ranjan's career shows that an IAS officer can succeed if he works with complete dedication, empathy and a desire to do good for the people at large.

YOGENDRA NARAIN
Retired IAS
Ex-Chief Secretary, UP
Ex-Defence Secretary, Government of India

Foreword

I have written this book five years after my retirement from the Indian Administrative Service (IAS) after serving for thirty-eight years and having enjoyed every moment of it, despite the occupational hazards, moments of frustration and the times things did not go according to plan. In balance, it is the memory of achievements, public service, making a difference, touching lives and acting as a change agent to transform society, that gives one the feeling of having had a worthwhile career and inner contentment. I feel this service gives you the opportunity to genuinely work for the common man and make life better for society. But I am worried that the service is at a crossroads and facing a lot of criticism and challenges for which, to a large degree, they themselves are responsible. Somewhere down the line, the IAS officer has got caught in the trappings of power and lost sight of his real goal of public service. This book aims to bring out the diversity, the opportunities and the challenges of a career in the IAS and also a roadmap of how an IAS officer can make a significant contribution to the Indian citizens. The IAS has to look within and reinvent itself, if it has to survive. It has to respond to the changing needs of the modern society and the challenges of the twenty-first century. The IAS has the calibre to do so and it has to keep its focus on professionalism, competence, creativity and integrity.

I am thankful to Mr Yogendra Narayan, under whom I worked when he was Chief Secretary, UP and then went on to become the Defence Secretary, for writing these kind words in the preface about me, this book, and about the IAS. He was one of the most remarkable officers I have served under and from him, I have learnt the art of keeping a smile on my face in any situation.

I also thank my seniors and colleagues for their good wishes and the inspiration that they have given me to write this book.

No words are sufficient to express my gratitude for the support, motivation and inspiration that I got from my wife Surabhi, and children, Shivam and Shikhar, to write this book and share my thoughts with the world around. They were always a part of my journey in the IAS and shared in my joys as well as my sorrows.

This book can be a great guide to the millions of young boys and girls who are aspiring to join the IAS because it will tell them about the right motivation to join the service with, and the way to prepare for the examination to ensure success. It will also motivate them to aspire for a career in the IAS. The book is also intended for serving IAS officers with whom I want to share my experiences as well as the leadership principles that a career in the IAS have given me. This book is not an autobiography but contains incidents from my career which were of great learning value.

My special thanks are due to Mr Rudra Srivastava and Mr Salil Kumar for having taken the pains of typing out my manuscript. I would also like to thank the Director of Jaipuria Institute of Management for giving me the facilities to write this book.

I would like to thank all the people with whom I have interacted during my service as they have given me an immense sense of satisfaction, which I have tried to bring out in this book.

Alok Ranjan
IAS Retired
Ex-Chief Secretary, UP

1

Challenges and Opportunities of the IAS as a Career

There are few careers which offer both the diversity of job content as well as the potential to make a difference to society like a career in the Indian Administrative Service (IAS). The cream of the country makes an effort to qualify for the IAS but very few succeed; from more than approximately 3 lakh candidates writing the exam, only about a hundred are selected in the IAS and about 700–800 are selected for all of the Civil Services taken together. From these statistics itself, you can understand the probability of getting selected in the IAS. It is such a fool-proof system that even today, nobody can raise a finger at the selection process conducted by the Union Public Service Commission (UPSC). The brightest and best, who prepare the hardest, are the ones who succeed in the examination. Just being selected changes the life of a person. It is not only a wish fulfilled or a dream realized for the candidate, but for their entire family. The status of the family takes a quantum leap and the selected person becomes a mini-celebrity. They become an object of envy amongst their peers and get instant recognition and admiration from all sections of society. Life is never the same after qualifying for the IAS. More than thirty years of unparalleled power, status and prestige flow for a successful candidate and they soon realize that they are VIPs.

I look back and can recall the day the results were declared and I had qualified. My joy knew no bounds; my normally reserved and serious father had embraced me with a look of extreme satisfaction and bliss on his face. This was the only time in my life that I had seen him so expressive. In a flash, it seemed as if the dreams of our entire family had been fulfilled. I remember trying to pen down my thoughts on this momentous occasion. Those months of hard work, the endless toil, those moments of frustration, elation and anticipation floated across in my memory. Yet, at that very moment, another thought started to take shape: what next? Is this career merely a means to status and power or something more? I felt then a deep urge to make a significant contribution to society, to 'make a difference'. I realize now, after over forty years, that a career in the IAS is worthwhile only if a person utilizes it to make a difference to society and the country. It has to be a career of transformational leadership and effective governance.

The IAS opens up a path to a lot of power, influence and immense opportunity. Yet, it is also the portal to numerous challenges. When we left the Lal Bahadur Shastri National Academy of Administration in Mussoorie, we were full of idealism, bursting with the desire and confidence to change the shape of the country. Now that I have retired, I look around and see that most problems of governance still exist, waiting to be resolved. I do not think that my career has not been a success. In fact, there are a lot of achievements which I can be justifiably proud of, where, through my actions, I was able to make a difference. Yet, the country is so vast and the problems so huge that one officer or an entire service cannot hope to resolve all the issues with the wave of a magic wand. At the time of entering the service, one feels as if they can do anything they want. Now looking back, I realize that this is far from the truth. The power of the IAS is not absolute and it has to work with the political executive who has the supreme authority in a democracy. The mindset and attitude of an IAS officer and a politician are very different; they come from different backgrounds and have different approaches to life. Then, the IAS officer never really gets the team they want and we all know that no leader can succeed with a team which is not the best.

Moreover, an IAS officer is not at liberty to change his team as he might often desire, as the political executive has full control on the transfers and postings of officers. An IAS officer has to work within the confines of a government system where rules and procedures take precedence over results and outcomes. Any non-compliance can land an IAS officer behind bars. At the same time, there are no special rewards for delivering results. A successful career is one in which an officer can go through their entire service without facing an inquiry or being subjected to allegations or controversies. Needless to say, some IAS officers adopt a 'Safety First' attitude which in simple terms means that you do nothing—take no decisions, not start anything new and sign as few papers as possible. Many people I meet in the outside world, hold the view that an IAS officer is all-powerful and that there are no constraints to his working. They feel that even ministers do what IAS officers want. This is not true and in fact, is far from reality. Many people tell me that if rules and procedures are obstructing action, then as IAS officers, we should be able to change them. This is possible but any change involves a number of processes and any officer doing so is at the risk of charges if some wrong decisions get made because of this change. I would like to give a simple example. Right at the beginning of my career, I was posted as a General Manager of an Industrial Manufacturing Unit and realized that we were getting substandard spare parts, simply because of the financial rule that an order should be placed for the lowest price offered. I used to call this 'the tyranny of the lowest' as this often meant that poor quality material was purchased and this in turn hampered the entire production process. I still recall the battles I fought to change the system to try and order on the basis of quality, but that was a herculean task as the finance department of the corporation simply refused to allow any such change. I admit that I overruled them and started my own system of technical evaluation on the basis of quality and only those who qualified, could have their financial bids considered. This greatly improved the performance of the plant but my Chief Finance Officer was always vocal about telling me that if there were to be an inquiry, I would have to face the music. It is by the grace of God that I didn't. Today, this system of technical bid and financial bid has been introduced in the government but this change required years of effort on the part of several officers and committees. Thus, my point is that it is not always easy to change government procedures which have been formulated to ensure fairness and accountability, even though they may not be serving a purpose. Besides, you may not be having the power to do so.

Yet, the IAS officer cannot be an 'I am sorry' officer. He has to deliver, whatever the odds might be and this calls for exceptional leadership qualities. He should be accountable to himself and also be conscious of the fact that efficient and effective public service delivery is what the citizen wants. It is the duty of the IAS officer to make this possible. The IAS as a service should look around to see the poverty, poor healthcare, low quality of education, poor nutrition and the poor quality of basic services in the country. The IAS is responsible if citizens are dissatisfied. Those desirous of joining the service must have dreams of creating a better society which is well-governed and where the needs and the expectations of every ordinary citizen are fulfilled. This should be the lifelong endeavour of an IAS officer.

Yes, the service should constantly introspect, and more so at the current moment, when despite seventy-odd years after independence, we are still a developing country with per capita income, human development and hunger indicators far below most countries. There has been a governance failure, somewhere. The IAS, being part of the system of governance, cannot escape responsibility. It is a service where you start as top management and it is your leadership that sets the tone for most organizations. Therefore, each IAS officer, past and present, must introspect and question oneself ruthlessly.

They have to improve governance so that outcomes are met and the country develops at a rapid pace.

The service needs to rediscover and re-invent itself, otherwise there will be visible dark shadows in the horizon soon engulfing it. Today, the IAS has few friends. A politician is not so comfortable with the IAS. They inhabit different universes and are often suspicious of each other. I have seen in Uttar Pradesh (UP) that most politicians prefer a promoted civil service officer rather than an IAS officer as District Magistrate and that they are more comfortable with departmental officers. The politicians constantly lament that the IAS officer is too rigid and creates obstacles in the path of governance. This is so despite the tendency of several IAS officers to bend over backwards before the political executive in order to get favoured assignments. But there are still numerous IAS officers who put forward their views without fear and insist upon rules and systems being followed, which is often not liked by politicians. The other services also resent the big brotherly attitude of the IAS and complain about the dominance of the latter. I have also experienced the media sometimes passing unjust and caustic comments against the IAS. Further, the ordinary citizens, though respectful of the IAS, can possibly also be jealous of the officers. And the arrogance and aloofness of an IAS officer only adds fuel to that fire.

In the scenario outlined above, an IAS officer has to constantly prove himself with his performance and ability. The service will survive only if its members can distinguish themselves by the work they do and outcomes they deliver. If the IAS lets things remain as they are and not exhibit the requisite qualities of leadership, then there is no raison d'être for its existence. The service has to survive on the strength of its ability to deliver results. Their work, conduct and output should be such that citizens feels their need. Individual IAS officers have been able to achieve this and many have been hailed as heroes and saviours but it is the entire service that should give such positive results to society. It is the responsibility of the IAS itself to weed out the black sheep from amongst themselves and hail the performers. The service needs to come together and deliver, otherwise it does not have a great future. Already, lateral entry into the government has started and this is just the beginning. But if the IAS does not watch out, then this will soon become the norm rather than an exception. The service is at the existential threshold of its life cycle and how it responds will determine whether it sinks or swims.

I often hear people talk about the Indian Civil Service (ICS) and compare the IAS unfavourably with it. It is important to understand in this context that the nature of the job, responsibility, working environment and expectations of the people from the IAS differed hugely from that of the ICS in the colonial days. It is, undoubtedly, the successor service to the ICS but it is not the same and cannot be the same. For those who are unstinted in their praise for the ICS, it is a sobering thought to be told that this hallowed service was considered neither Indian nor Civil nor a service by the great leaders of the nationalist movement. Yet it would be interesting to trace the journey of the ICS, its origins and contribution, and then try to understand how it evolved into the IAS. It would be relevant to examine how the IAS itself is evolving and undergoing change in its character, nature, diversity and reputation.

In the eighteenth century, the East India Company gradually spread its tentacles through most of India and from a professed trading company, it became an agency of governance on behalf of Britain. Naturally, administering such a huge country needed the Army and the Civil Service. Teenaged men were recruited into the East India Company Civil Service and they spent their time in India collecting revenue for the company and maintaining law and order. In 1800, Governor-General Lord Wellesley decided that teenaged recruits would have to undergo special training in India. For this, he decided to set up the college of Fort William in Calcutta, but this proposal had not been approved by the company's Directors in London. The Directors did however establish a college in Hertford Castle in England in 1806 and then moved to Haileybury three years later. The selection of candidates to Haileybury was by a process of nomination by the Directors. They had to be seventeen years old and come from distinguished families. There was no question of selection based on merit; family pedigree was considered the most important attribute. People joined the civil service for adventure and with a spirit of altruism. The salaries and the pensions offered were very attractive. After nomination and before joining Haileybury, the candidates had to take some kind of a written and oral exam where they were tested in history and mathematics as well as language. The foundational course at Haileybury was for two years and the candidate studied mathematics, philosophy, literature, law, history, general economics as well as Indian languages. Sanskrit, Persian and Arabic were also taught. It is a different matter that these languages were not of much use when the civil servant landed in India. They had to administer in the vernacular languages and learn them as soon as they were posted to the field. The educational atmosphere at Haileybury was not very demanding and most candidates focused on just clearing the exams. There were lectures for about two hours everyday and a lot of free time was available to socialize and indulge themselves in drink. There was, however, the minority who studied hard and were known as 'Steadies', much like the 'Keen Type Probationers (KTP)' of our time who took the training at the Mussoorie academy very seriously. Though discipline was lax at Haileybury, a feeling of esprit de corps was very visible and close friendships were formed which lasted for a long time. Haileybury continued till 1857 when the British Government took over the governance of India from the East India Company, and introduced a system of selection into the ICS on merit, through a competitive examination.

The British Government made this change as they felt that selection by patronage would no longer meet the needs of governance and that meritorious candidates were required. Initially, the ICS drew a majority of its entrants from the Universities of Oxford and Cambridge but this soon changed. The Macaulay Committee laid out the guidelines of the selection which prescribed the maximum age limit initially as twenty-three but subsequently brought it down to twenty-one. The committee designed an exam that demanded strong factual memory and a concentrated study of academic texts. The graduates had to study beyond their university syllabi to prepare for the exam and much like today, establishments like Crammer came up to prepare candidates for the exam.

There was a lot of criticism of this 'Crammer' system and many felt that unsuitable candidates were being selected just by preparing some questions that happened to appear in the examination paper. Still, many were of the view that the selection system provided better candidates than the earlier system that was based on patronage. This was followed by the Lord Salisbury Reforms which decided that candidates would take the exam at the school leaving age (seventeen to nineteen years) and then they would be on probation, studying in a university for two years. This system lasted from 1879–1892 but some leaders were of the opinion that candidates were being selected at too raw an age and they did not take their probation period in the university seriously. Another criticism was that it deterred Indian candidates from taking the exam. Since the 1830s, Indians had joined the Government of India (GOI) in the capacity of Deputy Collectors, Deputy Magistrates and bore the burden of governance supervised by a handful of British ICS men. Lord Cornwallis in the eighteenth century had excluded Indians from high positions in the government. The 1853 Act opened up the service to all natural-born subjects of the crown. However, it was near impossible for Indians to compete as it was expensive and there were religious considerations which did not allow Indians to go to London to attempt the exam. Satyendra Nath Tagore was the first Indian to have been selected. In 1869, four Indians qualified, including Surendra Nath Banerjee and Romesh Chandra Dutt. The Indian National Congress in 1885 appealed for a simultaneous exam at a centre in India. In 1886, the government appointed a Public Service Commission which raised the age limit for the ICS to twenty-three years, enabling more Indians to write the exam. Even then, till 1910, only 6 percent of the ICS were Indians.

As a result of competition, the social diversity of the candidates increased. Most people joined this service in a spirit of adventure, the idea of service and an imperial mission. They dreamt of riding in the countryside and dispensing justice under the banyan tree. Candidates from relatively less privileged backgrounds but academically good began to get selected. The selection process was also based on the premise that the formation of character was as important as the cultivation of mind for the administration of the empire.

The number of recruits each year was decided by the Government of India. Successful candidates were given the choice of province according to their rank in the open competition. North-western province and Punjab were favoured destinations, while Madras and Bombay were not as popular. The candidates selected through the exam were labelled as 'competition wallahs' and never respected by their seniors nominated based on pedigree. They were regarded as bookworms without any knowledge of the world and that these new recruits could probably deal with paper but not people. The Haileybury men often looked down on the new recruits assuming them to be of low birth, with vulgar minds and lacking manners. Doubts were expressed whether an examination focused on academics was the right way to select a candidate for the rough and tumble job of District Officer. However, the system continued as it was felt that by and large, these candidates were men of ability.

On joining the service in India, the officers were posted
to a district which was chosen on the basis of the personality
of the Collector. Their training was not scientific and they
had to learn everything on the job with some guidance from
the Collector. The young officer was expected to pay social
calls and leave his card with a helper. Warrant of precedence
was given the greatest importance. The young officer studied
for his departmental exams and did whatever job was assigned
to him by the District Collector, often accompanying him
on winter tours. They then became District Officers and
Collectors themselves and were vested with huge power and
responsibility. Their main task was the collection of revenue
and maintenance of public order and most of them took their
job very seriously. Natural calamities and famines brought
out the best in the ICS officers. The judiciary also had ICS
officers as Judges. An ICS officer did not start his career
as a Judge but after ten years or more, some of them were
pushed into the role or they opted for it. The ICS officers
who, though bright but not having the aptitude required of a
District Officer, became District Judges.

The structure of administration had the District Officer
reporting to the commissioner who in turn reported to the Chief
Secretary. The Secretariat did not have too many secretaries,
unlike today. Above the Chief Secretary was the Board of
Revenue, headed by the Chairman Board of Revenue, and then
finally, the Governor. The structure itself shows that the ICS
officer was largely concerned with the collection of revenue
and this is the reason for the status accorded to the Board of
Revenue. This board still exists in UP and many other states but
today, it is an ornamental body as land revenue is a negligible

percentage of total revenue collected by the government. Yet, traditions exist as the Chairman Board is still a highly respected officer who evaluates the performance of District Collectors and it is the revenue board that sanctions vehicles and other contingency expenditure for the district. It can be termed as the parent department of the District Collector. Generally, the Chairman Board is the senior-most officer of the IAS cadre, by virtue of which he is appointed as the inquiry officer in most matters involving senior IAS officers.

The Chairman Board of Revenue carries out regular inspections of the districts and these visits are always an event. More often than not, many of these 'Board Sahabs', as they continue to be called, are idiosyncratic in their behaviour and the art of handling their inspections is all about managing the quirks in their personalities. There was a Chairman Board in UP who loved his tennis and the Collector had to make sure that a good game of tennis was arranged for him, which implied that the player selected to play against him should give him a good game but ensure that he eventually lost! That game of tennis decided the tone and tenor of the inspection. Of course, their food habits had to be kept in mind as some chairmen liked all kinds of fruits and nuts for breakfast while others preferred eggs and toast. Cleanliness was often a major part of these inspections and weeks would be spent polishing and scrubbing walls and floors of the office of the Collector. Every Collector in UP would have his Chairman Board inspection story, as the Chairman was always an interesting person. Some questions have been raised about the relevance of such an institution today but then where would the government park senior officers who do not become Chief Secretary!

Though there was a great halo around ICS officers, not all of them were efficient or just. There were the deviants who drank too much or were just incompetent or abnormal. But the larger majority was dedicated to their job and had a strong sense of pride in what they were doing. Much like today, the Secretariat was generally resented by the District Officer who felt that they were doing the real work and not getting enough support from the Secretariat. The District Officer felt that officers in the Secretariat were out of touch with real India in a similar manner as a District Officer of today is often heard lamenting the attitude of officers from the state headquarters. In the days of the British, the Secretariat officer would move to the hills during summer months while the District Officers braved the heat. Such luxury is no longer available. However, it is true that officers of the Secretariat interfere far too much in the affairs of the districts sometimes. Too many reports and statements are asked for but strangely, the same was true in the ICS days. Then also District Officers complained that unnecessary paperwork kept them bound to their desks. As paperwork expanded, District Officers were unable to spend as much time with those they governed as they should have.

Junior promotions in the ICS were based on seniority and most rose to the positions of Collector or District Judge. However, incompetent officers would often be left to stagnate in remote districts. The next step of promotion to the post of Commissioner or Chief Secretary was based on merit. Even today, promotions are on the basis of seniority, subject to elimination of the unfit. However, since the performance is evaluated on the basis of performance appraisals which are generally not taken seriously by the evaluating officers, most officers manage to get promoted irrespective of their performance. However, the general reputation of an officer is well-known and he gets postings accordingly. There are a lot of changes like the 360 degree evaluation that has been introduced by the Government of India now to make the performance evaluation system more effective.

The salaries of the ICS were good, higher than in any other Indian service and also higher than what the Civil Service in Britain received. They ranged from Rs 4800 in a year for an Assistant Magistrate to Rs 1,00,000 for a Lieutenant Governor. Majority of the ICS officers would be earning about Rs 30,000 at the time of their retirement. And pension was an added advantage. Today, the Chief Secretary of a state or Secretary to the Government of India or equivalent retires earning about Rs 2.5 lakh per month and this clearly shows that the IAS officers cannot be considered well-paid if you compare them to those in the corporate sector. Top management in the private sector make salaries several times that of an IAS officer and this could be the reason a majority of the children of IAS officers do not join the Civil Service and opt for corporate careers. In Singapore, the bureaucracy is paid high salaries and Lee Kuan Kew, the leader of transformation in Singapore, is supposed to have said, 'If you give them peanuts you will get monkeys'. Low salaries do deter some of the best minds from opting for a career in the Civil Service but the service in India still carries a lot of attraction. The perks and the status make up for the low salaries to some extent;

however, over the years, there has been a considerable reduction in the perks available to IAS officers. In the Indian government, except for Secretaries, most IAS officers live in ordinary flats and the same situation is emerging in the state capitals. Domestic help is no longer available. A vehicle is made available but more often than not, there are limits to the amount of fuel you can use. Many departments have a system of sharing vehicles. Most IAS officers travel economy and stay in government guesthouses when on tour and are at the mercy of a lone chowkidar to provide you tea in unwashed cups and food that is just about palatable. When I joined the Government of India, I found that the biggest talking point was whether one had a toilet attached to their room. Generally only the Secretaries have this luxury! The common perception is that a person opts for a career in the Civil Services or private sector on the basis of money or power. Unfortunately the power of an IAS officer has depleted to some extent.

Many ICS officers did a lot of reading and observed a lot around them to write books. Kipling was a favourite and most District Officers had in their possession works of Kipling, for they found him echoing their lives. Some officers took up other hobbies too; some became botanists, ornithologists or experts on other subjects. There were many ICS officers who wrote poems, novels and books on various subjects and contributed articles to newspapers and periodicals. They generally wrote about the people they administered but some had more literary tastes and translated books from Sanskrit or Persian. Then there were the district gazetteers which were a profile of the land and the people, and written by

ICS officers. The ICS also produced a number of outstanding anthropologists, some of whom became University Dons on retirement. Despite many academically inclined officers in the IAS, this tradition of scholarship and writing is no longer there and most officers who do write, end up with autobiographies. During service, the schedule is so demanding that an officer hardly has any time for his family or for himself, leave alone attempting to write a book. I found that even reading habits take a beating and there are only a few voracious readers in the IAS.

Shikar, or hunting, was the most popular recreation of the ICS in British India. Indiscriminate shooting was also done sometimes but the general norm was to shoot for the pot. Indian jungles had abundant game for such a means to pass time. Pig sticking or hunting with greyhounds or dogs was a popular sport. Now, shikar is banned and some officers have taken up wildlife photography as a hobby but the call of the jungle is not as persistent or as glamorous as it once was.

The IAS as a successor to the ICS works in a different environment and its role has undergone a radical transformation. Even the District Officer today, though still known as Collector, has revenue collection at the bottom of his priorities. His entire focus is on development. The service is now geared towards this and several departments have been created for this purpose in the union government and in the states. So rapidly have these departments proliferated that they now work in silos and some of them are quite irrelevant. Frequent exercises are being undertaken to reduce the number of departments. Notwithstanding this, the job of an IAS officer today is in the sphere of bringing about economic and social development and the delivery of public services to the citizens.

At the time of Independence, the ICS faced a monumental crisis of existence because the service had served its colonial masters with dedication and efficiency, and were their main instruments for administering India. Naturally, many officers must have incurred the displeasure of the great leaders of the nationalist movement, for in the name of maintaining law and order, the ICS officers would have been at the forefront of arresting nationalist leaders and using firm methods against Indian citizens. There was a feeling of resentment against these officers as they were seen as oppressors. There was a loud cry for the abolition of the ICS and even Jawaharlal Nehru shared this view. The service found a saviour in Home Minister Sardar Vallabhbhai Patel, who spoke up in their favour, complimented them for their efficiency and administrative skills, and was clear in his opinion that India needed a Civil Service. No doubt Patel is regarded as the patron saint of the Civil Service and his birthday – 21 April – is celebrated as the Civil Services Day in the country. Had the ICS ceased to exist, its progeny, the IAS, would not have been born. Many state leaders preferred the State Civil Service to the all-India service.

In a speech on 15 October 1949, Patel said, 'You can realize what a year-old government has to do to maintain peace and bring about prosperity. The steel frame on which India relied so far is now broken – 50 per cent of which was foreign, went across the seas. Partition further weakened it – we have only a small number of Civil Servants left – outsiders cannot appreciate their work. Many of them are loyal workers and patriots and are working with us night and day. All we have been able to achieve, whether it be in the sphere of states or in Kashmir or in any other theatre, have been possible only because of their loyalty and whole-hearted support.' In those turbulent times, Patel found the officers of the Civil Service to be an asset. They were always doing their job and Patel had the vision to realize that they would serve the Government of independent India in the same manner as they served the British regime. How different is his view from that of current governments! As soon as a different political party comes to power, it removes officers supposedly 'close' to the earlier Government. They must realize that the IAS officer is trained to carry out policies and programmes of whichever government is in power.

Civil Servants should feel proud that at the time of Independence, while addressing the constituent assembly on 10 October 1949, Patel had these words to say about the ICS: 'I wish this to be recorded in this house that during the last two to three years, if most of the members of the service had not been serving the country efficiently, practically, the union would have collapsed'. However, to remove the psychological barrier that people may have against the ICS, he introduced the new service of IAS. It was also decided that it would be an all-India service under central control, and that IAS and IFS officers would be recruited through a common exam.

Sardar Patel laid down the proposed character of the IAS while addressing the first batch of officers in 1947 when he said, 'You are the pioneers in the Indian service and the future of the service will depend much upon the foundation and tradition that will be laid down by you, by character and abilities and by your spirit of service.' He highlighted five characteristics that the IAS should have:

1. Impartiality and incorruptibility. It was clear that a Civil Servant cannot afford to and must not take part in politics. 'Nor must he involve himself in communal wrangles,' Sardar Patel said.
2. Integrity
3. Work without any expectation of extraneous rewards
4. Sovereignty
5. Spirit of service

Patel said, 'Along with discipline, you must cultivate an esprit de corps without which a service has little meaning. You should regard it as a proud privilege to belong to the service— covenants of which you will sign and uphold, through your service, its dignity, integrity and incorruptibility.'

The IAS today has to ask itself whether it has lived up to the lofty ideals with which it was created. The answer would be mixed. The service has produced outstanding and dedicated officers who have contributed to building the nation. Officers of the Civil Services conduct elections with total fairness and impartiality as well as great efficiency; they do outstanding work in handling natural calamities and they have stood for the values enshrined in the Constitution as well as worked with a sense of service for the people. Yet, a large section of people bear animosity towards these officers and consider them remnants of the colonial regime, insulated from the real citizens of India. Some of this criticism is valid but it is not true in all cases. Like in any other discipline, individuals have different styles of working and differing mindsets. Clichés like the IAS is rule bound, resistant to change, overbearing, arrogant, self-seeking, obstructionist and not suited for the twenty-first century are thrown around. Such critiques ignore or turn a blind eye to the yeoman service rendered by the IAS in building the nation, and many of these criticisms are ill informed. However, there is a decline in the quality of the IAS with respect to its basic values of integrity, impartiality and incorruptibility. The service must retain its prominence or else it shall be consigned to history.

The charge of elitism is often placed at the doorstep of the service but I believe this is misplaced. So many changes have taken place in the recruitment process over the years that the service is no longer accessible only to the urban, well-off, English-speaking youth. The percentages of marks allocated for the interview have been reduced and the written examination has also undergone changes. You can now write the exam in Hindi or any other language mentioned in the schedule of the Constitution. There is a 50 per cent reservation for schedule castes, schedule tribes and other backward castes. The net result is that a large number of officers are now from rural backgrounds and they are not English-speaking or products of elite colleges. Most of them now belong to the middle or lower-middle class. Gone are the days when largely, only students of history or political science or philosophy would qualify. Today, a large majority of them are engineers and also from other professional disciplines like management. The IAS today is a truly diverse body of individuals and its members are in a much better position to understand the problems of real India.

The service is equipped to deliver but it must realize that it exists to change India for the better. It has to be result-centric, outcome-oriented and have a strong foundation of values. It has to live by the code prescribed for it by Sardar Patel. Introspection at the level of each individual officer and service as a whole is essential. If there is a negative perception about the service in the eyes of the people, then it should work actively to change this image. It has to ask itself whether it is upholding the standard of integrity expected of it. Is it impartial or politically neutral? And more so, is it accountable for its performance?

The problem is not so much with the members of the service as it is with the system of governance. You may replace the IAS with experts and through lateral entry but if you do not change the system, you will find that the results are not forthcoming. Of course, many people point out that the IAS is in a position to change the rules and processes which might be dysfunctional but this is true only up to a point. The service also functions in an environment of constraints and it is not free to do whatever it wants. Governance reforms on a much wider scale are required if public service delivery has to be improved.

The role of the IAS has increased over the years, and so have the complexities of the entire governance process. Long hours have to be put in and voluminous amounts of paperwork have to be dealt with. The task is diverse and the level of expectations high. There too many oversight agencies like the CAG, Courts and CVC, leading to a culture of ensuring personal safety rather than focusing on results. The IAS officer today has to be a leader in this extremely volatile environment. He has to multitask, achieve multiple objectives and respond to pressure and stimuli coming from various quarters. Despite the hazards and obstacles, he has to deliver and be accountable for his performance. He has to be a true team leader, having the confidence of his team and should lead by example and communicate the right way with all those working with him. He has to combine the skills of a strategic planner with that of an effective implementer and prove his mettle by his performance. That is the only way the service can survive and make a difference.

2

Preparing for the IAS: Selection and Training

In the seventies, when I wrote the IAS exam, it was the cherished dream of almost every young boy and girl. Career options were not as plentiful as they are today and the IAS was what everyone aspired for. It was an obsessive desire not only of the candidate but parents, relatives, neighbours and the community. So all-pervasive was this fascination for the IAS that taking the exam was akin to a national hobby. Irrespective of academic ability or talent, every young person tried their hand at the IAS exam. Success in the exam meant sudden alleviation to the top-most level in society and failure meant frustration and sadness. Today things may be different with multiple career avenues and different definitions of success but it still remains the dream for countless youth. In UP, Bihar and Odisha, which are economically backward, this fascination for the IAS is very intense.

Right from childhood, parents would start indoctrinating the mind of their child so that they make getting into the IAS their only ambition. It was the same for me. My father, an officer of the Indian Forest Service, used every opportunity to impress upon us the virtues of making it into the IAS. My brothers and I often countered by giving contra examples but he would not relent and tell us stories of those who had succeeded in the IAS and the great life that they enjoyed. Many of these discussions became heated but my father always had the last word. He would tell us stories about a mythical character called the DM (District Magistrate) who would be just a boy but would preside over meetings with other departmental officers who were twice his age. It was during these discussions that we realized the DM was the fulcrum of all authority in the eyes of the citizens, and that any post in the IAS carried with it an aura of immense power and exalted status. I learnt from my friends and course mates that this line of conversation, discussion and persuasion was taking place in nearly every household. I recall that on the day my results were declared and I had been selected, my father pulled out a bottle of scotch that he had kept for two decades for such an occasion and was in a state of bliss. When I wrote my first book on district administration, titled *The Collector Today*, I dedicated it to my father whose dream it was that I became a Collector and whose inspiration had converted this dream into a reality.

The lure of the IAS is greater in more backward states and which are more feudal in outlook. The power, pomp, status and respect for the IAS in these states need to be seen to be believed. On a lighter note, getting selected in the IAS can become a passport to a 'decent' marriage. As the territory comes with the promise of status, many young men and women find this appealing.

Things are different in progressive and industrialized states like Maharashtra and Gujarat. In Gujarat, the spots fill up with officers from outside Gujarat as not many young people from Gujarat write the civil service exam. There, a young boy or girl would prefer to become an entrepreneur or join the private sector. The same is true for Maharashtra. In Mumbai, an income tax officer is far more powerful and well-known than an IAS officer.

I was serving in Mumbai after doing my MBA from IIM Ahmedabad and was surprised to find that none of the Mumbai newspapers even published the Civil Services exam results. An interesting anecdote is that when I resigned from my private sector job at Mumbai to write the IAS exam, my landlord, a Gujarati gentleman, was unable to understand why I had made this decision. He asked me whether IAS was another company that was offering me a better salary! Despite all my explanations, he could not comprehend and till the very end believed that I had been thrown out of my job and was just spinning a yarn.

One must have their goal in life clearly defined in order to realize it. This is true for all aspects of life. This applies to a person who wants to write the IAS exam too. Just becoming an IAS officer is a nebulous goal. One should know why one wants to join the service in the first place. Only if the goal is clear can one work towards it and make a professional choice. Unfortunately, I have found that people want to join the IAS for the wrong reasons. They see the IAS as a passport to unbridled power and status, and attaining this seems to be a goal in itself. They are enamoured of the trappings of power like being given police guards, cars, escorts, red beacons on cars and huge offices with lots of staff, official housing and household staff. These factors are not unimportant but they should not become the driving force. Also, great effort is required to prevent power from going to one's head. Power has the uncanny ability to insidiously enter a person's character and personality and give him a swollen head. This is true for any organization. I have even seen people who are members of spiritual organizations change completely the moment they get appointed to position of power. 'Power corrupts and absolute power corrupts absolutely,' wrote Lord Acton and there could not have been a truer statement.

The IAS does give you immense power. You have to make an effort to remain level-headed and work for the people otherwise your entire personality will change. You will reek of arrogance and become insufferable. You will throw your weight around much to the chagrin of the citizens as well as members of other services. In the process, the real goal is lost sight of.

The goal of joining the IAS has to be to transform society. An officer should dream of making a difference in whichever job he is given to handle. Any IAS job gives you the power to take a lot of initiatives, formulate policies, work out strategies and implement action plans. You have to use your power and status to make the lives of the people in your state and country better. If you have this desire in you, if you are fired by this passion, then you are joining the IAS for the right reason. You should want to use the power for the greater benefit of all.

No job in the world can give you the variety that the IAS provides. You run districts, head diverse departments like health, agriculture, education, etc. Everywhere, your approach and initiatives set the tone for the department. You are always in a leadership position and can be transformational. It is this variety, diversity and job satisfaction one must want if he or she desires to join the IAS.

Nowadays I find that people want to join the IAS for the worst possible reason. My son works in the private sector. A colleague of his wanted to try his hand at the IAS. My son asked him if he was okay with making less than fifty percent of his current salary. The reply was shocking. He said that he would be able to make much more on the side in the IAS so the salary was not important! Anyone having this kind of motivation should not come anywhere near the IAS. He would be doing a great disservice to himself and to the country. Sadly, he is not the only one. Many boys and girls now opt for the IAS with very flexible views on moneymaking. The IAS is the successor service to the ICS and amidst its core values is integrity. A person lacking integrity should not think of the IAS as a career. One of my batchmates was the Deputy Director at Lal Bahadur Shastri National Academy of Administration, Mussoorie, almost a decade and a half after we joined the service. He once told me that there was a big difference in attitude between probationers of our times and the current lot. 'They are worldly wise,' he told me, compared to the wide-eyed innocent youngsters in the woods that we used to be. We had come straight from college to the IAS. We were brimming with idealism and had visions of changing the world. The candidates joining the IAS now have greater exposure to the real world and have their idealism tempered with real-life pragmatism. They see the IAS as a launch pad to power and status and some, unabashedly, see it as a route to amass wealth. This could well be a matter of perception and reflective of the typical syndrome that 'things were better in our times'. However, there are cogent reasons for this kind of a scenario. The average age of the person joining the IAS has increased significantly. From an average age of twenty-three to twenty-four, it has now risen to almost twenty-seven to twenty-eight years and you can write the IAS exam up to the age of thirty-two. Quite a few selected candidates have previous work experience where they have seen the world at close quarters. Their brush with reality has softened their notions of morality, integrity and selfless service. The maximum age permissible for writing the IAS exam used to be twenty-six in our days. This is an issue which merits the serious attention of policy makers. I am of the view that general candidates taking the IAS exam should be between twenty-one and twenty-six years of age. This will ensure that boys and girls fresh from university will join the service with their idealism and dreams for the future intact. Also, joining at an earlier age guarantees a longer service career and with it, the prospects of rising to the top post of Secretary to the Government of India or Chief Secretary of a state. It is much easier to mould candidates from this age group into the kind of Civil Servant they should be.

A career in the IAS is very enriching. The quality of the job you get is excellent and very rich in content. In a career spanning thirty-five years or so, you get to hold charge of a district, divisions, and look after various departments like finance, home, health, education and so on. Every moment of your career you are learning something new and responding to new challenges. Each assignment gives you the opportunity to touch the lives of ordinary people and bring about a positive qualitative change. Your jobs take you to villages and hamlets and if you implement schemes well, you see the benefits reaching every household. This gives an immense feeling of satisfaction. The scale of your operation is huge. NGOs do good work but on a limited scale, whereas the government works on a large canvas and the impact of its activities affects a larger number of people. If you work with integrity, dedication and passion, you will make a truly significant contribution to society.

I have already stated earlier that the service puts you in a top management position from the very day you join. The first posting of an IAS officer is as SDM (Subdivisional Magistrate) or Sub Collector, depending upon the state cadre allotted to you. When I joined as SDM on completion of my training, I was surprised that I was referred to as 'Hakim Pargana'. Literally translated, this means ruler of the subdivision. Of course, one must not get carried away by the literal translations of such things. That will detract you from performing your duties towards the people. You have to realize that you are a public servant who is expected to solve the grievances of the people and ensure proper delivery of public services. The right attitude is very important to keep you in a proper frame of mind and stop you from falling into the abyss of arrogance.

To keep your balance, you need to be emotionally mature and rational. I have seen officers not behaving properly with officers from other services. I have also seen officers who make a constant show of their power and become insufferable. Power is not the easiest thing to handle, particularly at an early age. You are in a leadership position so you have to be a genuine team leader. Your team must respect you and want to work with you. They will do so if they perceive the presence of higher qualities in you, those of honesty, integrity, dedication, diligence, intelligence and above all, humility. I feel humility is the greatest asset of an IAS officer. The comment from people that I most cherish has been when people tell me that I do not behave or act like a 'typical' IAS officer and they complement me on my simplicity, openness and genuineness. If you are humble, you will listen to others, otherwise you cannot empathize with the grievances of the people, leave aside providing a resolution. Humility will also enable you to learn. It is important for an IAS officer to have the attitude of a learner. The diversity of his job is such it has to be a lifelong learning experience. He has to learn fast, comprehend, understand key issues, prioritize and then plan and execute.

Most IAS officers, when they join the service, are full of energy and dynamism. Yet as the years go by, I found that a large number of them mellow down to such an extent that they stop taking decisions. They give up their initiative and passion and get embroiled in the labyrinth of rules and procedures. Too often, the officers make the processes an end in itself. This is such a waste of a brilliant career opportunity that the IAS provides you with. In fact, you should consider yourself specially chosen to do something big for society, to make a difference to the lives of millions.

A question people often ask me is when should a person start preparing for the IAS? There is no doubt that it is one of the toughest exams in the country, having a large number of written papers and personality test. Several lakh aspirants vie for the coveted hundred-odd vacancies in the IAS in a particular year and about 700 in all the Civil Services put together. The competition is intense and requires massive preparation. It requires a lot of determination to work long hours for several months at a stretch to be able to compete. In fact, most people prepare for years as a large number of candidates do not succeed in their first attempt and may make several attempts, consuming three to four years of their life. I would say that at least one full year of uninterrupted preparation must go into getting into the IAS. A prospective candidate has to be of a certain academic level to even think about being selected. Most boys and girls write the exam as a compulsive obsession, even though they do not have the required academic credentials. That is why I feel that out of the lakhs who write the exam, the serious competition is amongst the academically proficient 10,000 candidates.

Now luck is definitely a factor and cannot be ruled out. However, it is not just pure luck and not just anyone can get selected by chance. Apart from those who possess the true academic calibre, the rest are simply wasting their time. People will tell you all kinds of stories of how 'third divisoners' or very dull students have got selected. Do not believe them. Most stories like this are false. It could be that some student has not performed very well in their graduation exam but if you look beyond this, you will find that he has been brilliant at the school level. The basic competence and intelligence is there. In fact, when we were in college, we could predict who would succeed in the IAS exam and who would not. More often than not, our predictions turned out to be true. When we joined the IAS and I looked around at my batchmates, I found them all to be exceptionally bright and with a distinguished academic record. We did have some doubts about a few of them who did not appear to have the requisite personality or communication skills. Yet, as one got to know them better, it was revealed that one was a mathematics wizard who had scored more than 90 per cent in mathematics and another was a walking encyclopedia on political science, which was his optional subject. It is a matter of great satisfaction that the selection system of the UPSC is absolutely fair and selects only the right candidates. No one is there who does not deserve it. It could be that some really deserving person missed out in the IAS and got some other Central Service. Here, luck can be a factor in bringing about the difference of a few marks.

Taking this line of reasoning further, it is clear that you have to be a good student right from when you're in school to stand a chance in the IAS exam. It is true that one may decide to join the IAS at a much later stage but the academic foundation laid during this time is very important and vital. You must develop an interest in the environment around you and pickup early habits like reading the newspapers, especially the editorials. One should also do a lot of general reading from the school stage. It is not possible to pick up reading at a later stage or closer to the exam. In the same vein, one must give attention to their communication skills too – both written and oral – from early stages. These skills are very difficult to acquire just before you decide to attempt the IAS exam.

The point to make is that the IAS exam is a serious affair; one must start orienting oneself mentally long before the actual preparation starts. Also, focused attention is required. You cannot take this exam along with the other diversions. In particular, I strongly feel this exam cannot be taken while working. Any job can be demanding and your entire day is spent in the office. Just preparing after office hours will not suffice. Moreover, the preparation requires single-minded dedication and commitment, which is difficult along with a job. When I resigned from my private sector job to write the IAS, many eyebrows were raised. Family and friends questioned my decision and they pointed out that there was no guarantee that I would succeed. A retired ICS officer who was well-known to my father, rather caustically remarked, 'A bird in hand is better than two in the bush'. Logic and caution is definitely on the side of not throwing your job away to write an extremely unpredictable IAS exam. However, the stark reality is that if you keep your feet on two boats, you will fall into the water. Taking the civil service exam as a part-time endeavour is a sure shot recipe for failure. One should give everything they have to that one complete and dedicated effort. If you have the basic potential, then success is bound to come.

How many hours should one study? There cannot be any one number that can be quoted as it depends on an individual's capacity to concentrate and be at his highest mental level. However, the question can be answered by simply saying that one has to work extremely hard. At least eight to nine months before the exam, serious preparation must begin and it should take up the better part of your day, leaving time to exercise your body and get a good night's sleep.

It is not what you study and how much you study but how you study that is more important. The preparation has to be systematic and focused. The syllabi of the various papers have to be studied in detail as well as the previous year's question papers. This will make you aware of the style and content of the papers so you can prepare accordingly. Writing skills are of utmost importance. Nowadays there are as many as four general studies papers of 250 marks each. In each paper, you have to answer twenty questions and there is a word limit of 150 to 250 prescribed for each answer. One has to bring out all the points within this word limit. So it is clear that the preparation requires a lot of writing work. Questions need to be attempted while adhering to the word and time limit. The papers are generally lengthy and if one does not manage their time effectively, they will inevitably run out of time. This is the worst-case scenario—you know the answer to the question but are unable to put it down because of the shortage of time. If you miss out on a couple of questions, you miss out your chance of succeeding in the exam. This is because in the final result, the total score attained by candidates is very close to each other and even one mark makes a difference. Therefore, there is no substitute to rigorous practice of writing answers with a clock on the table.

The scheme of the main exam at the moment is that there are four papers in general studies of 250 marks each; one essay paper of 250 marks, one optional subject having two papers of 250 marks each. However, not everyone is eligible to write the main exam. The candidates have to first clear a preliminary exam in order to qualify for the mains. There is only one paper of general studies on the basis of which you qualify for the main exam. There is a CSAT paper as well but one has to get only minimum qualifying marks in this paper and these marks are not added to your score. Somehow the pattern of examination has undergone a lot of change over time. In our days (the 1977 exam) there was no system of preliminaries. We had to write three compulsory papers of 150 marks each – essay, general English and general knowledge. This was followed by three optional papers which were known as the lower papers and the knowledge expected in these was up to the graduate level. Each lower paper carried 200 marks. Then there were two higher optional papers that a candidate had to offer and were supposed to test their knowledge at a postgraduate standard. These papers were also of 200 marks each. For the Indian Police Service, your scores in your compulsories and two optional papers were added. The optional ones had to be indicated in the form beforehand. Then for the central services like Income Tax, the third lower optional paper was also brought in to the calculation. Only if you qualify at this stage would you be eligible to have your two higher optional papers evaluated for the purpose of selection to the IAS or IFS. It was indeed an extremely rigorous exam which forced candidates out of their comfort zone as they had to select optional subjects which they had not studied at the college level. This system changed in 1980 but it definitely had its merits. The very fact that a candidate had to offer optionals which he had not studied earlier was a test of his grasping power of new subjects which is definitely a required quality in a diverse and versatile career in the IAS. In any case, every scheme of exam has its merits and demerits. The main point is that it is a fair, competitive exam and only the best get selected. So, you have to be better than the others to make the exam a success.

The prelims were introduced in 1980. There was one general studies paper and one optional paper of choice. This scheme underwent a change with the optional paper being replaced by a CSAT paper to test the general aptitude and ability of a candidate. This led to a furor as it was felt by some people that this scheme favoured professionals like engineers and MBA graduates who scored well in the CSAT as the format was more familiar to them. It was argued that there were questions on quantitative aptitude which worked against the students of liberal arts and humanities. I personally feel that this was not a valid criticism. The paper carried just a few elementary questions on numerical aptitude which could easily be answered by non-engineers and non-science students. In fact, a job in the services now increasingly requires more and more data analysis and dealing with graphs, tables and charts, and so a certain amount of quantitative aptitude is necessary. Somehow, it was also felt that this paper had an urban bias because there were some questions which required a basic knowledge of the English language. The advocates of this viewpoint argued that candidates from rural areas were not able to make the grade because of this inherent bias in the system. Mass agitations took place all over the country and the government succumbed to the pressure and prevailed upon the UPSC to alter the system once again. Now there is only one general studies paper in the preliminaries while the CSAT paper has become merely a qualifying one. This is a rather strange compromise which does not improve the selection process in any way. The irony is that even after this change, the number of engineers qualifying has gone up every year. I feel the value of the preliminary examination has been lowered by this change and would advocate going back to the earlier system. If there are still some problems of having the CSAT paper evaluated, then even the earlier system of having one general studies and one optional paper should be reverted to in order to maintain some sanctity of the preliminary exam. Also I strongly feel that the UPSC with its experts is the right organization to decide the nature of the examination and the government should not interfere in the process. I recall that as Chief Secretary of UP, I received a proposal submitted by Uttar Pradesh Public Service Commission to have a CSAT paper in the preliminary exam for state civil service on the analogy of the Union Public Service Commission to the Cabinet. I was absolutely shocked to find that one minister after another strongly opposed it, using the same arguments mentioned above. No amount of persuasion from my side could succeed in pushing the proposal through. I feel that politicians should not intervene in issues like selection to the Civil Services. The value of the entire selection system is based on the fact that it is merit-based, which is decided upon by impartial experts. Recently I was informed that the UPSC model has been fully adopted by the State Public Service Commission.

As already pointed out, the first hurdle is the preliminary exam which, for all practical purposes, has only one paper, which is general studies. The CSAT paper is only for qualifying. The marks are not added. This paper is a test of your aptitude and the topics covered are comprehension, interpersonal skills, logical reasoning, decision-making and problem solving, general mental ability, basic numeracy, data interpretation (charts, graphs, tables, etc.). The knowledge level required for basic numeracy and data interpretation is only that of the Class 10 level, which makes it very elementary. This paper is similar to aptitude tests like SAT for entrance to universities or CAT and GMAT used for management exams; however the standard is much lower than CAT or GMAT. Since one has to only pass this paper, not much time is required to be spent on this. A candidate may practice half a dozen mock tests which are readily available to prepare for this. Even at the risk of repetition, I would like to strongly reiterate that this paper should be evaluated for considering qualification for the main examination. It is after all a basic test of mental ability which is absolutely essential for a civil servant. If our education system is unable to equip our students with these basic skills, then it certainly needs urgent attention. Lowering the standard of an examination is not the answer.

The other paper in preliminaries relates to general studies. The syllabus for this consists of current affairs—National and International History of India and Indian National Movement, India and world geography, Indian Polity and Governance, Economic and Social Development, Environmental Ecology, Biodiversity and General Science. Current affairs can be handled by regular reading of newspapers and general awareness. However, there are some good magazines focusing on current affairs which can be of great help. Many people have found The *Hindu* and *Frontline Magazine* very useful. *The Manorama Year Book* and *The India Year Book* give a complete review of the current affairs. The Internet can also be used to get valuable information. Regarding the other topics, school-level knowledge is required and the best way to prepare is by using the NCERT books on these subjects, especially those which are for Classes 10, 11 and 12. With a significant number of questions on Indian National Movement, Indian geography, Indian Polity and Indian Economics, these are areas that must be prepared thoroughly. One should attempt the previous ten years papers to get an idea of the type of questions being asked. Also various good coaching institutions have their mock test series. It would help a candidate to try out a few of these papers in the required time limit. The questions are generally deceptive and the alternative answers given are very close to each other. An important thing to remember is to read the questions very carefully and also the alternative answers so that in a hurry, you do not commit an unnecessary error. I would recommend that one go through the paper and keep answering those questions which they are absolutely sure of. Then one should take up those questions where you can narrow down the answer to two alternatives. There is a 50 per cent chance of getting the answer right. Other questions where you are not sure at all should not be attempted. The reason is that there is negative marking which a candidate must avoid. This paper is of 200 marks and the cut-off marks for qualifying for main examination are generally around 110 for general candidate but it varies from year to year. For instance, the cut-off marks for the years 2015, 2016, 2017 and 2018 for general candidates were 107.34, 116, 105.34, and 98 respectively. The marks for the OBC category were 106, 110.66, 102.66 and 96.66. The corresponding figure for SC candidates was 94.00, 99.34, 88.66 and 84.00. The figures for ST candidates were almost similar. I feel a candidate should prepare in a manner that they score at least 125 marks. This way qualifying would be assured. As you can see, the qualifying level for the general candidates is about 55 percent which is not very high but indicates the level of difficulty of the paper and the fact that a very detailed and specific knowledge is required; one has to be extremely careful in choosing the correct alternative for an answer.

For those who clear the preliminary, the main examination, or the mains as they are called, is the next big hurdle. An important point to be kept in mind is that there is very little time between the announcement of the results of the preliminary examination and the main examination. Generally, a candidate would get about three to four clear months to prepare and this is not sufficient to clear the main examination. It is clear that a candidate has to start preparing for the main examination along with his preparation for the preliminaries. Normally, the preliminary examination is held in the month of May and the results are declared by the end of June. The main examination is in the month of October–November. My recommendation would be that a candidate start his preparation at least from the month of January and focus on the preliminaries and the mains together. There are a lot of common topics between the general study paper in the preliminaries and in the mains. Thus it is possible to design your study schedule in a manner that the course material for both the exams is covered far as general studies is concerned. The one-month time period between writing the preliminary and the declaration of results should be utilized to prepare for the optional paper. However the important point is whether you have studied the optional paper before as part of your graduate or undergraduate studies. In case the optional paper is absolutely new to you, then it is advisable to start preparing for it at least three to four months before January.

The current pattern of the Civil Services main examination is that you have to qualify in English and one Indian language. This actually does not require any preparation as you have to only pass the examination and the level of it is quite elementary. If you are not confident about English then you should give some time to this paper. Then there is an essay paper of 250 marks, four papers in general studies of 250 marks each and two papers in the optional you select of 250 marks each as well. This new scheme attempts to bring all the candidates to an even platform as there is a strong feeling that candidates scored higher in some optional as compared to others. In fact some people are extending this logic further to argue for the elimination of this one optional subject. However, I am not in agreement with this and strongly recommend the continuance of the optional subject.

The essay paper is general in nature and a candidate is expected to write two essays from a choice of subjects. The general studies first paper is about Indian heritage and culture, history and geography of the world and society. This paper lays emphasis on ancient Indian culture, modern Indian history with specific reference to the freedom struggle, Indian society, the role of women, social empowerment, world history and geography. The second general studies paper concentrates on governance, constitution, polity, social justice and international relations, with special emphasis on the Indian Constitution and the working of the Indian political system, issues relating to development and management of schemes related to health and education and the role of Civil Services in a democracy. The general studies third paper comprises of questions on science and technology, economic development, biodiversity, environment, security and disaster management. The fourth general studies paper is the most interesting and relates to ethics, integrity and aptitude. I will discuss this paper in greater detail at a later stage. Then you have to choose one optional subject which will have two papers of 250 marks each. There is a wide range of optional papers to select from. There are Indian languages and various subjects in humanities, science, mathematics, engineering, management, medicine and law. Almost all disciplines are covered.

In the IAS exam, the candidate is expected to write two essays. The time limit is crucial. Equal time must be given to both the essays. The essays test your ability to present your views cogently, logically and with clarity. Two essays have to be chosen from two sections carrying equal marks. It is indicated that each essay should be of about 1000 to 1200 words. The first section is general in nature and there is no material from which you can prepare for this. For instance, the 2000 Civil Services essay papers had topics like 'values are not what humanity is, but what humanity ought to be' or 'courage to accept and dedication to improve are keys to success' in Section-A. As you can see, these are general topics and you cannot possibly prepare for them as the examiner can ask you to write on any subject. Section-B is a little more predictable as topics are concerned with current issues. For example, the 2019 paper had topics like 'neglect of primary healthcare and education in India are reasons for its backwardness' and 'rise of artificial intelligence: the threat of jobless future or better job opportunities through reskilling and upskilling'. For these topics, you need a very good understanding of contemporary issues. It is advisable to make short notes or points on current topics from your readings, otherwise it will not be possible to remember. The content in your essay is of great importance. For instance, if an essay is on some aspect of democracy, then the candidate attempting it should have a sound knowledge of the institutions of democracy and the various facets of the actual workings of the government.

There are elementary rules to be followed in writing an essay. There should be an introduction which should be interesting, introducing the topic. Then there should be a conclusion which should sum up the ideas discussed in the main body of the essay. In between, different paragraphs should present the various viewpoints you wish to communicate. One should present both sides of an argument and have a balanced approach, and then logically arrive at the viewpoint you want to advocate. The essay should flow logically and smoothly from one point to another. Your ideas should follow each other, showing clarity of thought. There should be a sense of continuity in the essay and the material should not look disjointed. It is therefore important that the candidate spends at least ten minutes in planning their essay.

The topic must be clearly understood. The worst thing that a candidate can do is deviate from the topic. This is a sure recipe for scoring poorly. Just to illustrate this point, I would like to narrate a story that went around when I attempted the IAS. In the exam the essay topic was 'To a man with an empty stomach, food is god.' (MK Gandhi). There was a candidate who was a very bright student and was expected to make it into the IAS. When the results were out, he was stunned to find that he had failed to qualify for the personality test. Later on it transpired that he had got zero marks in the essay paper. It seems he had attempted this topic but had overlooked the fact that MK Gandhi had been written in bold after the quotation. This candidate did not even mention Gandhi in his essay, whereas the Gandhian thought should have been the essence of the essay. This emphasizes the point that the topic should be fully understood and your essay should not stray from it.

It must also be understood that a body of experts sit down to decide what kind of answer they expect and the marking scheme is laid down in great detail. A candidate is expected to bring in original thinking and show a width and breadth of knowledge. I will illustrate this with another example. During our time, we used to have a general English paper which had a question on paragraph writing of about 150 words. I happened to meet a professor who had been an examiner for this paper. He explained to me what was expected from paragraph writing. In the exam, the candidate was expected to write a paragraph on 'All that is beautiful is not useful'. The marking scheme expected the candidate to give both sides of the picture. Surprisingly, the marking scheme mentions whether the candidate has talked about spiritual beauty. If the candidate had done so, he would get three additional marks! The examiner expected the candidates to think of spiritual beauty when he visualized beauty. What an amazing depth of thinking the examiner was looking for!

This clearly shows that preparing for the Civil Services is not a matter of cramming for six months or so. A very deep and broad level of awareness is required, which cannot be inculcated in just a few months. Years of reading, thinking, analyzing is essential to have the right kind of mental makeup. The essay is a test of your general awareness, logical reasoning, power of analysis, command over language and depth of knowledge. Memorizing essays given in self-help books will not help much. One should read widely, and also attempt writing a few essays on topics of contemporary relevance. However it is not possible to write too many essays. The best things is to write down points related to various topics and also make notes from your readings from the newspapers, magazines and the Internet. This paper is important because you can score high marks in it which will boost your overall score in the written exam. As I point out later, by and large candidates do not score very high marks in general studies and the marks obtained in the essay paper can be a game changer.

There are now four papers in general studies. Earlier, there was more emphasis on the optionals but it was increasingly felt that some optionals were easier to score in than others. Having common papers brings everyone to the same playing field. Four papers in general studies cover a wide range of topics and are more than enough.

Once again the art of writing an answer is of utmost importance since all the general studies questions have a word limit. It is important not to exceed this limit and at the same time, give due weightage to all the important points within the confines of the word limit. The answer has to be analytical and have a logical flow. The general studies papers are by and large not very scoring. In fact, a score of

50 per cent is quite reasonable. There are about twenty to twenty-five questions in each paper and there is no choice with these questions, making it quite difficult. There is a word limit ranging from 150 to 250 words for each question. I personally feel that this is a little unfair. It is difficult for a candidate to think and write answers for so many questions within the prescribed time limit. Also, I feel that a choice must be given. However, the candidate has no choice but to respond to the system as it exists today. The best method to tackle the situation is to go through the paper and select the questions you know well and answer them first and in the best possible manner. You have to keep in mind that your answer has to be balanced, giving both pros and cons and then arriving at a conclusion. The civil service does not encourage an extreme viewpoint. For instance, some magazines give a leftist interpretation of issues. Your answer should have both the 'left' and 'right' viewpoints. You may ultimately support a particular viewpoint in your conclusion.

When preparing for this exam, it is important to remember that you need knowledge that is expected of a class 12 student. Do not make the mistake of excessive preparation by studying material that is of a graduate or postgraduate level. Conceptual understanding is important. Mere rote learning will not serve the purpose. It would be best for a candidate to make short notes. He should also attempt important questions and have them fully prepared.

The fourth general studies paper is a little tricky. It has a very general syllabus on ethics, aptitude, attitude and integrity. There is no defined course and not much material is available in the market. Recently, a couple of good books might have been made available but a candidate will still have to use a lot of his common sense when answering this paper. The report of the second administrative reforms commission is a great source material. Further, you can access the Internet for material on corruption, values, attitudes and ethics. This is basically an applied paper. Too much learning or memorizing is not required. A basic understanding of ethics, morals and values is required and then the candidate can frame his answers accordingly. The best thing to do would be to go through the previous papers and tailor your preparation accordingly. 50 per cent of this paper is devoted to case studies. A candidate should first read the case study properly and understand the issues involved, and then look at the various alternatives given, discuss them and then arrive at the best alternative, giving sufficient reasons for his choice. One rule of thumb is that the basic ethics required of a civil servant is public service and welfare, and the civil servant must be financially and intellectually honest. The candidate should apply these rules while attempting a case study. The golden principle to be followed is to think about what kind of behaviour you would expect from an officer as a citizen and then apply that to the case study. Another rule which will never fail is to apply is Mahatma Gandhi's thought which says, 'I will give you a talisman. Whenever you are in doubt, or when the self becomes too much with you, apply the following test. Recall the face of the poorest and the weakest man (or woman), whom you may have seen, and ask yourself if the step you contemplate is going to be of any use to him (or her).' Then we move on to the optional subject which has two papers of 250 marks each. The first major decision to take is regarding the choice of the subject. This is very important as the optional subject is one where you can score reasonably high marks which will increase your score in the written exam and ensure your selection. The weightage of the written exam in the overall marking scheme is disproportionately high. The total marks for the written examination is 1750, while that for the interview is 275 only. It is thus clear that a candidate who scores high marks in the written exam has a much higher chance of being selected. One guiding factor when selecting your optional could be to choose the subject in which you have done your graduate or postgraduate degree. However, another method is to select an optional where candidates tend to score high marks. It is also important to see the syllabus of an optional. Some subjects have a very vast syllabus which makes it difficult to prepare. It is always better to choose a subject which has a well-defined and specific syllabus. For instance, history used to be a favourite of most candidates but the current syllabus is huge and unwieldy. History, thus, is not a great optional paper now. I have noticed that very few people with history as an optional are making it into the Civil Services. Subjects like philosophy and public administration or political science and international relations have a compact syllabus and are good subjects for the services. Of course, science students can prefer subjects like physics, chemistry or mathematics. By and large, even when I wrote the IAS, mathematics was a tricky subject and still is. It can take you to the top of the selection list or completely ruin your chances. Mathematics should be attempted by only that candidate who is exceptionally good at it. Physics has always been a good subject. However, I have noticed that these days a lot of engineers are getting selected and most of them choose a humanities subject as an optional. Another factor that can influence your choice of subject is the commonality of topics in that optional and the general studies papers. There is a lot of geography, political science, history and economics in the general studies papers. Above all, it is important that you should find the subject interesting.

The most important aspect of the written paper is that one should know the art of writing an answer. First, the question must be understood properly and then the candidate should answer the question and not the topic. If she does the latter, then she would be writing a lot of irrelevant things. This may sound obvious but very few people know how to answer a written question. They tend to write everything they know about the topic and end up scoring poorly. I remember when I wrote the IAS exam, I took a short three-week course at the RAU's Study Circle in Delhi. Many of us had opted for European history. Mr Rau gave us a question to write on – 'Napoleon was a child of the French Revolution but was ultimately devoured by it. Critically discuss'. He liked my answer and praised it but was scathing in his criticism of the rest, who had written everything they knew about Napoleon. The correct answer would show the situation created after the French Revolution which brought Napoleon to power but ultimately, arrive at how the change the revolution had set in process became his undoing. The answer has to move from the French Revolution to the rise of Napoleon.

It is also important to write lucidly, covering all aspects of a question. The way you write an answer in the Civil Services is different from the way you would do in a postgraduate exam.

In the latter, you have the liberty to take off and forcibly argue your viewpoint quoting from various authors. In the Civil Services, you have to be restrained in your answer and concentrate on raising the all-important points in a balanced manner. Many students criticize the Civil Services selection system on this ground. However, I feel that this is how it should be. In your job as a Civil Servant, you are expected to weigh the pros and cons before arriving at any decision and should have a sense of balance and perspective. This is the reason why many engineers and science students score higher marks in humanities optionals than students of Humanities. Just to share with you, I had done my BA (Hons) in Economics from St Stephen's College, Delhi University. I had chosen optional papers in European history, public administration, international law and economics. I got very high marks in all the optionals except economics, which was my main subject! In any case, let me warn students of economics that it is a disastrous subject for the Civil Services. In particular, the syllabus of Economics Honours at Delhi University is very different from the one prescribed for the Civil Services.

Once you qualify in the written exam, the personality test or interview follows. Normally candidates two to three times the number of the vacancies are called for the interview. The interview has been downgraded in importance over time with the argument that it favours the English-speaking, urban youth educated at good colleges and it works against those from rural areas. There can be different views on it. The interview now carries only 275 marks against the total of 2025 marks. If one does very well in the written exam, then the interview does not make much of a difference. I find many candidates woefully saying that they had qualified the written but could not clear the interview. This is more often than not, wrong. Actually, their written marks are normally on the lower side and they are not able to make up the deficit in the interview. Of course, it does matter if your interview has been a disaster. Also, the marks in the interview can make a big difference to your rank and in turn the service that you are selected for. In the days of the ICS, it was compulsory to pass in the interview and the pass marks were 50 per cent. Even when I wrote the IAS, the proportion of the interview marks was higher, especially for the IAS and IFS.

The interview is essential to test the communication and logical skills of a candidate along with his general awareness and bearing. The personality of an individual makes a big difference in the way he performs his job and can take on leadership responsibilities. Of course, there is the limitation of language but now the UPSC allows you to take your interview in any recognized language. Moreover, it is not merely the fluency or style that matters but the content.

The interview board is not expected to test your knowledge about your subject. This has been done in the written examination. They are expected to assess how you analyze issues, your viewpoint, your ability to communicate and convince. The board also assesses your attitude, behaviour, bearing and other personality traits. Believe me, twenty to thirty minutes can reveal a lot about the personality of a candidate. However, interview board members are human beings and hence have their own attitudinal issues. Some members want to impress others and will ask questions only to show off their own knowledge. Others might prepare questions and keep asking them, irrespective of the background and experience of the candidate. Some members can be very strict whereas others are lenient. Despite the attempt at moderation by the UPSC, the perception remains that some interview boards are tougher than the others.

There are some basic principles that need to be followed. The first impression is vital. You must dress well and conservatively. Besides that, you should be comfortable in what you wear. There have been cases where a candidate wears a new suit or a sari for the interview and is conscious of their dress all through the interview. This should never be done and can be counterproductive. The next important thing is to enter the interview room smartly and walk up to the table with confidence and with a smile. You should then warmly greet the members of the interview board and sit down once they ask you to do so. The posture you adopt while sitting says a lot about your personality. You should not lean backwards or slouch forward. You should sit with your spine straight but not appear tense. You should look and feel comfortable. Normally, the chairman of the board will ask you some introductory questions and then ask the other members to engage with you. The candidate should realize that it is not necessary to answer all the questions. The marks in an interview are decided on the basis of your overall impression and it is not as if marks are being awarded for each question. It is thus important to capitalize on questions which are well-known to you and if you are unsure of the answer to a question, then it is best to say, 'I am sorry, sir, I do not know'. You should not allow your confidence level to come down at any stage so it is important not to brood over questions that you have not been able to answer correctly. In fact, the art of interviewing is to bring the discussion around your strong points. Moreover, often the questions asked do not have a specific correct answer and more often than not, the board evaluates the way you process your question and how logically you analyze it and come to a reasoned conclusion. It is important to avoid guessing answers and the worst thing you can do is to tell a lie or try to bluff your way through. Sometimes the board asks you questions which are not in your comfort zone. If you attempt to respond, supplementary questions will follow going deeper and deeper into an area you do not know much about. This leads to a visible loss of confidence in the demeanour of the candidate—she starts hesitating, her voice becomes slow and unsure, and her body language exhibits diffidence. The moment this happens, you can be sure that your interview is going downhill. I will narrate my experience of the IAS interview where I committed this mistake and it was only with great difficulty that I was able to salvage the situation.

Before that, it is important to remember that one should never contradict any member of the board. Even if you feel that you are right and possibly the member is not, it is best not to become argumentative. Statements like 'I do not agree with you, sir', should be best avoided. The best response would be to say 'Okay, sir', and move on. However, at times you might feel very strongly about something. It would then be best to say that possibly there is another way of looking at it and then put forward your views. The tone should be always polite and respectful. Sarcasm and cynicism have to be avoided at all costs. Some candidates try to prove their point by counter-questioning. One should refrain from doing so.

The interview board is looking for a positive, balanced, poised and analytical personality, who is aware of the environment around him. A candidate must show a spark of energy. The answers of the candidate should also show that he has a strong value system and sense of ethics. At the risk of repetition I would like to add that it is not about *what* you answer but *how* you answer. A candidate must have good knowledge about India, his state and district. The candidate should be fully aware of all current issues of national and international importance. He should be prepared to answer questions where scenarios are given to him and he is asked how he would handle the situation. Some questions can always be expected on the optional subject that you have chosen if one of the board members is from that discipline. If you have mentioned a hobby in your application form, then questions will be asked about that and you are expected to have a deep knowledge about the subject. Stating reading as a hobby can be most dangerous as most of the board members are very well-read.

As promised earlier, this is the story of my IAS interview which nearly became a disaster till I was able to turn it around to some extent. I nearly lost the plot before recovering at the end. My interview started beautifully with some general questions asked by the chairman and then the first member, who was a retired ambassador and started talking to me about books, as reading was my hobby and I eloquently spoke about authors and my favourite books. Authors like Ernest Hemingway and Gabriel Garcia Marquez were discussed and I performed brilliantly as this was like batting on home turf for me. He even favourably opined that I should have considered the Indian Foreign Services (IFS) as my first option but I persisted by saying that I preferred the IAS. The next member was an astrophysicist of great repute. He started by asking me if I had read any books on science. I told him that *Origin of Species* by Charles Darwin was my favourite. Evidently, this was not in his area of interest. He then asked me if I had read any science fiction. I told him that I was not a great fan of science fiction but I had read a couple of books by Arthur Clarke and had particularly liked *Rendezvous with Rama*. He had not read this book and so he did not respond. He then asked me to name top Indian scientists. I mentioned CV Raman, SC Bose and JC Bose. He asked me about the contribution of Raman and I answered 'Raman Effect'. The next question was least expected. 'What is Raman Effect? Please explain'. I had read generally about Raman Effect and I made the mistake of answering. I was not very confident and a little hesitant in my reply. He said, 'You are right but something more'. I tried to clarify that I was not a student of science but of economics and management. Yet I hazarded to answer further and got myself into a tangle. At this stage, instead of answering I should have said firmly, 'I am sorry, I do not know, sir. I am not a student of science'. This could have put an end to this line of questioning. My continuous attempt to answer was encouraging the board member to persist. He then moved to SC Bose and asked about his contribution. Again, due to my general awareness I answered by saying 'Bose–Einstein Statistics'. The board member continued and asked me about Bose–Einstein

Statistics. I told him that it predicted the behaviour of an elementary particle called Boson. He then proceeded to ask me further questions and I began to get extremely tense and started losing my confidence. I was clearly not in my comfort zone. He persisted by asking me some technical questions on satellites, as he was an astrophysicist. I could not handle that question and weakly mumbled something about not being a student of science and my body began to slump, showing my confidence dropping.

Then came the turn of the next member, who was a retired IAS officer but my luck was running out and he asked me to explain the scientific principle on which a pressure cooker works. I had worked with Hawkins Pressure Cooker after my MBA from IIM Ahmadabad and so could answer this question. Evidently, this officer must also have been a student of science for he continued by asking me questions about science. I answered but was clearly out of my depth and losing confidence with every moment. The next interviewer was a lady, who was a professor of political science. I began well with her before she asked me to name some regional political parties. Since at this stage I was low on confidence and my mind was not working at its full level of alertness, I mentioned Jharkhand Mukti Morcha of all the parties, which led to her asking me some probing questions about this party, leaving me high and dry. The last member was a retired Air Chief Marshal, a Sikh gentleman, who took off on agriculture, asking me detailed questions on cropping patterns, soils, agro-climatic zones and fertilizers and insecticides. Now I was an urban-educated youth having little direct knowledge of agriculture. I answered him but clearly I was out of my depth and not exuding confidence and control. In fact, at that stage, I was feeling in my heart that my chances in the IAS were over and I was becoming a little despondent. Some more questions followed and then it appeared as if the interview was over. Except for the first board member, all the others had asked me questions in areas where I was not well-versed and had not given me a chance to speak at length on any of the topics which were my strong points as I had the ability to articulate well. The chairmen of the board could have ended the interview at this stage but he also felt that maybe I had not been given a fair chance, looking at the nature of the questions being asked. He decided to extend me an olive branch and asked for my views on the Rhodesian crisis (later called Zimbabwe) which was an international issue very much in the news, those days. I jumped at it and spoke as much as I could on this as I was aware of all aspects of the problem. The interview ended and I came out of the room with mixed feelings. At the RAU IAS study circle, I used to be a favourite of Mr Rau and he had predicted that I would score more than 70 per cent in my interview. But as you have seen, the interview was not as per my desire. Except for one member and the question asked by the chairman, I felt I had not been able to leave the kind of impact I wanted. Things could have gone much better had I not tried to answer questions which I was not very sure of and had clearly impressed upon the board that I was not a student of science. However, I fared much better than I had expected I got around 55 per cent.

My experience as narrated shows that interviews can go wrong even if you are well-prepared. The art of doing well in the interview is to focus the discussion on your strong points and if a board member is asking you questions about which you are not very sure, then it is best to manoeuvre your way out of it as quickly as possible. The important point is that you should remain very agile and alert, and also appear extremely confident. Your shoulders should never droop and you should come through as a well-informed, articulate, analytical, logical and balanced person with original and deep thinking.

The IAS exam is a test of one's endurance, determination, capacity for hard work, intelligence and communication skills. The beauty is that the UPSC as a body has been able to preserve its integrity and nobody can question the fairness of the selection process. There is a total commitment to impartiality and transparency, leading to the entire process having unquestioned credibility in the eyes of the people. The civil service is an extremely tough exam but it is a fair exam and you get selected based on your merit. I was very surprised to read a book recently, that said the best do not get into the Civil Services and many with mediocre academic records get selected. There are people who have got selected without being 'first divisioners' but then there are subjects like history and literature, in which not many get a first division. The selection process selects the best.

It could be that the best do not opt for the Civil Services and prefer the private sector. Many top students go into management, engineering, medical and academics. Before the economic liberalization of 1991, the cream used to go for the Civil Services. In fact at that time, you would rarely meet a person who had not tried their hand at the Civil Services. This did change after 1991 with excellent opportunities being thrown up by the private sector. However, there was an economic slump in 2009 leading to students gravitating towards the Civil Services once again. The Coronavirus crisis leading to stagnating growth and reduced avenues of employment will propel more students towards a career in the Civil Services.

Increasingly, the number of engineers writing the exam and getting selected has gone up to the detriment of liberal arts students, who used to hold the majority at one time. There is nothing wrong with this, though I feel that this phenomenon should be studied to understand whether the current system is working against the students of humanities. It is true that when the CSAT was started, more students from engineering and management backgrounds began to write the exam and so more of them qualified. The civil service exam has to choose the best – it is a merit-based exam and the UPSC should not bend to any pressures that try to influence the selection process.

Further, the weightage given to the personality test must be increased. The job in the Civil Services requires communication skills of a high level and your success depends on your ability to put forward your views in a rational, logical, analytical manner. It also requires the ability to take a comprehensive view of a problem. Then there are certain qualities like commitment to democracy, secularism and the Constitution of India, which are essential. A spark of idealism is a desired attribute in the Civil Services. The personality test gives an opportunity to test all these factors and also assesses the administrative aptitude of a candidate. As a District Magistrate, when you have to stand before a mob and address them, you need a personality. You also need communication skills if you want to convince a minister or the cabinet about a policy.

My father was selected in the Indian Forest Service during the British days and used to often regale us with an anecdote from his interview. There were two rounds of interview and after the first, a few candidates were shortlisted for the second interview and my father was called in first by the interview board. The moment he entered the room, he was asked to go and stand in a corner. My father complied and stood straight and confidently. One by one, other candidates were called in and the same drill was repeated. Most of them were confused, became nervous and stood, not knowing what to do and started fidgeting around. My father caught hold of their hands and guided them to the corner and asked them to stand straight. For a few moments, the interview board members kept staring at the candidates and then thanked them and asked them to go. When the results were announced, my father had stood first in the exam. Years later at a dinner at the Nainital Club, my father met one of the members of that interview board and asked him 'I always wanted to know what you were testing when you made us stand in the corner of the room.' The reply from the interview board member was classic. He said, 'We wanted to see if you could stand on your own feet!'

The lesson of the story is clear. The personality test tries to gauge whether or not you have the requisite qualities to be an officer of the Civil Services and as such, its importance in the selection process should not be reduced.

It is true that there are many bright students from rural or disadvantaged backgrounds who are academically bright but not able to express themselves. This, then, is the fault of the education system which concentrates on subject knowledge rather than soft skills. In any case, the interview board definitely has the ability to understand the potential of a candidate even if he/she is not very fluent in a language. Thirty minutes of interview time is enough to plumb the depths of a candidate and assess her true potential. Of course, the members of the interview board also need to be counselled on their approach and type of questions to ask. Often, the board members try to impress by asking difficult questions and are keen to prove the candidate wrong. The members should be clear that the interview is not a test of memory. Also political questions should be avoided. There is no denying the element of subjectivity and luck in the selection process but then that is true of most things in life.

The essay paper is also very relevant but I feel having four papers in general studies is a bit too much. We could do with two papers. Actually, by increasing the number of papers and the curriculum, the exam becomes out of bounds for many bright students who cannot give so much time. I find that many candidates who are selected have attempted the exam several times. Even the toppers are those candidates who are writing the exam for the third or fourth time. Repeated attempts are not everybody's cup of tea. Boys and girls gravitate to good jobs elsewhere, rather than attempting the Civil Services exam year after year. The current selection process appears to be more of a test of endurance rather than aptitude or mental ability. The UPSC should examine the selection process in this light. At the moment, I feel many bright students stay away from the civil service exams because of the vastness of the course and time required to master it.

Further, I feel that there must be a restriction on the number of attempts allowed to a candidate. There should be maximum three attempts. There should also be an upper age limit which should preferably be twenty-six years or in any case not more than twenty-eight. It is not good for the candidate also to join at a late age, as then his chances of reaching the top posts gets adversely affected, impacting his overall job satisfaction.

An issue often raised is whether the civil service exam tests administrative acumen. While the exam does test many attributes, I feel it is very difficult to test administrative aptitude. A student writing the civil service exam has hardly any exposure to real-life situations and so it is hardly feasible to make out whether he has the basic attributes required for administration. For that matter, I do not think even the CAT exam is able to test whether a student has an aptitude for management or leadership roles. Even the IIT entrance exam focuses on subject-matter knowledge and does not in any way test the aptitude for engineering. It is also true that many Civil Servants would perform better in academics or other disciplines rather than administration. I recall the case of an IAS officer who was the topper of his batch and, I believe, his marks in the written exam have not yet been surpassed but somehow he could never get things done and alienated almost anybody who came into contact with him. Similarly, I have seen examples in my career of IIT students who got selected in the civil service and were extremely sharp and brilliant, but poor at decisionmaking and relating to people. This proves the point that all those who get selected in the IAS do not have the necessary aptitude for the job. This was equally true in the days of the ICS. In fact, ICS officers who did not show much aptitude for executive work were often shifted to the judicial side and they became excellent Judges. Your rank in the IAS exam does not have anything to do with your success as an officer. I have seen many toppers adopting deviant behaviour or suffering from a lack of integrity and falling by the wayside in their career. Also many colleagues in my batch who seemed to be indifferent and even cynical towards the demands of an administrative career, turned out to be legendary officers when they were actually posted in the field. Aptitude, thus, is an individual-related phenomenon and it evolves gradually during the course of one's career. Even then I have found that not all IAS officers are suitable for all assignments. Some are excellent at regulatory work while others perform well in development jobs.

The CSAT paper does have some objective questions on administrative aptitude but I do not think they are of any use. Objective questions can never test your aptitude. Maybe some sort of psychological test can be designed that could throw up some idea of your personality. However I am not so sure how a candidate can be evaluated on this basis. In the main examination, the General Studies-IV paper is on ethics, aptitude and attitude for public service and I feel this serves a useful purpose. More than 50 per cent of this paper is on case studies based on various administrative scenarios. This would throw light on a candidate's process of thinking and his approach to resolving issues.

Sometimes the government and often, some intellectuals needlessly want to tinker with the system of recruitment. One model that was proposed was for a student to choose the civil service as a career after Class 12 like they choose engineering or law. Thereafter, the selected candidate undergoes a three-year training programme and then is allotted to a service on the basis of his performance. I feel this would be most inappropriate. It would shut out a large number of students from the ambit of the selection process and, moreover, no student at that stage really knows whether they want to opt for the Civil Services or any other career. Today engineers, doctors, lawyers and MBA students are getting into the Civil Services and they are definitely enriching it.

Another idea that was floated was not to allot cadres or service on the basis of the UPSC marks but to add the professional course marks in the training academy and then decide. This would give rise to nepotism and favouritism and completely play havoc with the sanctity of the selection process. The current selection process and system of allotment of service and cadre suffers from no major infirmity and there is absolutely no need to interfere with it. The UPSC exam has stood the test of time for its fairness and no effort should be made to bring down its image.

The candidate selected in the IAS proceeds to the Lal Bahadur Shastri National Academy of Administration (LBSNAA) in Mussoorie for a two-year training programme. It comprises of a four-month foundational course in which members of all services participate, and is followed by a professional course at the academy for the IAS. All other Civil Services have their own professional academies. The IAS professional course includes a one-year attachment to the state cadre which primarily involves an attachment to a district to understand the fundamentals of running a district, which is by far the most interesting and challenging job that an officer handles in her entire career. Again, I feel the programme is well-structured and does not need any major change. Minor adjustments are always required in any system. The foundational course affords a wonderful opportunity to bond with officers of other services and many enduring friendships are built that last for life. This course develops a sense of camaraderie amongst all services which is an enriching experience. Constitution of India, principles of political science, Indian economy and public administration are some of the subjects taught. Since officers from all over India are there, culture programmes and musical evenings enliven the experience. There now being no tension of qualifying for the Civil Services, this is truly an enjoyable experience. The Mussoorie academy is a beautiful place. The infrastructure has vastly improved now, compared to our days and boasts of all modern facilities. Mussoorie itself is a beautiful hill station and the long walks to the market and back are memories to be cherished.

There is a one-week village visit during this period when officers go to the districts and spend time in a village trying to understand the real India. Those of us who were not from rural India found the village visit to be a revealing experience. The evenings at the Government guest house were, of course, full of mirth, jokes, stories, laughter and a lot of drinks and food. Then there is also a trek to different destinations in the Himalayas. The more adventurous chose difficult treks. However, all treks are interesting and exciting, and once again the bonding and camaraderie is long-lasting.

The one event I recall fondly is the election to the post of PMC (President Mess Committee). PMC is regarded as the representative of all probationers in all matters, apart from managing the mess. I don't know how but somehow, my friend Jawed Usmani, who was the topper of our batch convinced me to stand for the elections. There were four candidates in the fray and one of them was the acting PMC as he had prior experience of running a mess at the income tax academy in Nagpur and seemed to be the candidate most likely to win. To my utter surprise, the election became a serious political affair. The candidates began to rely on officers from their university or from the same geographical region. Politics is a language of its own. We had to make speeches which nobody heard seriously and there was lot of hooting and leg pulling. I found that I did not have a base which would ensure group votes. I was from St Stephen's College, from where a reasonable number of officers were at the academy. But one could never be sure whether Stephanians would come for voting as they had their typical contempt for such mundane activities. Jawed and I decided that personal contact with the maximum number of people would help and we also decided to focus on the silent category. Our strategy paid rich dividends and I won the elections. It was an elevating experience to become the PMC for the foundational course.

I remember that towards the end of the foundational course there used to be a 'formal dinner'. There was a high table where the PMC sat with the Director and his wife. Other members of the faculty and the mess secretary were also at the high table, with other officers sitting according to seats reserved for them on other tables. This was a formal occasion and you had to attend in formal dress. I had to give a coded signal to the mess manager to start serving the soup. The moment the soup was removed from the high table, after the director finished his helping, it was removed from the other tables, irrespective of whether they had consumed it or not. The same drill was repeated for the various courses of the dinner. Most officers complained bitterly of remaining hungry as they got very little time to eat and very small portions of the dish. At the end, there was a toast to the President of India, to the nation and to the service. Then the PMC gave his speech talking about the experiences of the foundational course and the camaraderie that developed between officers of different services. This was followed by the speech of the director. I recall that many officers came for the dinner in high spirits and laughed uproariously, long after the director had cracked a joke in his speech. So much for a formal dinner!

Thereafter, each service went to its professional academy and the IAS continued at the Mussoorie Academy. The professional course is quite well-structured with an emphasis on law, public administration and economics. There was a tribal study in which we went to the interior parts of the country to understand the life, culture and problems of the various tribes. There was also a Bharat Darshan with the objective of familiarizing the officers with various parts of the country. There was also an Army attachment where we were sent to the border areas to live with an Army regiment for a week to understand the conditions in which the defence forces live and work to safeguard the country. It was a truly humbling experience. On a lighter note, I remember some of us were invited for a drinking session and soon it became a test of how much alcohol civilian officers could tolerate compared to the armed forces officers.

I feel that the entire professional course has been well-designed and focuses primarily on district administration which is what would occupy the officer in the first ten to twelve years of his career. As a result of various expert committees, there are now three more phases of professional in-service trainings at various levels of an IAS officer's career, focusing on the skill set most relevant for that level with a special focus on the intricacies of public policy formulation. The experience sharing in these training programs is a great learning opportunity. Of course, one can argue for more domain-specific training programmes but that would have to follow a major reform which brings domain specialization into the careers of an IAS officer.

The professional course has almost a one-year-long district attachment. During the course of this, one goes through about four weeks of training at the State Academy of Administration where they are exposed to state laws, policies and problems of the concerned state. Special focus is on revenue administration. For some time the officer is attached to the state Secretariat with a particular department and also gets to meet the Chief Secretary, the Chief Minister and the Governor. We were also sent to Government of India to understand the workings of the parliament and the executive. We called upon the Prime Minister and the President of India. I recall we felt so proud of ourselves on such occasions. Recently, I believe, probationers are being attached to ministries in the Government of India for a couple of months to understand their working. I do not know if this is a great idea as it is too early in one's career to spend so much time in the Government of India. However, I guess the best thing to do would be to take the feedback of those who have gone through this attachment.

District attachment is real-life experience which no classroom training can substitute. I found it to be an interesting though quaint experience. Actually everything depends upon the district you are attached to and the personality of the District Collector. If the District Magistrate (DM) takes interest in your training then it can be a great learning experience otherwise it may be quite frustrating and you may feel that you are not learning much. Also, I feel officers should be sent to smaller, more rural districts because they will get in touch with the real India and get firsthand knowledge of the problems of the people. There is a disconcerting tendency these days for young officers to be using influence to decide their district training postings and often, they try and get posted to big cities. As Chief Secretary UP, I found that many officers wanted to be attached to district Noida, Ghaziabad, Agra or Lucknow. I made it a point to decline such requests, resist the pressure and post the young officers to backward districts like Bahraich, Gonda or Maharajganj. Of course, I did check who the DM was. A direct IAS officer is always a better training DM than a promoted officer but there have been a lot of exceptions. Even though the district training is structured with assignments to be submitted, it is largely dependent on how the DM treats you and guides you.

I was posted to Gorakhpur for my training and my friend Jawed Usmani was posted to Basti (the adjoining district). We had very similar experiences often leading to a weekly get together where we drowned our frustration in drink and food. We did learn how a probationer should not be treated or trained. That itself was quite a learning!

I recall that the moment I reached Gorakhpur, I walked to the office of the DM smartly and was ushered in by the peon with a red turban, who immediately recognized me. He called me 'Junt Saheb' (an acronym for joint magistrate which is what a young ICS/IAS officer was designated since the times of the British). My DM was a venerable old gentleman by the name of Balwant Singh, who was close to retirement. I smartly introduced myself. He raised his white, bushy eyebrows and looked questioningly at me. After some time, it dawned upon him as to who I was and he said in an irritated tone, 'These academy people do not even consult us and send officers for training.' Sensing my feeling of shock and utter dismay, he relented and motioned to a chair. He said, 'Now that you have come, make yourself comfortable'. He immediately addressed my creature comforts by asking for a room in the officer's hostel to be allotted to me and a cook and a peon made available. I could share a Jeep with a state civil service officer. He felt that he had done enough. I started explaining my training and my attachment to different offices and courts. Mr Balwant Singh was not too impressed and by now it was clear that I was wasting his time. He however spoke to the Additional District Magistrate (ADM) concerned and asked me to meet him. 'You can attend my meetings sometimes,' he told me as a final act of dismissal.

I came out of the room hugely disillusioned. I had notions of how young Joint Magistrates were treated by the DMs during the ICS days. I had read about how they stayed in the

Collector's Bungalow and had their meals with the Collector and his family and accompanied him to all official events.

I had no option but to organize my own training. The ADM was respectful and kind. However, after several months I felt that I was not learning enough and wanted to do some real work. I went to the DM and requested him to give me some office charges so that I could actually learn on the job. He readily agreed. A few days later, an office order was issued designating me as 'officer in-charge Bills'. I was shocked as this charge meant signing a lot of bills which were put up to me by the office. I only had to sign and there was no other involvement. I was quite furious and went up to the DM to complain. He looked as if I was really testing his patience but then recalled the order and gave me a Court to decide cases as additional subdivisional officer and also made me officer in-charge of the record room. This made me happy and I started working and actually began to learn something. It so happened that after some time, one SDM went on leave and I ran to the DM requesting him to give me charge of the subdivision. He looked at me for a long time but then relented and appointed me SDM, a charge I held for three months and this became my real learning period about district administration as I toured extensively in the villages and stayed at the tahsil and decided revenue and criminal cases.

The district training is followed by another couple of months at the Mussoorie Academy and then one is ready to start one's official career. The two years, training is a great learning experience, apart from being extremely enjoyable. It gives you some of the most memorable moments of your life.

The training is also very useful and though there is always room for improvement, it is on the whole, very well-structured.

There are those who take this training very seriously—PT and horse riding included. There are others who enjoy themselves to the hilt. Most use this period to get used to the idea of being an IAS officer and build lasting friendships with other colleagues. The amazing thing is that I found very little connection between the behaviour of the officers during training and their ultimate performance on the job. I remember an officer who was most cynical about the IAS and took no interest in his training, read books on religion and Tantra and submerged himself in liquor and tobacco. We wondered whether he would last. Imagine my surprise on being told a few years later that this officer was one of the legendary collectors of the North-east where he mingled completely with the culture and society and was revered. Similarly, some really hard working, serious officers surprisingly exhibited deviant behaviour in their careers and the most carefree ones became symbols of responsibility and dedication. Destiny plays a great part in how the career of an officer unfolds. It was amusing to see some really ambitious probationers look at the age and the cadre of their compatriots and try to work out the path to becoming Chief Secretary or Cabinet Secretary. They made a lot of predictions. None came true! You can never predict how far you will go and in which direction. So one should not worry about it at this stage and focus on doing their job as well as possible. In fact it is a waste of a career in the IAS if one is always planning for the future and not getting the maximum out of the present.

Getting into the IAS is just the beginning. It opens the gates to a career full of amazing possibilities and immense diversity. It is a job rich in content and experience but it all depends on what you make of it. Your attitude and desire to learn and grow further enriches the job. The job can give you a lot. It all depends what and how much you can take from it.

3

Life in the Districts

Every civil service aspirant is enamored of the halo around the post of the Collector and District Magistrate (DM) who is also called Deputy Commissioner in many states. An IAS officer reaches this post within five to six years of his career and moves further ahead after fifteen to sixteen years of service. Yet every officer fondly and proudly recalls his days as District Magistrate. One senior officer very candidly told me that there only three posts that matter: DM, CM and PM. Such is the authority and power that is vested in the institution of the DM! You meet any retired IAS officer or a very senior IAS officer and get him to talk about his career, and you will find that he will regale you with stories of his days as DM and how he resolved a law and order problem or settled a contentious issue. There was one very senior officer who retired as Secretary, Government of India but for some strange reason had never held charge of a district. But even when he would talk of his service days, he would reminisce about his time as Subdivisional Magistrate (SDM)!

At the time of joining the IAS, perhaps the one post that an aspirant is aware of is that of the District Magistrate. I remember my father always talking of the powers vested in the DM when he would try and motivate me to write the IAS exam. He would never tire of saying, 'At the age of less than thirty, the DM is virtually the king of the district.' Officers of other services resented this. My father who belonged to the Indian Forest Service was no exception. However, his experience only strengthened his desire to have his son become a DM. When I succeeded in the IAS exam, he was simply ecstatic.

The aura of the post may have dimmed over time but it still remains one of the most powerful jobs that one can aspire to and that too at such an early age. There was a time when the DM was the government at the district level and all the departments worked directly under him. This has now changed. He still represents the government at the district level but most departments have their independent departmental lines of reporting. Today, he is the Chief Coordinator and his powers are drawn from the fact that an adverse report by him against any departmental officer is enough to mar the career of the latter. Besides, every department of the government keeps the DM in the loop while implementing any of its schemes. Moreover, in the eyes of the citizens the DM is perceived as being powerful enough to get anything done.

The British ran this country using the ICS, whose basic foundation pillar was the institution of the Collector and District Magistrate. The two main responsibilities of the government in those days were collection of revenue and the maintenance of law and order. Both these functions were performed by the Collector and the District Magistrate at the district level. The work of the DM was supervised by the Commissioner who was the senior-most officer at the divisional level and such was the importance of this post that often the Commissioners were of an equal seniority to that of the Chief Secretary.

Prior to 1861, when the Indian Police Act came into existence, the Police's function was looked after exclusively by the DM. It was only after 1861 that the post of Superintendent Police (SP) came into existence. Normally at the district level, there would only be a handful of British officers – the DM, SP, Civil Surgeon and the District Judge. They worked hard and then socialized amongst themselves. I found in the remotest districts of UP, an old ramshackle building that was known as the officers, club. The clubs are functional only in a few districts now but were active during the British rule where officers played tennis with their families and later in the evening, had a drink and a good game of bridge. Their life definitely appears to be very idyllic and romantic.

It was the institution of the District Officer that held the empire together. It was a model of decentralized administration. In fact, I read a book by Peter Drucker, the modern management guru, and he analyzed this system of administration and rated it very highly. He says that this was a perfect example of governing large organizations through decentralization of power, authority and responsibility. The District Collector was the government at the district level and he along with the SP and DJ carried out the entire working of a district using their own initiative and administrative acumen. There was full autonomy and delegation of powers but they were accountable for the results. We can say that this system was made out of a necessity as the means of communication were archaic and there was little option but for the man on the spot to take a decision and be accountable for it. Today centralizing tendencies have become the norm in administration. Various levels want to exercise authority without bearing the responsibility. The entire governance gets diluted in this manner. The departments are fond of issuing government orders, making the DM personally responsible for results yet they bind him in fetters through numerous instructions and guidelines. The DM no longer enjoys the freedom and autonomy that he used to yet he still remains very powerful and the dream of every officer on entering the service is to hold charge of a district. When I was the Chief Secretary, I found most young officers and also those promoted from the State Civil Services meeting me and requesting to be posted as DM.

The supreme power of the DM in the British days can be illustrated by a few stories. I read somewhere that a DM in northern India, on going through his official correspondence, came across a government order that he did not agree with. On the margin of the government order, he firmly wrote that this order would not apply to his district! Imagine a DM trying to do this today. Even if a scheme is irrational or not relevant for his district, he has to implement it and send reports in countless monitoring formats. A classic example is the Mahatma Gandhi Rural Employment Guarantee Act (MGNREGA) in western UP, where the market wage rate is far higher than that prescribed in MNREGA and no labour is likely to turn up for jobs under this scheme but the poor

Collector has to strain his innermost resources to meet the targets given to him.

A supposed story relates to Mr Wyndham, who was Collector of Mirzapur District of UP for almost eighteen years. Mr Wyndham obviously loved his district and used to tour extensively to the remotest areas. File work obviously suffered. It is said that his poor Personal Assistant (PA) found that unattended paper and files filled a couple of rooms in the Collector's bungalow. The PA hesitatingly brought this to the notice of the Collector. Mr Wyndham was unruffled. The district at that time was facing floods and the River Ganga was in spate. 'Keep all the files in the boats and accompany me on my visit to the flood-affected areas. I will dispose of the files during my inspections,' is what he is believed to have told the PA. The PA acted accordingly. Once on the river, the Collector began to clear files in earnest. As the PA read out each file, the Collector asked him to throw the file into the river. Soon the entire lot of files found a watery grave for itself. The poor PA was trembling as he realized that he was responsible for the custody of the files. Mr Wyndham had an ingenious solution to this. 'Take down a letter to the Chief Secretary.' He is believed to have said and dictated how his boat had almost capsized in the floods and a whole lot of files had fallen into the river. However, his PA had risked his life and jumped into the river to salvage the papers but did not succeed and for his act of exemplary courage and dedication to duty, the Collector strongly recommended that a state-level award should be given to the PA!

Well, the story could be a product of one's imagination but does indicate the kind of independence and autonomy that a Collector held at that time. It is said that so enamored was Mr Wyndham of the post of Collector that he refused promotion and proceeded on tour whenever his transfer orders came and did not return to his headquarters till the orders were cancelled.

Even when I was in a district before the telecom revolution, one could get away with a lot. I recall that when an incident of police firing killing a student took place in Ghazipur district of eastern UP in the early 80's, the Home Secretary rang me up and sounded very agitated. 'Why have you young officers become so trigger-happy?' He asked in a voice dripping with sarcasm. I mumbled some explanation but the grilling went on. I then adopted the evasive method. I shouted 'Hello' a couple of times and then said, 'I am sorry, sir, but I cannot hear you. I will send a detailed report immediately,' and put down the receiver. The report was then prepared at leisure, covering all possible queries and sent. I may add that the report was prepared by a seasoned Deputy Superintendent of Police whose ticket to fame was the ability to draft brilliant reports in such sensitive matters which would stand scrutiny from the most difficult inquiry commission.

I cannot help but relate another story told to me by a senior officer. I doubt its authenticity but it highlights the romance and halo surrounding the institution of the District Magistrate. There was a district which was perpetually plagued by communal riots. The DM was a brilliant officer who worked very hard to control the riots, which lasted about a week. After things became normal, a complaint about the DM reached the state headquarters. It was said that the DM was spotted in an open jeep with a pretty girl driving around the city which had just witnessed such a major riot. The Chief Secretary rang up the DM asking him to explain his behavior. The DM said that the reasons were both official and personal, and wanted to know which one the Chief Secretary wanted to know. Amused, the Chief Secretary asked him to give both the reasons. The DM replied that the official explanation was that the riots had greatly affected the sense of security of the people and they were still unsure if everything was normal. There was no better way to give a message of normalcy than the DM driving a jeep with his girlfriend by his side all over the city. The Chief Secretary saw the logic in this rather strange explanation but then wanted to know the personal reason too. The DM is supposed to have said, 'Sir, I was exhausted after a week of handling riots and wanted to relax. What better way of becoming stress-free than driving around in an open jeep with your girlfriend?' I do not know how the Chief Secretary reacted nor do I know how long after this conversation did the DM last in the district. However, what mattered was that the DM had controlled the riots, and also that the personality, behaviour and attitude of a DM has a tremendous impact on the psyche of the people.

There is no doubt that the District Magistrate has, by tradition, unquestioned authority in his district and if he has leadership qualities he can get almost anything done. A very senior officer who was my boss told me how he had been posted as District Magistrate of a distant, difficult hill district called Chamoli when there was a major cloudburst and the connecting roads to the district and its towns had been washed away. It was a very critical situation and no assistance could come from outside the state. He had with him a couple of Deputy Collectors and Tahsildars (revenue department officers). He called them and gave them full authority to take decisions and carry on relief activities and told each one of them to behave as if he was the Collector. The result was that without any outside help, excellent relief measures were carried out and the people of the district still remember the work done and often talk about it.

In most states, the DM is the support system of the administration. I have found that if you want to make any scheme a success, you must involve the DM and if the DM is committed then the rest follows. I recall that as Chief Secretary, I made it a point to associate the DMs with the priority programmes of the states. For instance, we wanted to improve the power position in the state and a record number of transmission substations and transmission lines had to be constructed. The progress was slow. We decided to make the DM the Chairman of the committee to monitor this programme, and I reviewed it every fortnight with them over video conferencing. The result was that all the required substations were constructed and operational within a year. Similarly, we wanted to control line losses (power transmission and distribution losses), a major reason for which was power thefts. We involved the DMs and started a drive against illegal power connections. More than 50,000 new connections were granted within a week and line losses reduced significantly. In fact, a Collector of district Shravasti, which was amongst the most backward districts of UP, did such outstanding work that this became known as the Shravasti model. Nikil Shukla, the DM, brought down the line losses to 15 per cent from over 40 per cent. In return, we gave twenty hours of uninterrupted power supply to the district, as had been promised.

I had my own personal experience of what is possible; we were able to implement a total literacy programme in district Agra in 1992–93. As DM I was committed to the project and mobilized the efforts of all the stakeholders and citizens of the district. This was a volunteer-based programme and I went personally to block headquarters and villages to address the people and motivate them to join the movement for literacy and also recruit young boys and girls as volunteers. I roped in all the administrative officers and allotted them a block each. They went and engaged with the people of the allotted blocks and personally supervised the literacy classes. It was clear that the literacy project would succeed only if the proper environment for it was created. The volunteers, under the guidance of officers and teachers, moved from village to village to create the awareness for literacy. Door-to-door visits were arranged. Street plays, songs and dances were created by these teams of young people to focus on the positive effects of literacy. We commissioned mobile vans which went to each village and along with movie shows and dance performances, gave the subtle message of literacy. We honoured the volunteers by calling them soldiers for literacy and gave them badges to this effect. This allowed them entry into government offices and they got respect from the rest of society. The new learners were motivated by using novel methods. For instance, we encouraged new learners to write postcards to the Collector about any grievances of their village, like the problem of drinking water. I would respond to that new learner by writing a personal letter to her. Imagine her joy when the village postman went around announcing that the Collector had written a letter to 'Shanti Devi'. Her respect in the village shot up by a mile. In this manner, I was able to create a learning environment which was essential for literacy classes to run effectively. This was possible only because I led from the front as the Collector and all the officers, Pradhans and others realized that they would be in the good books of the Collector if they performed well in this project.

Officers toured villages extensively to inspect literacy centres and ensure an adequate supply of books and stationery. Books were especially developed for new learners by having workshops at the district level where education experts and teachers were involved. Thereafter, the volunteers who were to actually teach were imparted extensive training by master trainers who had in turn been oriented by resource persons. The volunteers not only taught the new learners but they visited each home to ensure attendance. The zeal of these youth, especially girls, had to be seen to be believed. We allowed them to be innovative at their level and they did it so beautifully! It became a matter of pride for these volunteers to see that the learners in their class did the best they could.

The net result was that within a year, the Agra district was declared totally literate—5.5lakh people in the age group of fifteen to forty-five—after an evaluation done by the Government of India. All this was possible only because it had become a passion for me as Collector. This only proves the point that such is the capacity of the institution of the Collector that anything that he or she puts their weight behind is bound to materialize.

Often I find that people argue against the institution of the Collector and tend to brand it as colonial. We should not look at all institutions created during the colonial regime with coloured glasses. As I already elaborated, this institution is time tested and conforms to the highest principles of management. Some argue that an elected functionary would be a better option. However, we have seen from the experience of the Panchayati Raj that an elected functionary finds it difficult to remain neutral, impartial and objective. Also their approach tends to be localized and short term, and it may often be in their interest to perpetuate the status quo. The Collector belongs to a cadre service (IAS) and he is able to have a broad vision and keep the development of the state in totality in his focus. Besides, there is no need to tinker with a system that is delivering results. The most recent examples of this has been the handling of the Coronavirus pandemic by the District Magistrate who is the person authorized under the Epidemics Act to take all possible action.

The IAS service would not be able to deliver if the officers are not posted as Collectors during their careers. It is in the district that the young officer experiences the reality of India. He is confronted by the socio-economic reality, the extent of poverty and extreme backwardness. He also gets to realize how the problems can be tackled and how and why the lofty and idealistic schemes fail. This practical grounding provides the IAS officer with a very strong base and this is the basic upper hand that he has over other services and specialists. In all my senior postings, I used my experience in the districts as a frame of reference to formulate policies and projects. It would not be an exaggeration to say that the essence of IAS is the district posting.

I feel thrilled when I see so many young Collectors using innovative approaches to deliver public services. Nowadays, a large number of engineering and management graduates are joining the IAS and whereas questions may be raised about their wasting the technical knowledge that they acquired, I find that such diversity only makes the IAS stronger. These young engineers are technology savvy and I find that many of them have developed apps and monitoring systems which have made the administration stronger. I recall that one Collector started Lokvani in UP which was an IT-based grievance redressal system where a complaint could be registered and responded to within a specified time period. This model was replicated throughout UP and also won the Prime Minister's Award for Governance.

Another Collector in district Badaun of UP started a movement called 'Daliya Jalao' through which he eliminated the scourge of manual scavenging in his district, and motivated the community to build and use toilets, leading to a major transformation in the health and hygiene of the district. This happened before the 'Swachh Bharat Mission' was launched. There are many examples like this which only go to show that the Collector is around whom the entire administration revolves and he can deliver anything if he is committed to it and has the right qualities of leadership. I have found that this post makes leaders out of seemingly ordinary officers. The motivation and the power and public acclaim is such that even a subdued, meek and introverted officer changes into a dynamo, powering the various schemes and projects in his district. Some of the most outstanding Collectors have been boys and girls from rural backgrounds who look simple, do not talk much, are not very articulate but understand the pulse of the people and deliver brilliant results. In fact, no serious efforts have been made to document the innovations and achievements of young Collectors and this is the reason why the common citizen is unaware of the tremendous contribution that they are making.

A stint in the districts involves posting as Subdivisional Magistrate (SDM), Chief Development Officer (CDO) or equivalent. Normally, the posting as SDM is for two years but prepares the grounds for an officer to take over as DM later on. I recall the pride I felt when I joined as SDM straight after training at the Mussoorie Academy. I found myself being addressed as 'Hakim Pargana' which literally means king of the subdivision. It was great to inspect villages and development works, attend to court work, meet people and solve their problems. It was deeply satisfying and uplifted one's self esteem.

Things have changed now to some extent but at the time one joined this service, the subdivision was a shocking exposure to the realities of rural India. I recall that I was posted to Derapur subdivision of Kanpur district of UP which happened to be the most backward subdivision of the district with very poor connectivity. I was put in a ramshackle, dilapidated Public Works Department (PWD) guest house which had no electricity or running water. Dutifully in the morning, my help would bring me two buckets of water from a nearby well. For lighting we used lanterns and slept outside in the open air. Despite these apparent hardships, for even a person like me who had grown up in an urban setting in the midst of all amenities, did not resent this life. There was a uniqueness about it which made it quite exciting.

One tends to learn many lessons which assist you in your future career. For instance, I remember holding an internal meeting when I was told that the local MLA had come to see me. He sent in his name. Since I was in the midst of a meeting I did not call him in for at least half an hour. The MLA was furious and made quite a scene and I realized my mistake. I learnt that you must extend all possible courtesy to an elected public representative as he has been elected by the people and if his ego is hurt he will complain against you and make your life miserable. There was yet another MLA, a dashing young firebrand, who was known to be very rude and rough in his behaviour. It so happened that my subdivision was severely affected by floods which damaged all the roads and bridges and there was no connectivity to the district headquarters. I was on my own and put in all possible effort to provide relief to the people. I was going around from one marooned village to another, evacuating people and providing them with food, shelter and medical assistance. I got a message from the young MLA to come and meet him. I sent a reply that I was touring the flood-affected areas by boat and on foot, and would not be able to come to his village but that he was welcome to accompany me. He did so and he was amazed at the round-the-clock relief work that was being undertaken. His entire tone and demeanour changed and he became one of my greatest supporters. The lesson I learnt was that the public representatives, when they see the kind of work that is being done with total integrity, impartiality and dedication, they begin to admire and support you.

I also learnt a rather unhappy lesson. I remember the state government had ordered a month-long drive to give the schedule castes possession of land which had been allotted to them by the government to alleviate their condition of poverty and landlessness. It was a tough task as the socio-economic structure of the village was such that the strong and powerful upper caste would forcibly take over this land and begin cultivating it. I took this assignment very seriously and went from village to village personally and ensured that the original person allotted got back the possession of his land which had been taken away from him. At the end of the month, I had achieved 70 per cent of my target. The commissioner held a meeting to review the progress. Every subdivision in the district had reported 100 per cent achievement except me. Naturally the commissioner was wild and would not listen to any of my pleas. He was caustic in his comments towards me and said that he expected a young IAS officer to perform better. I felt humiliated after all the hard work that I had put in and had genuinely given possession to the landless by personally visiting the spot. The others had relied purely on reports passed on to them. After the meeting, I approached my Collector and spoke to him about how I was feeling. He patted me on the back and said, 'Alok, I know you have done excellent work but you must learn "*duniyadari*" also.' What he meant was that along with work, you have to be worldly-wise too. I narrated my tale of woe to my Tahsildar, a white-haired old man and veteran of several administrative battles. He smiled at me kindly and asked me for three days' time to recheck the figures. After the stipulated time, he came to me with a revised statement showing 100 per cent achievement. 'There was some mistake in the earlier statement,' he told me and I realized what 'duniyadari' meant. I signed the amended statements and sent it to the Collector but did not relax in my efforts and kept visiting villages and actually delivering possession of the land to the landless.

The fact here is that whenever there is a major drive ordered by the government on an important scheme which is monitored at the highest level, the content of the reports filed is far more important than the substance of the actual work. Nobody wants to face the realities and instead expects 100 per cent performance. If a young officer out of missionary zeal wants to report the truth, then he is likely to be singled out. I strongly feel that it is the duty of the senior officer to insist on a factually correct position being reported; otherwise the entire objective of the scheme or programme is lost in bundles of paper. It is the outcome at the field that should be the focus and not imaginary statements being put up on monitoring formats to appease senior officers and ministers. Sadly, I find that today the reverse is true and instead of allowing the Collector to function as a field officer, he is buried under volumes of paperwork and reports which tie him to his desk and lead to the detriment of the welfare of the citizens.

As a Collector one must realize that your subordinates will always give you the information that you want. The Tehsildars and Block Development Officers are real magicians for whom the word 'impossible' does not exist and they are adept at meeting targets. However, they respond to signals from the top and if a Collector encourages honesty in reporting them, then they will comply. Whenever a Collector inspects a Tahsil or a Block he would have a beautifully bound booklet depicting targets and achievements under various programmes put up before him. If you glance through it, you will get the impression that everything is in perfect order. But if you go deeper and question it, then the truth will come tumbling out. It is important for a Collector or a supervisory officer to have the ability to perceive the reality hidden behind the maze of tabular statements dished out to him. He should also be careful of the efforts to distract him by the serving of sumptuous snacks and tea!

It is imperative to ensure that actual development takes place and the people benefit. Regular inspection of development works is an absolute necessity. There is no substitute for this and a system of inspection down the line by all officers needs to be designed and monitored. There is no better way of improving the public service delivery than by actually inspecting the realities at the field level. I would reiterate that anything that the DM and his team start inspecting and focusing on begins to give immediate results. For instance we all lament the poor state of primary education in the state, and teacher absenteeism is often highly prevalent. I have seen many DMs themselves inspecting schools and making education department officers, CDO and SDMs do the same. Action against errant teachers is taken and the result is that teacher absenteeism goes down significantly, improving the quality of primary education. Similar is the case with doctors and primary health centres and district hospitals. Regular inspection and monitoring of attendance leads to significant improvement in the healthcare services being offered. However, I feel that inspection needs to go beyond merely checking attendance. The inspecting officer should try and ascertain the learning achievement levels of the students and the accountability of the teachers can be fixed according to the outcome of these inspections. The inspection reports need to be uploaded onto a computer for others to see. In the same vein, inspection of a district hospital to see the condition of the patients being treated, availability of medicines and the status of the wards, operation theaters and functioning of other equipment and the general cleanliness and hygiene in the hospital can considerably improve things. Inspections must look at all aspects to ensure better public service delivery. Every monitoring of a development programme should be done with the outcome in mind. The entire administration has to become outcome-oriented if the Civil Service has to justify its existence.

Technology is a game changer and leads to much better monitoring. Photographs can be uploaded; videos can be put up in specific WhatsApp groups for regular and continuous review. The citizen is also much more empowered. I find that armed with a smartphone, the ordinary citizen takes pictures or videos of development schemes and sends it to the authorities. Much better supervision is possible in this manner. Moreover, biometric system of attendance, IVRS system of monitoring schemes like midday meals have proved greatly beneficial. I find young officers developing specific apps which greatly enhance the flow of information and lead to better redressal of grievances. I recall my days as Collector when we used to go from one village to another to see if the state tube wells were functional or not. However, during my tenure as Chief Secretary, the irrigation department developed a state-of-the-art command centre where real-time monitoring of each and every tube well was being done. Technology gives information but there have to standard operating procedures to ensure prompt and effective action on the inputs provided. Young officers need to be encouraged to use technology to come up with innovative methods for monitoring government schemes. It must be remembered that a district is a basic unit of implementation of all policies. Recently I read a statement that three things are required to bring about faster and affective development— Implementation, Implementation and Implementation!

Often we hear people saying the policies are good but the implementation is poor. I have reason to quarrel with this statement. I feel policies are often designed without taking into account the intricacies of implementation. A good policy must factor in all the details which can make it succeed at the execution level. I will come to this later when I discuss policy formulation. For now, I want to emphasize that the Collector should mobilize his team to implements schemes according to his intent. He has to conduct structured meetings to monitor and review various projects and schemes. It is important that these meetings are effective and have a problem-solving approach. Today in most states, the Collector is the Chairman of more than 100 committees and it thus becomes extremely important for him to prioritize his time according to the signals emanating from the state headquarters and, of course, the local-and district-level imperatives. There is also a disturbing trend these days for the departments at the state level to put responsibility of the Collector for almost everything and making little effort to make their own departmental officers accountable. As Chief Secretary, I took great pains to amend government orders which sought to make the Collector personally responsible. It is true that the Collector is the core of all that happens in a district yet his role is supervisory and that of coordination. Basic responsibility for the content and quality of development schemes must be with the departmental officers. Besides, making the Collector personally responsible for various aspects of implementation leads to a situation where the Collector can be subjected to enquiries and has to suffer for no reason. This kind of attitude creates apprehension in the mind of the Collector who becomes wary of signing papers and starts raising all kinds of objections on file to protect his interests but in the process, government work suffers.

A very sad incident took place in UP where a couple of young, bright and honest Collectors had to face the ordeal of a CBI enquiry simply because they approved a contract related to midday meal distribution in schools which was put up to them, duly recommended by a committee of officers. I found that this was a big blow to the self-confidence of these outstanding officers. I feel we must not involve the District Officer too much in approvals and sanctions as he does not have time to go into the details and has to append his signature on the basis of trust. If the District Officer is dishonest, he becomes party to the corrupt activities and the administration suffers and if he is honest then he becomes vulnerable to enquiries and related harassment. In either case, it impacts his ability to perform his true role of supervising, monitoring, coordinating and leading the development of his district. The Collector, therefore, has to be kept away from detailed processes so that he can keep any eye on everything like a watchdog. If he finds some wrongdoing then he can, at his own level, order an enquiry which he would not be able to do if he is himself made a party in each and every decision and process.

In the government there is always a strong tendency to create more and more paperwork and I found that every department is extremely fond of developing and prescribing endless monitoring formats. The District Officer is made accountable for signing and sending these statements with the result that development on paper takes precedence over real work. We started a system in UP of having a development agenda for the state. The idea was, indeed, laudable because it gave a sense of direction to the entire administration. However, as Chief Secretary I found that more than 200 formats were developed to monitor this agenda and the crushing burden of this fell on the hapless District Officer. In review meetings I could sense the frustration of District Officers and I had to intervene personally and override strident objections of departments to make sure that no more than 20 per cent of these formats were relevant and needed to be signed by the District Officer. Any other information required could be taken directly from the departmental officers.

I strongly feel that the District Officer must be given a lot of space to use his initiative and innovative skills to bring about development of his district and set his own priorities. There is no need to force everything down on the District Officer from the top. Some untied funds must be kept at the disposal of the District Officer to be used to attend to local problems as the resolution of these would have a far greater impact on the people than uniform schemes for the entire state. Some years ago, with this purpose in mind, the concept of a district plan came into existence where resources were meant to be allotted to the districts to encourage them to plan for the district and take up projects which were most relevant for them. However, the way these district plans have worked in practice leaves a lot to be desired. The district plans are not reflective of the district reality at all.

I still vividly recall the day when district planning was introduced in UP. The year was 1981 and I was a young SDM in district Chamoli holding charge of the district, as my DM had gone on a long leave. We were palpably excited by the project and I planned several meetings with officers and consulted public representatives and other stakeholders, and prepared a comprehensive district plan. The Divisional Commissioner took a review which went on for several days as we presented our plans and there was a lot of discussion and debate, and it certainly gave us a great sense of empowerment. But slowly, over the years, it has been converted into a routine annual exercise. There is a minister incharge of each district who visits the district and holds a meeting with all officers and public representatives to give final shape to the plan. I found that most ministers take this very causally and often nearly the entire year goes by without the meeting being convened. As Chief Secretary, I tried to re-establish the glory of the district plan but I found there was so much delay in district plan proposals reaching the state headquarters that they were not reflected in the annual budget at all. Despite my best effort, a couple of powerful ministers did not hold the district plan meetings till December and the budget proposals were finalized without the crucial inputs from district plans. Further, I found that rather than leaving it to the districts to formulate schemes, as was the intention, the schemes were designed at the state headquarters by the departments and mechanically made a part of the district plan. This created a situation when most of the funds of the district plan were already committed to fulfill the objectives of the state-level schemes. I feel that the District Officer along with elected representatives is most suited to prepare a district development plan and he should be allowed to do so and sufficient funds should be allocated for the purpose. This will lead to a decentralized model of development which is essential today.

There have been recent amendments to the constitution, devolving a lot of functions and powers to the urban and rural local bodies, and there have been changes in the Panchayati Raj Act and recommendation of Finance Commissions which have devolved a lot of funds and functions to the Panchayats. This has greatly changed the complexion of development at the district level. Local planning to resolve local problems now becomes possible. In fact, one spin off of this has been that the post of the Pradhan has become greatly sought after. The elections to the three-tier Panchayat structure are fought bitterly using a lot of muscle and money power, which eventually leads to frequent charges of corruptions against the Pradhans and others. It is in the interest of good governance to decentralize development work and so there is nothing wrong with the

District Zila Parishads and the Village Panchayats being flush
with funds. It is true that there are allegations of financial
impropriety but this is the direction that development must
take. Village-level democracy should and would ensure
utilization of resources in the interest of the maximum number
of people. Today, an enlightened Pradhan can convert his
village into an oasis of development. Many Pradhans have
done so but it is important that systems are put in place to
ensure accountability. It would be better if instead of vesting
all the powers in one person, the Pradhan, other members of
the Gram Panchayat who are dormant and powerless should
be made accountable and vested with powers to enable them
to contribute to the development process.

In the above context, the role of the District Officer
and his team becomes all the more important as he has to
guide, mentor and provide leadership to these nascent
Panchayati Raj Institutions. Any citizen having a grievance
with the Panchayat can approach the District Officer and
he has to play a balancing role. He should not become
trigger-happy and start taking action against Pradhans on
the slightest pretext. The Collector should not interfere too
much in the functioning of these institutions of democratic
decentralization. There is no doubt that he has to ensure that
public money is spent properly.

The district level developments administration structure
has been greatly affected by this increased flow of funds
directly to the Panchayats. Earlier, the Chief Development
Officer or CDO of the Zila Parishad was the top official in
the development hierarchy and he was assisted by a District
Development Officer and Project Director. The basic unit of

development was the block, headed by a Block Development Officer. Now the powers of District Panchayat Raj Officer (DPRO) and field-level Panchayat functionaries has greatly increased, leading to a certain dysfunctionality. For obvious reasons these post have become greatly sought after and now the District Panchayat Raj Officer does not want to report to the District Development Officer or the CDO. The major negative fallout of this has been the erosion of the power and authority of the office of the Block Development Officer. It is important to empower the institution of the BDO so that he becomes the principle coordinator at the block level for all development departments.

Despite the thrust on democratic decentralization, the devolution of powers to the urban and rural local bodies is likely to remain on paper as the state-level politicians and bureaucracy are opposed to this since they see it as a dilution of their powers. In UP, numerous committees have recommended democratic decentralization but their reports, being inconvenient, are gathering dust. In reality, functions, functionaries and funds have not been delegated to the local bodies. Some states like Kerala, Maharashtra and Karnataka have taken the initiative to strengthen their rural local bodies but this is not the case in the larger states like UP and Bihar where, possibly, such governance reforms are very much required. I feel that the District Officer today must have a healthy respect for the democratic and elected local bodies and he should facilitate their working. This requires a change in the mindset of the District Officer as he will have to relinquish a lot of his powers but it does not mean in any way that the responsibility of the District Officer towards the development of his district is reduced. There is a lot of work that he can still do and it is his duty to guide and mentor these local bodies. I personally feel that despite the necessity of democratic decentralization, the Collector should continue to be involved in development work. In fact, this is the most exciting part of the job of a District Officer and he cannot truly claim to be a leader in the district if his role in development is minimized. We may like it or not but the truth is that in our country, development still revolves around the institution of the District Officer/Collector. The common man perceives that the Collector is a single point for ventilation and resolution of all grievances and this faith of the ordinary citizen makes the involvement of the Collector in development works inevitable.

Just like in revenue (land) matters it is the Lekhpal (Patwari) who matters and in Police it is the local police station incharge, in rural development it is the Village-Level Officer (VLO) around whom all development schemes rotate. Far too much is expected of this functionary who is not adequately trained or motivated to carry out this job. They have to be conversant with details of various government schemes and should have basic computer skills as most monitoring systems now require the use of computers. Training of the elected village-, block- and district-level Panchayat functionaries is also very important to enable them to perform their duties properly.

The Collector has to involve himself not only with the schemes related to rural development and agriculture but he has to be concerned with monitoring all other aspects of development like education, health, social welfare, environment and power situation in the district. The Collector has to be a leader and have all the qualities of team building, motivating and inspiring officers, interacting with various stakeholders, planning and implementing projects and creating a result and outcome-oriented work culture. The responsibility is onerous and challenges multifarious but no other job in the public or private sector gives this kind of diversity, scope for innovation and ability to bring about a positive change in the quality of life of the people.

Urban development has now become a major area of focus for the government as realization has dawned that cities are the engines of growth. Cities are governed by elected local bodies with the larger municipal corporations having an elected Mayor and the smaller ones having an elected Chairman. In the larger Municipal Corporation there is the post of Municipal Commissioner and also that of the Vice Chairman of Development Authority. In most states, these post are held by the senior officers of the IAS perhaps of the same seniority as the District Magistrate. The services offered by these local bodies are generally not of the required standards as they suffer from a shortage of funds and poor governance. The Jawaharlal Nehru Urban Renewal Mission and the Smart Cities project have provided funds and ideas to bring about a qualitative change in municipal governance, finance and the level of facilities offered by them to the citizens. I would like to point out that the assignment of the Municipal Commissioner is an extremely challenging and rewarding one. The citizens are vocal and demand immediate attention to their problems and the Municipal Commissioner has to be alert, responsive, dynamic and have a total hands-on approach. In some ways, this assignment is far more difficult than that of a District Magistrate as it does not carry with it the statutory powers which the post of a DM has. Besides, the DM has the support of the police whereas the Municipal Commissioner is more often than not on his own. The job is also more demanding because in urban areas, issues like the garbage not being removed, failure of water supply and sewer overflowing or street lights not being functional are directly connected with the daily lives of citizens. The urban public is also more educated and demanding, and the Municipal Commissioner has to constantly be on his toes. The results of his actions are also immediately visible with there being public satisfaction if the decision succeeds but a lot of resentment if things do not work out. The officer then has to face the fury of the people and the media, which is also very alert and sensitive to issues relating to urban development. There are a large number of elected corporators putting pressure on the Commissioner and often they are more concerned about getting contracts or employment for their people. The Commissioner has to wade through these pressures and deliver public services to citizens. Often the interference of the elected corporators can make life miserable for the officer but then it also provides great training in the functioning of grass-root democracy. I feel with the increasing trends towards urbanization, an IAS officer should have the field experience of the posting of a Municipal Commissioner, without which it would be difficult for him to formulate policy for development of the urban areas. Sooner rather than later, despite the reluctance, the state governments will have to devolve functions, functionaries and funds to the elected local bodies in line with the amendments made to the constitution. I feel there is a crying need for professionalization of the municipal cadre. The municipal service officers now need to have a qualification like an MBA so that they actually function as city managers and they need expertise to handle issues like solid and liquid waste management, water supply and others.

The District Magistrate is not directly answerable for issues relating to urban services in big cities, where there is a Municipal Commissioner. However, because of the inherent nature of the post of the DM and the propensity of the people to go to him for every grievance, the DM cannot ignore urban problems. Moreover, issues like removal of encroachment would require complete support of the DM. Further, more often than not, there are agitations relating to water supply or poor sanitation or any other urban problem and these tend to become law and order issues, the resolution of which requires an active role for the DM. The Municipal Commissioner, thus, has to work in close coordination with the DM.

In smaller cities, where there is an Executive Officer incharge of the corporation, the DM has to own the entire responsibility of urban administration and he fulfills the role of a Municipal Commissioner in these cities. Once again it's clear that the quality of being sensitive to grievances of the people and being prompt in taking decisions will enable a DM to handle this responsibility properly. With the right approach, he can bring about change in the quality of life of the citizens.

The term Collector emanated from the basic nature of the job during the colonial regime, which was to collect land revenue which at that time was the most important source of revenue for the government. Today land revenue is so marginal that it is almost negligent, yet revenue administration is still the foundation of the institution of the Collector and District Magistrate. The system of revenue administration involves settlement of land in rural areas, ensuring title of land holder, resolving disputes and handling litigation related to all matters of land. Even though land revenue is insignificant today, the entire revenue collection machinery is deployed to collect other dues like bank dues, and electricity charges using the power vested in them through the mechanism of arrears of land revenue.

Nowadays, revenue administration is often ignored by the Collectors and their team because it is actually routine and not as glamorous as development or law and order which gives the Collector far more publicity than the grind of revenue case work. Yet it cannot be denied that most people in rural areas have grievances directly related to the Tahsil. In UP, we have a 'Tahsil Divas' once every week to resolve the problems relating to land and other related issues. The crowd on these days is to be seen to be believed which shows how important the problems related to land are in the lives of the people.

A large number of people require income certificate, birth certificate and other similar documents and these are provided by the revenue administration and are essential for getting jobs and admission in universities or getting benefits of government welfares schemes. Perhaps the most important document is a copy of the record of rights (Land Title). This document is central to the life of people living in rural areas. There is a remarkable book by an author who was also a civil servant titled *Raag Darbari* by Shrilal Shukla, which is a beautiful satire on the working of the bureaucracy and the politico-economic structure of a village. In this book there is a lame person who wants a copy of his land records and persistently tries but does not succeed till the end of the book. This is just an illustration of how revenue administration is inextricably linked to the lives of the people. Good revenue administration makes a big difference to the satisfaction level of the people. It is a well-known fact that the perception of how a government is working depends upon the response a citizen gets at the Tahsil, Thana and the Block. Governments come up with grandiose schemes but ignore the basics, where a lot of improvement is possible without spending huge amount of funds. The role of the Collector and the efficiency with which he works is a major determinant of the satisfaction of the people with the day-to-day activity of administration.

Computerization of land records has been a game changer. Transparency and easy availability of land records has reduced the pernicious influence that the village Patwari had on the lives of the people by having the power to manipulate the entries in the land records. This computerization was first taken up by the 'Bhoomi' innovation in the state of Karnataka and was spearheaded by the IAS officers of the state including District Collectors. This only goes to show how a creative Collector can transform governance at the field level. Digitization of village maps is at an advance stage and will further demystify land issues. Computerization of the court work relating to revenue matters has also greatly reformed revenue administration at the district level. Now obtaining the essential certificates has also been made possible online, reducing the interface with the Tahsildar and Patwari and eliminating harassment and corruption to a large degree.

Revenue court work is an area which receives a lot of neglect from Collectors and Subdivisional Officers. Court work requires the discipline of sitting in the court, listening to lawyers, passing orders and dictating judgments. It certainly is hard work and not very glamorous but it is extremely vital and a young IAS officer as Collector, if he pays attention to court work, can bring about a sea change in the work culture of the district and satisfy people. Unfortunately despite the computerization of revenue courts, the pendency of cases remains huge, largely due to the fact that the presiding officers rarely sit in the court and also because of the tendency of some lawyers to continuously ask for adjournment. It is a sad commentary on the governance to see cases pending in revenue courts for years, sometimes as much as ten years. Imagine the tension it must be creating for the litigant and the unrest and the conflict it must be leading to at the village level. There is a simple principle of administration—that which is monitored and evaluated gets done. At the state level and that of the board of revenue, the revenue court work needs to be monitored strictly and diligently, and it should invariably form a part of the performance appraisal of the Collector. After the amendment to the criminal procedure court, the power to try criminal cases has been taken away from the District Magistrate and given to the judiciary. If Collectors ignored revenue court work then this power will also be taken away from them sooner rather than later and ultimately lead to the demise of the institution of the Collector.

Land acquisition is another major responsibility of the Collector and this is the basis for various infrastructure and industry-related development projects. A delay in declaring the compensation award by the Collector and subsequent court cases often derail a project completely. The new land acquisition act has made the process simpler by prescribing reasonably high rates of compensation but then one also has to prepare a concrete relief and rehabilitation plan. Direct negotiation with the farmers is often the best way of deciding the compensation and prevents litigation. As Chief Secretary of UP, we implemented the 328 km Lucknow–Agra Expressway within twenty-two months and the work was of very high quality. This was possible because within six months, the local Collectors who were empowered by us went from village to village and fixed the compensation through negotiations. The role of the Collector and his team is very important in deciding the compensation rate and distribution of the money to the affected people. The Collector has to be careful otherwise there are several vested interests involved in this and there is a lot of scope for corruption at various levels. I recall when I was district magistrate of Ghaziabad, a rich western U.P. district, land acquisition was one of the major activities of the Collector due to the industrialization of the area. One day, as I drove to my office I found a large number of private cars lined up outside the gate of the Tahsil. My curiosity got the better of me and I tried to ascertain the cause and was pleasantly surprised to find that the cars belonged to the Patwaris of the district who had come for a meeting. Land acquisition was the obvious explanation for their affluence.

The most onerous responsibility of the District Officer is to maintain law and order as the District Magistrate. He does this in collaboration with the Superintendent of Police. If everything is peaceful, the DM may not get any credit for it. However, in the event of a communal riot, he is liable to be transferred, suspended and almost always faces a judicial inquiry. Law and order disturbances can happen due to communal or caste tensions or often there could be student or labour unrest. The most vicious of these is a communal riot. There are districts which are more prone to such riots owing to historical or demographic factors. The DM and SP have to work together to prevent or control such situations. They have to be constantly on their toes to see that any small incident does not trigger a major riot. In fact, the DM and SP can only do so successfully if they have a complete understanding of their district and its people. A riot does not take place in a vacuum and there is always a series of events or disputes which if not resolved in time lead to an escalation of distrust between communities and if an officer is alert, he can discern the seething undercurrents of frustration and anger. A vigilant DM or SP who has credibility and has channels of communication open with important people and leaders gets valuable information before an event which helps him to tackle the situation.

The 2013 Muzaffarnagar riots began in UP as a fight between Jat (Hindu) and Muslim boys over a trivial matter which got blown up into a large-scale communal issue. Normally, it is the urban areas which are affected by the riots but in this case, the tensions spilled over into the rural areas. If prompt action is not taken at the initial stage then the situation is always likely to get out of control. Prompt, strong and impartial action is the best way to prevent a major riot. And the worst thing to do is to follow a policy of appeasement because such behaviour on the part of the administration gives the signal of weakness to the troublemakers, who then become more aggressive. Politicians, also then get the time and space to jump into the fray and complicate matters further, as they did in this case.

The key is to get information on time and if the DM and SP are accessible, then it is the people who will inform them in time about any communal or law and order situation developing. There are a lot of people in different communities whose help can be taken to defuse situations and peace committees of such eminent citizens is a powerful tool that can be used by the DM. I remember when I was DM in Allahabad, I got a call from a responsible citizen about a particular animal having been killed and the dead body laying at the entrance of a place of worship. Obviously, someone was intent upon creating a disturbance. I immediately contacted eminent citizens of both communities and requested them to rush to the spot and defuse the issue. The police and the magistrates also reached the spot and within minutes, the offending body of the animal was removed before the news could spread. A major riot was prevented.

However, if despite all precautions, an incident with communal overtones occurs then immediate action against the guilty is the best response. Potential trouble is nipped in the bud in this manner. It is also important to constantly brief the media so that there is no rumour mongering. These days the most pernicious tool of spreading hate and misinformation is social media, and the DM and the SP have to take steps to see that fake news or hate-inciting content is not circulated.

In recent years, I have perceived a strange tendency in the District Officers for not acting promptly after assessing a situation at their level but looking to the state headquarters for instructions. Worse is when the DM and SP start talking directly to the office of the Chief Minister and asking for instructions. Actually, they do this to be on the right side of the government in power. Some influential people with close links to the ruling party may be involved in a dispute and by referring the matter to state level or the CM office, the district administration only manages to create complications. Politicization of the disputes takes place immediately and multiple instructions start flowing to the districts which inhibit the DM from taking affective action. Only the DM and SP are aware of the ground realities and they are the best people to assess the situation and decide upon the course of action. Nobody from state headquarters can or should give instructions. The district responds to the signals that emanate from the conduct of the DM or SP and any delay, dithering, procrastination, nervousness or hesitation on their part sends the wrong kind of signals and emboldens troublemakers.

The desire of the DM to curry favour with the party in power to prolong his tenure in a district and get further good postings is often the weakest link in his armour; it inhibits him from acting as per the rule of law. Governance collapses when the DM or SP looks at the face of an individual and then takes action in their overwhelming desire to take politically correct action. This, however, leads to the erosion of their credibility as they are perceived as being partisan.

Even the smallest action of the DM is observed carefully by the people and they form an opinion about the officer and the administration. Law and order is not a matter of statistics but that of perception. I recall that when I was District Magistrate of Ghaziabad, the police had to open fire at a crowd of majority-community people who were using the worship of an idol of Lord Shiva to settle property scores with members of the minority community. An idol of Shiva had emerged on a disputed piece of land overnight and men and women began to offer prayers and bathe the idol in milk and water. The Additional District Magistrate and the Rural Superintendent of Police tried their best to find a peaceful solution but could not succeed and had to resort to forcible removal of idols. This led to a huge mob collecting on the spot and pelting the police force and Magistrate with petrol bombs and stones, and women lay down in front of the police vehicle. There was no option but to resort to police firing in which five people died. By the time the SSP and I reached the spot, imposed curfew and began intensive patrolling, the majority community had struck back by knifing three members of the minority community. With great effort, we controlled the riots and after about a week, when things normalized, Chief Minister, Mr Kalyan Singh visited Hapur. After assessing and reviewing the situation, he was persuaded by his party functionaries to go to the household of deceased majority-community victims and distribute compensation money to them personally. He, however, was dissuaded by his party people to go to the homes of the deceased of the minority community. The SSP and I immediately realized that this would send a very bad signal and the situation could again get out of hand as the minority community would lose faith in the administration. The fact was that we had been able to control the riots through our impartial, objective and fair handling which had built up the credibility of the administration. We persuaded the Chief Minister to visit the houses of the deceased of the minority community and hand over compensation money personally and we assured him that there was no problem of security. Fortunately, the Chief Minister had a lot of faith in us and so he agreed. He was welcomed with slogans of 'Kalyan Singh Zindabad' and the situation became absolutely normal. The point I want to make is that in a law and order situation, the most important thing to do is project an image of neutrality and impartiality to gain the trust and faith of the people.

Maintenance of law and order in the district depends a lot on the relationship between the DM and SSP. Even in recent times in Uttar Pradesh, there have been incidents of tension between two functionaries and the issue taking the shape of an IAS–IPS rivalry. Nothing could be worse than this as it sends a negative signal to the citizens and also to other officers. This relationship is not based on any written orders or government instructions but on mutual respect and understanding, and on the mental attitude of both the functionaries. It is important for both to look at the larger picture and not make an issue of small and insignificant matters. A major bone of contention is the power to post the Station House Officer (SHO). The SP feels that as commander of the team, it his prerogative to make the postings but the convention as well as regulations say that the DM is the head of the criminal administration and as such, he should decide on the postings of SHOs. I would agree with the SP that because he has to lead his police force he must decide on who would be incharge of the police station but it is always advisable to have a system where both the DM and SP discuss the postings and then the SP formally issues the order as per the discussion. Moreover as a DM I can recall that I fully agreed with the proposal of the SP and also never wanted him to send the file to me for approval in writing as most often, the matter was discussed over the telephone. This is a sensitive issue and has to be handled with a lot of emotional maturity by both the officers. It also helps in deflecting political pressure as both the officers can pass the buck from one to another. I recall that when I was DM of Allahabad, my SSP and I used this strategy to blunt a high-profile politician who was insisting on a particular officer being posted as SHO. Also, in one of the districts, the Deputy Inspector General (DIG) and Inspector General (IG) wanted a particular SHO to be transferred out as he was creating a lot of trouble for a local mafia politician who was in turn pressurizing the IG and DIG. The SSP was not in favour of shifting the SHO as he was an outstanding officer and had taken on the mafia politician but he wondered how he should respond to his superiors. We discussed the issue together and as per our mutual agreement, he finally told his bosses that the DM was not agreeing. The matter rested at that and the SHO made life miserable for the mafia politician.

One of the most dashing SSPs that I have had always said that magistracy was the shield to protect that police from getting into trouble. There is no doubt that the system works beautifully and to the mutual benefit of both if there is a healthy relationship of trust and confidence between the DM and SSP.

Often the question of introducing a police commissioner system in UP and other states keeps cropping up in addition to the various big cities where it exists. Unfortunately this becomes an IAS vs IPS issue with members of each service supporting a viewpoint that is favorable to them. The IAS does not want dilution of the authority of the DM while the IPS looks at an opportunity to get several more powerful posts in their cadre and total independence. I feel that we should change something if it is not working. There are no alarm bells that the present system is failing and as such there may not be any need for a change. The law and order and crime situation is as good or as bad in districts having police commissioner systems as those not having them. It cannot be denied that large cities need a different, upgraded and modernized system of policing with more senior police officers at the helm of affairs and specially trained for the demands of urban policing. However, this is possible within the existing system, too. As far as the citizen is concerned, the institution of the DM provides an alternative channel of grievance redressal as police being a uniformed force tends to support its junior officers in order to maintain their morale. There has to be somewhere that a citizen can go if he wants to complain against the police. However, I would not say anything further as being from the IAS, my views may be coloured. The important point is that we have to assess what is good for the citizen and go for a system which delivers better law and order and security for them so that the public has greater confidence in the working of the administration.

Law and order disturbances and sensational crimes like rape threaten the fabric of a society. No development can take place in the absence of a sense of security amongst the citizens. Different political parties in power are critical of their predecessors regarding the handling of law and order and they cite statistics to prove their case, yet it cannot be denied that it is the political ramification of a dispute or incident which leads to unwarranted political interference and paradoxically leads to adversely affecting the law and order situation.

Further, the law and order and crime situation cannot be assessed on the basis of statistics. It is actually a matter of perception which is a complex phenomena. If people see the police and administration acting as per law and impartially, they develop a positive perception towards them. Unfortunately most political parties, when in power, try to misuse the police for their political gains and that is why even senior ministers lobby hard for posting of SHOs. When I was in the CM Secretariat, a particular minister was insistent on getting an SHO transferred and replaced by a particular officer, and when I questioned him about this, he brazenly told me that if he had his own man as SHO he will use him to file criminal cases against his political opponents and correspondingly no FIR would be lodged against his supporters. He told me that this gives a big signal to the people and determines which way they would vote in the elections.

Often I found that even when there are no instructions from the ruling party in power or any senior officer, the

Thana-level police officers or even the District Officers look at the political affiliation of a criminal or lawbreaker and then take action. Sometimes just because a person belongs to the same community as the Chief Minister, district-level administration is reluctant to take action even though the Chief Minister may not have intervened at all. This leads to a negative perception about the administration in the eyes of the people and the rule of law breaks down if applied selectively. In fact I would go as far as to say that maintaining law and order is not rocket science. If only the police and administration are fair, impartial and objective, then rule of law is ensured and law and order maintained. However, these days this is easier said than done.

Sensational crime, particularly those against women, catches media headlines and colours the perception of law and order. In such situations if the FIR is written immediately and action taken as per prescribed procedure and criminals are arrested early, then damage control is possible. A careful handling of the media is an absolute must. The district administration is accountable for prompt and effective action and not allowing things to spiral out of control.

Surprisingly, it is not the bigger crimes like murder but smaller incidents of crime and people getting away with breaking the law that has the biggest impact on perception about law and order. It is the 'Goondaism' at the street corner that has the greatest impact on perception. Incidents like chain snatching, eve teasing and harassment of women, and violation of traffic laws, create an atmosphere of lawlessness. Extortion from shopkeepers, businessmen and industrialists is also very detrimental to the perception about law and order.

If petty crime is controlled then the citizen definitely feels more secure. An oft-repeated comment is that FIRs are not being registered. Repeated instructions from state level have little impact on this pernicious phenomenon. One reason behind this tendency is that all the police stations compete with each other to show how they have reduced crime in their jurisdiction and the higher officers also review the performance on the basis of the statistics relating to FIRs being lodged. Thus, it pays the local police officer not to lodge an FIR and is also one of the main reasons for people resorting to the greasing of palms at the police station and the inevitable corruption. As DM, one should always order registering of an FIR even though the local police station may not be happy with this. Sometimes the matter gets so serious that people approach the courts for lodging of FIRs. Once an FIR is lodged, the matter has to be investigated and everything taken on record, so the ease of lodging an FIR is the basic indicator of the quality of criminal administration. The best remedy would be to evaluate the workings of the police not on the basis of crimes registered but other parameters which may also include the perception factor, the nature of crimes, the investigations done, the number of chargesheets filed, the follow-up at the court level and behaviour with the citizens as well as general reputation. The DM and SSP have enough knowledge about their area to be able to design such an evaluation system. Technology can also become a saviour by filing of FIRs through email. During my tenure as Chief Secretary, we started this practice of registering FIRs on emails in cases where the accused had not been named. This is a good beginning and one can build on this further.

Utmost sensitivity is required in matters relating to crimes against women as these incidents are taken up by the political parties and media and also create a very poor impression of the district administration. A great degree of sensitivity and promptness is required when dealing with such crimes. There should be no delay in registering an FIR, making arrests and carrying out the investigation. The victim has to be shown a great degree of respect and there should be a detailed Statement of Procedure (SOP) to deal with such situations. As Chief Secretary of UP, I had taken an initiative of having the Home and women welfare departments coordinate their activities. Asha Jyoti Kendras were setup in twenty-six districts which provided a one-stop solution to women who were victims of such crimes. Under one roof, FIRs were registered, medical attention given, medical investigation done, psychological counselling made available and financial aid distributed. These Kendras were managed by women and have the potential to be an excellent model for providing relief for crimes against women. Technology can help by having a dedicated website for tracking the action taken on crimes against women and the complainant should also be able to find out the status of her case. Moreover, every police station must have a woman police officer and there should be a woman police officer of a very senior level who should be put in charge of monitoring and reviewing such matters.

As Chief Secretary, I had a few very dynamic police officers who successfully used technology and there was a helpline number 1090 where any women or girl facing harassment could register a complaint on her mobile phone and immediate action was taken so that the harassment cases stopped. The 1090 was a remarkable success story and during the two years I was Chief Secretary UP, more than 5.5 lakh complaints were lodged at 1090 and more than 90 per cent resolved to the satisfaction of the complainant. Similarly, we implemented the UP 100, the largest technology platform for calling up the police and getting immediate attention. It was a real game changer as it enabled the police to reach a complainant within twenty minutes, leading to a remarkable improvement in the law and order situation. A team of professional, talented police officers and home department worked relentlessly to make UP 100 a reality. The command centre at Lucknow should be seen to be believed. More than 3000 new vehicles with complement of police force were put on duty round the clock. Detailed SOPs were drafted and the police personnel fully trained in acting as per these SOPs. Curiously, the major opposition to this innovation came from the police department itself, where the Thana saw itself losing its paramount power and resented it. However, the political will backed by administrative determination and strong leadership provided by senior police officers the UP 100 has become a major success story. Today it has been rechristened as UP 112.

Land disputes at district levels are often the main reason for offences against the human body, like murder. The best way to handle this is by registering all such complaints and then categorizing them according to their severity, and joint teams of police and magistrates visiting the village and resolving them on a regular basis. The DM and SSPs themselves should visit villages in this connection and I am confident that remarkable results will be visible in a very short period of time. Of course it all depends on the level of monitoring and coordination.

For effective law and order, the criminal justice system should work in a manner that action is taken against criminals without delay. For this there is an institutional mechanism in UP called the monitoring committee which is presided over by the District Judge and has the DM and SSP as members. This gives a wonderful opportunity for a free and frank discussion on the status of all criminal cases as well as preventive action and also leads to close coordination with the judiciary, which is essential. Recently, because of a lack of coordination, matters have come to the forefront where judicial officers have gone to the extent of directing the lodging of FIRs against the DM, SP and other officers of their team. Such a conflict situation would ultimately lead to a breakdown of law and order at district level and the solution has to be provided by the DM by not thinking of his ego and going out of his way to cultivate good relations with the District Judge. The DM has to be the pivot around which the entire relationship between the judiciary, police and magistracy revolves. A high level of emotional and social intelligence is required of the District Magistrate.

Holding of fair and impartial elections is one of the most important duties of a District Officer. During the course of the elections, the DM works under the Election Commission and carries out the mammoth task of conducting elections even in extremely difficult situations. Those who are critical of the working of the government would do well to study how elections in such a large country are conducted in a fair, transparent and organized manner. This is truly a success story for the IAS and the post of the DM in particular. S.K. Sen was the Chief Election Commissioner who conducted the first elections in 1952 on universal suffrage in such a large country successfully. All of you must have heard the name of Mr T.N. Seshan, IAS retired, who through the force of his personality and toughness in implementing the law, has made elections a very fair and transparent process in the country. The IAS is certainly proud of officers like Mr Sen and Mr Seshan who have done invaluable service to ensure a working democracy in the country. The entire election process is conducted by the DM. Right from preparing the voter list to preparation of election booths, categorizing booths as sensitive for deployment of additional police force, making arrangement for law and order and security, requisitioning vehicles for transporting polling parties and ballot papers to even the remotest areas, deploying personnel on election duty and then arranging for the actual polling and counting of the votes is a herculean task which is performed smoothly and effectively by the District Magistrate. It only goes to show that if the IAS officers are given sufficient freedom of action and there is no political interference at each step, then they can surely perform wonders. Conducting of elections brings out all the leadership qualities of a DM and gives a great sense of satisfaction for having contributed to the functioning of a democracy.

Handling natural calamities like floods, drought, earthquakes or any other disaster is another major function of the District Collector. The DM has to galvanize his team of officers to carry out immediate relief work to save the lives of the people and to provide them with food, shelter and medical aid. These are crisis situations which bring out the best of the Collector as a leader and many officers have performed wonderfully in these situations. Even I recollect that at the time of floods, how I had to move throughout the day and night from one marooned village to another providing relief to people and moving them to safer areas. There were times when one had to wade through waist-high water at great personal risk but these are the moments which give you an opportunity to provide dedicated service to the people. A lot of monitoring is required to see that the funds provided for relief are not misused and that there is no corruption in relief work. People in the districts remember the District Collectors who without caring for their safety worked tirelessly to provide relief to the people and their names become a part of the stories of the district.

There has been no greater disaster in my living memory than the Coronavirus pandemic which is still claiming lives and has severely damaged the economy leading to large-scale unemployment and distress. The District Magistrate is the officer empowered under the Epidemics Act to take all possible actions for managing, regulating and controlling any pandemic, including Coronavirus and its various side effects. It is a different matter that the DMs have been working silently while the limelight is on the political leaders and the doctors. There is no doubt that the doctors and other medical staff have done outstanding work exposing themselves to the infections at considerable danger to their lives as well as that of their family members. They deserve the same respect and gratitude as we feel for our soldiers who are prepared to lay down their lives for our security. However, the DM who does all the coordination and management work and provides leadership to the team of officers and is also responsible for declaring lockdowns, implementing lockdowns, identifying containment zones and ensuring that people follow safe practices like wearing masks and social distancing, is often not even mentioned in media reports and the people are not aware of the dedicated service that these officers are putting in. It is a tribute to the working of the District Magistrates that Coronavirus has been handled with a reasonable degree of success in India. It is the DM who has been doing the day-to-day monitoring of the number of people falling sick, the fatality rate, the availability of ICU beds and ventilators and other medicines, and also getting a large number of tests done and then carrying out the process of tracking and tracing to reduce the spread of the pandemic.

There is definitely a great degree of romance attached to the post of the DM. I recall carrying out extensive tours of the interior areas of my districts during the winter months and solving the grievances of the people. It is really touching to see the kind of faith that the ordinary person has in the DM. I remember visiting the remotest villages and sitting on the cot with the villagers all around and discussing their problems and issues. The innocence of the rural people was really amazing and some of them used to even discuss personal problems like the in-laws of a girl not allowing her to come home. They expected that the DM has the capacity to solve all problems and the reality is that if the DM takes genuine interest, he can resolve most issues. I remember camping in the night in these villages and sitting till midnight with the people talking to them and understanding their lives and feeling like a part of them. Early in the morning, I would go and take around of the development work being done with the crowd of village people following and the poor householders offering tea, jaggery and sweets as a token of their respect and affection.

I am sure many of you would have seen photographs of the District Officers sitting under the tree dispensing justice to group of village people surrounding them. This is not a mere figment of imagination but a reality and this is how it should be. The DMs must go to the people to solve their problems. I will narrate a small incident which happened when I was SDM and handling severe floods. I was sitting in the marketplace of a town asking the traders and businessmen to contribute wheat, salt, gram for distribution in the marooned villages when a lady came to me weeping bitterly. On inquiry it transpired that she was from the state of Bihar and her daughter had been abducted by the tribe of snake charmers and they had brought her to a nearby village and kept her in captivity and were torturing her. The local police station incharge briefed me that the girl had come of her own volition and was very happy and did not want to go back but the women insisted that this was a false story. I then constituted a team of my police and revenue officers and sent them to the concerned village. Sure enough, it was found that the girl was locked up in a room tied up with ropes and crying for food and water. We freed the girl and gave her back to her mother and then I arranged for a vehicle with security to take them back to their village in Bihar and also took immediate action against the snake charmers. The look of gratitude on the face of the mother of the girl is something I will never forget as these are the moments which make you proud of being the member of the IAS and, in particular, a DM because you can touch the lives of the people so closely and significantly. This is the reason why if an officer performs his duty with empathy and compassion then he is remembered for long by the people of a district. And emotional bond develops between the DM and the citizens of his district.

Even today, after my retirement, and almost twenty-five years after I last served in a district, people from those districts come to meet me and pay their respects. Their affection and warmth really makes you feel that you have done something worthwhile in your life. Such has been the impact of Collectors who have done their job in the spirit of service that there have been cases when communal riots have broken out in a district with situation going out of control and the state government having no option but to once again post the same officer as DM who has served in the district earlier and has earned the love and respect of the people. The moment such an officer reaches the district, peace prevails. I have personally experienced standing on a rickshaw and addressing a mob of more than 5000 and being able to calm them down because of their immense faith in the institution of the DM, and also if the person holding the post has been able to build a reputation of credibility.

Unfortunately, the tenures of the District Officers have become very short in many states and my own state of UP is amongst the worst offenders. Such short tenures make it difficult for any officer to provide leadership to the district and it is important that at least a two-year tenure should be given to the DM. Even after this period, continuity is required and for this there was an old system of an outgoing officer writing a charge note giving all the details of the problems and issues of the district, including his comments on the officers and the influential people. This helped the new officer settle in fast. I recall in many districts, reading charge notes written by officers who had served in the district almost a hundred years ago and found them to be extremely incisive and perceptive. This system has fallen in disuse but should be made a mandatory practice. There was also a wonderful institution of a document called the district gazetteer which gave a detailed description of all aspects of a district—its history, culture, geography, economic issues, demographic factors and problems. These were mostly written by the District Officers in the ICS days and can be a great source of information for the new District Officer. Unfortunately, in UP most of the gazetteers have not been updated since the early twentieth century. They are a veritable treasure house of knowledge and must be regularly updated and now digitized.

The DM is perhaps the most exciting and rewarding assignment that an IAS officer gets during the course of his or her career. It provides a tremendous opportunity for an officer to do well, to help people resolve their problems and to bring about all-round development in the district. There is tremendous scope for exhibiting qualities of leadership and this post has enough freedom for an officer to be creative and innovate. It is important to maintain the sanctity of the institution which is suffering today because of some officers becoming corrupt and also not being transparent, open, accessible and accountable. This job gives you the kind of experience and opportunity that very few jobs in government or the private sector would provide. Your actions touch the lives of the people and your decisions make a difference to each and every household of the district. It is indeed an experience of a lifetime which no officer ever forgets.

4

Working with the State Government

IAS officers need to be prepared for a shock the moment they move from the heights of a district posting to the harsh realities of Secretariat life. In the districts, the IAS officer is under the illusion that he is the head of all he surveys. The moment he enters the state Secretariat, he is rudely brought down to the ground level. He becomes a part of the crowd. Now he has to start searching for a house, make a desperate effort to get an office room and has to plead before his seniors to get a proper vehicle. Coming to the Secretariat is a great leveler for any officer but it is also a great learning experience. You come to realize how the wheels of the government move and why the bureaucracy is labelled as obstructionist. Joining at the Joint Secretary (JS) or equivalent level accentuates these problems but once an officer reaches the Secretary or Principal Secretary level, things become much better.

In the Secretariat your work is largely paperwork-driven and you are bound by rules, procedures and precedence. You come to realize that each bit of paper is sacred and that there is an established way in which the paper moves. You will be in great trouble if you choose to interfere with the existing way of working. Yet times are changing and the bureaucracy has to move fast to meet the expectations of the people and also be held accountable for actual performance. The officer must then impose his will on the system and make it move at a pace he wants it to, and also make it more and more result-oriented. It is with this in mind that as Chief Secretary, I made it mandatory for the Principal Secretary to tour for three to four days in a month to understand the ground realities and similar instructions were given about the heads of departments and their teams. This was necessary as I found that the Secretariat officers rarely moved from their offices and were constantly submerged in mountains of files.

I came to the Secretariat after sixteen years of field experience and joined as Secretary Basic Education and remember feeling quite depressed about it for a while. However, soon I realized that handling a department at the state level can be quite exciting and absorbing. You can have a vision for the department and be in a position to implement it. Rigorous monitoring of schemes, projects and budgets makes you aware of the intricacies of the subject you are handling and it can be most interesting.

Most of the establishment issues of a department get referred to the Secretariat, where the Secretary as well the head of department at the state headquarters spend a disproportionately long time on these matters rather than focusing on the development aspect. Control over establishment is all about power and all those concerned are continuously playing this power game. The minister is no exception to this and you often find the ministers excessively concerned with transfers and postings rather than policy issues. Confronting this reality, a very colourful and outspoken Principal Secretary once remarked, 'I keep on making polices but the minister does not implement them!' This reversal of roles is a matter of a joke but also an unfortunate reality. Ministers are known to be involved in the transfers of officers and employees below class-one level, which should normally be the exclusive domain of the head of the department (HOD). Often the HOD develops an unholy nexus with the minister and conveniently bypasses the Secretary. Some secretaries resent this but the majority accepts it without raising their voice. The result is that allegations of corruption are abound and some posts are openly sold, adversely affecting the image of the department in the government. In order to strengthen governance, it is important to allow space to the HOD to function and he should be given the power to choose his team but the reality is that many departmental officers realize where the power lies and develop close links with the ministers. This anomaly is difficult to eradicate as no minister will willingly relinquish his power and only if the Chief Minister has the political will, can this problem be tackled. The Secretary is involved in the transfer and the postings of class one officers but here also there is a lot of political interference and many battles between the minister and Secretary are the result of this confrontation. The net result is that governance suffers.

I would like to narrate two incidents which exemplify the conflict between the minister and his Secretary on transfers. Of course, there are exceptions and I have seen ministers who do not put a foot out of line with their Secretary and there is a lot of mutual trust and faith. Inevitably, the performance of the departments is at its best. Then there are IAS officers who surrender completely and become yes-men and lead to the detriment of the overall governance system. A balanced approach is required and not every battle needs to be fought. Moreover, rarely does a minister interfere in other governance matters and the Secretary is left free to conduct the workings of his department.

An incident occurred when I was Principal Secretary Technical Education and trying my best to improve to quality of education. The interviews for the posts of Directors of two premier government engineering colleges were to take place. We wanted to select professionals who would take these institutes to the next level. However, in UP at that time the board of governors of government colleges was headed by the then-minister. The minister promptly appointed himself as Chairman of the selection committee and soon, unsavoury rumours started floating around. I responded by selecting a strong selection committee of professionals like Directors of IIT Kanpur and IIM Lucknow, and I too became a member. After a prolonged interview, throughout which the minister kept silent, the committee zeroed in on two names. The minister then very clearly told us that he disagreed and gave the names of two other persons to be selected as Directors. Incidentally, both of them had performed very poorly in the interview and the committee said so in plain terms. But the minister would not budge despite my effort to use all my communication skills to convince him. Suddenly, the situation turned bitter. The minister thumped the table loudly and threatened to walk out if his wish was not met. 'As a minister, I cannot even select a Director!' He thundered. We were dumbfounded and were forced to keep quiet and make conciliatory noises. We lost the battle and the institutes suffered. However, I approached the Chief Minister's office and briefed him and succeeded in having the minister removed from the post of Chairman Board of Governors and appointing professionals in his place. The war was won. Then again, to improve the quality of the intake on the recommendation of the Vice Chancellor, we had proposed a minimum aggregate in physics, chemistry and mathematics for a candidate to be eligible to take the engineering entrance exam. When the file was put up to the minister, he wrote a long note about this being unfair for children from rural backgrounds and directed that the figure should be kept at 33 per cent for General and 25 per cent for SC/ST. Once again I had to take up the matter with the CM Office by sending a note directly to him through the Chief Secretary which led to a compromise solution: 45 per cent minimum for General candidates and 40 per cent for SC/ST.

The above two examples illustrate the kind of differences that can arise because of a different view. The minister was concerned with disseminating technical education to maximum students, especially of the under-privileged class and felt that the quality issue could be tackled later on with proper teaching, while we were clear that the quality of intake is of vital importance. I would like to point out that he was a very fine minister who was courteous and gave a lot of respect to officers. I still have an excellent relationship with him. It is just that often the bureaucrat and the political executive look at the problem from different perspectives and neither of them are wrong. It is important for IAS officers to appreciate that the minister is elected and has to be responsive to his constituency. However, an IAS officer should never become a part of any corrupt or illegal practice that some ministers may desire.

I found that the problem in the state government is more prominent because the minister is often left to fend for himself. Files are put up to him and he is expected to go through a maze of paperwork and make decisions even though he has never been trained in file work. At the central government level, the minister has an IAS officer as a special assistant who puts up the files to him, briefing him on all relevant details. In UP, the minister is assisted by a PA from the Secretarial personal assistant service, and he has to depend on him to guide him about file disposal. These PAs do not have the requisite calibre for this kind of job and more often than not, have a different agenda in these postings and utilize their time in exploring the various avenues of corruption that are possible. It would be advisable to have a senior officer of the State Civil Services to assist the minister. Often the Secretary of the department has to personally get the files cleared from the minister. Politicians have a lot of ground-level knowledge and are very comfortable with people but it is a rare politician who enjoys wading through the dusty and crumpled Secretariat files. I have been Secretary to the Chief Minister for several years and found that even at that level, not many CMs like to deal with paper. However, there are great exceptions, for I remember that Kalyan Singh as CM of UP was a super bureaucrat and enjoyed nothing more than going through the papers and offering his written comments.

Another incident that comes to mind regarding this politician–bureaucrat divide, took place when I was Chief Secretary UP. The Principal Secretary Agriculture, a young and dynamic officer, realized that the subsidy for seeds that was being given to the farmers was reaching only a small segment of intended beneficiaries. He decided to implement a direct cash benefit transfer scheme after enrolling the eligible farmers online. I agreed with his proposal and we decided to go ahead with it. Soon there was huge opposition to this from the Directorate of Agriculture, which wielded a lot of power in making purchases of seeds and more often than not, there used to be allegations of rampant corruption. They briefed the minister who took up the issue by sending the file to the Chief Minister opposing the proposal of the Principal Secretary. Meanwhile, I had briefed the CM about the enormous benefits of this scheme. The CM asked for my comments as Chief Secretary and I wrote a long note supporting the Principal Secretary and the CM approved it, much to the chagrin of the minister. The scheme succeeded and we saved money and also the subsidy reached the intended farmer. The Government of India also appreciated this initiative.

Similarly, we implemented the Samajwadi Pension Scheme stipulating a monthly pension of Rs 500 to the women in the eligible family. The Principal Secretary wanted to ensure that there be no corruption in the scheme and he used the PMFS system (the financial system prescribed by the government of India for DBT schemes). We ensured that on the first of every month, the pension would be transferred to the bank account of the beneficiary. A very fair and objective system of selection of beneficiaries was put in place. Unfortunately, the minister did not appreciate this and he developed serious differences with his Principal Secretary. His logic was that implementing the scheme in this manner would not give any political advantage to the ruling party, and the selection of beneficiaries should be left to the discretion of the public representatives. He made an issue of it and prevailed upon the CM to have the officer transferred. However, I briefed the CM about the brilliant system that the officer had implemented and got the transfer order cancelled. With the approval of the CM, we then implemented the scheme which became a huge success.

In both these matters, the minister was motivated by the fact that the elections were around the corner and he wanted to satisfy as many people as possible rather than focus on reforms. As I have pointed out earlier, it is not that the minister is always wrong and the civil servant right. It can always be the other way round. Nor am I advocating an adversarial relationship between the two which would be detrimental to the workings of the government. In fact, things move smoothly if only there is harmony between the minister and his Secretary but this harmony should not become a euphemism for collusion or corrupt practices. If the situation is untenable then the safest course for the officer is to opt out of the department unless he has the backing of the CM. My experience has been that, but for a couple of incidents, the ministers have always given me a lot of respect and listened to my views and generally, given me a free hand to act. If there is mutual trust, then this kind of relationship is the outcome. Officers should avoid trying to deliberately create a hostile environment. It is catastrophic to treat the minister lightly and ignore him. The minister should be well and properly briefed on every issue by the officer, and he should be very courteous and polite in his manners.

The Principal Secretary has to prepare answers to assembly questions and brief the minister on possible supplementaries. There was a minister of mine who had become a cabinet minister for the first time and assembly questions made him nervous. The minister would take repeated briefings and take down copious notes yet flounder when supplementary questions were thrown at him in the assembly. On such occasions he would helplessly rummage through his papers and then look at me sitting in the officer's gallery and I would promptly send him a slip with the possible answer which he would read out with a sigh of relief. One fine morning, there were a lot of questions and this spectacle had been repeated a few times. Finally, a senior member of the opposition got up and raised a point of order. He requested the Honorable Speaker to ask the Principal Secretary to come down to the assembly hall and answer all questions rather than continuously send slips of papers. This caused huge embarrassment to both the minister and me. The practice of sending slips to the minister is well-established but should be done furtively.

Assembly questions are often treated as a necessary evil by most officers but they should be given the highest importance as they are essential tools of a vibrant democracy. I personally found that questions raised helped me get an idea of various issues in my department and how I could deal with them. Answering the questions requires great parliamentary skills and the answer is normally kept as brief and to-the-point as possible. Often the assembly questions can be a wake-up call.

When the assembly is in session, points of honour are raised, urgent issues crop up for immediate reply and debate, and the Principal Secretary has to respond promptly and with accuracy as he is personally responsible for the information he furnishes. Dealing with assembly-related matters is one of the most important aspects of the job of a Secretary.

Most Principal Secretaries/Secretaries are not very happy when they are called to give evidence before various committees of the legislature. The roles get reversed here and the very same MLAs who seek an appointment to meet you, become the honourable members who seem to be intent on tearing you and your department apart. Utmost preparation has to be done before making a presentation to these committees. You have to avoid making even one wrong statement even though the issues raised often relate to several years in the past. The principle in government is that of continuity and so the Secretary has to try and defend his department, even though he may not be personally aware of the matter. Sometimes the committee members can become very aggressive. Informal channels and your relationship with several members is a great help, for then the members help you get out of tight situations. The greatest asset is the chairman and if the principal Secretary apprehends that certain issues are likely to be difficult, it is best to meet the chairman before the meeting and place the facts before him. I found in most cases, the chairperson would then support you in the meeting and ugly situations could be avoided. The worst thing that one can do is not attend the meeting in person and depute your second-in-command for the purpose. The situation becomes potentially explosive as the members take it as a personal affront.

Once again on a positive note, one can learn a lot from the grilling of these committees and you realize the kind of mistakes that have occurred in the past and which one has to be careful about in the future. These are all institutional mechanisms of a democracy and their functioning is essential to ensure the accountability of the executive to the legislature. This is the spirit in which the officer should respond to these committees.

Preparation of cabinet notes and presenting them before the cabinet is an important part of the job of a Principal Secretary. I have noticed that the standard of cabinet notes in the state governments is vastly inferior to that in the government of India. The drafting is often poor, the note too lengthy and the quality of paper indifferent. Often the Principal Secretary just initials a cabinet proposal that comes from the HOD without the application of their mind. This can be counterproductive, for at the time of presentation to the cabinet, the Principal Secretary has nobody to assist him and if he does not respond properly to the queries raised then he presents a very bad impression of himself. As far as possible, the Principal Secretary must dictate the cabinet note himself and prepare thoroughly. It is also very important for the Principal Secretary to personally monitor the action taken on cabinet decisions.

Legal cases take up a large amount of time of the Principal Secretary. More often than not the officer would find that he has been summoned by the court on contempt charges. The moment a contempt notice is issued the department becomes hyperactive and the midnight oil is burnt to comply with the court orders and draft a response. Not complying with the court orders when contempt proceedings have been initiated against you is an unwise step. I have often found that there is a nexus between the lower-level Secretariat officers and the petitioner, which creates the situation of contempt and often the officer sees the file for the first time on the receipt of a contempt notice. Either the earlier order of the court has by some stratagem not reached the department or it has been deliberately kept lying submerged in the files. The best course of action in these matters is to hold the concerned officers accountable and take action against them for non-compliance of court orders. It is always advisable for a Principal Secretary to keep a register with his Personal Secretary (PS) in which all such notices and orders are entered and personally monitored.

The officers must take court matters very seriously and monitor them regularly. The situation is often so bad that even counter affidavits are not filed in most cases and the proceedings remain pending. The government is the largest litigant and the state must have a litigation policy that should focus on avoiding unnecessary litigation. Often there are a lot of cases on the same issue which can easily be clubbed together with the permission of the court and if a particular government order or rule is leading to numerous cases, then the officers concerned should examine the order or rules and amend them accordingly.

Establishment issues are often the most agitated before the courts. For this the department has only itself to blame. Most officers are insensitive or unresponsive to genuine grievances of their employees and issues of seniority, promotion, postings, inquiries or punishment keep flooding the Secretariat, where the unfortunate tendency is to keep them pending, bound in red tape. There should be no need for employees or officers to rush to the courts in such matters as it is the duty of the Principal Secretary to engage with them and resolve their issues in a time-bound manner. Needless to say, the performance of a department greatly improves if establishment matters are properly organized and handled in a transparent manner. As Principal Secretary Urban Development I found that no promotions had taken place for almost twenty years and we resolved the pending issues and introduced regular departmental promotion committees to bring promotions up to date. There was a sense of euphoria all across the department and the entire working environment changed for the better.

The more the government tries to regulate by issuing a plethora of instructions, the more the litigation piles up in the same proportion. Often contradictory or impractical orders are issued and it is worthwhile to keep reviewing such instructions and remove those which have no further relevance. In the name of building systems, the officers keep creating a labyrinth of orders and instructions which confuse the ordinary citizen and help in defusing the accountability of the public servant. The elaborate and often contradictory instructions issued during the Covid-19 pandemic are an illustration of this malady. Some departments in the government are more prone to litigation than others and I found that in UP, the education department and especially the secondary education department are the worst affected.

This is because the strength of teachers is very large and also the government has got itself involved unnecessarily in matters relating to private or government-aided colleges. In fact, the District Inspectors of Schools and even the Principal Secretary of the department spends more than half the time in the courts. I was once summoned before the honourable High Court when I was Principal Secretary Urban Development and to my utter surprise, I found that outside the court room, in the verandah, a table and a few chairs were laid out and I saw seated on them the very colourful and innovative Principal Secretary of Secondary Education. He invited me to have a seat and a cup of tea and he told me that since he has to spend a lot of time in the courts, he had decided to make himself comfortable and dispose of his files while waiting for his cases to be called out! Who says that the IAS is not creative!

Sensitivity of the departmental officers towards the genuine grievances of their employees can remove the need for people to rush to the courts. As it is, the courts are saddled with a high volume of cases and such matters only tend to increase their workload. Each Principal Secretary must frame a system whereby grievances are addressed in a time-bound manner. Some will still go to court but a large number may not.

Another factor causing the litigation piling up is the idea of going for an appeal to a higher court against any adverse order. The correct course of action would be to examine an order and see if there are any valid grounds for appeal and whether an appeal is likely to succeed, then higher courts should be approached, otherwise compliance should be done and matter closed. The reality is that the concerned department and the law department play a game of throwing the file at each other and finally after some time, the law department opines that an appeal may be filed taking it as the safest course of action. Litigation mounts, government money is wasted and grievances remain unaddressed. This tendency is even more evident if a court order is leading to any financial liability on the government.

Another interesting aspect is the flexibility of the legal opinion that the law department provides. I had my first experience of this when I was Secretary to the Chief Minister and the CM wanted an urgent legal opinion on an issue. For quite some time, the file did not surface from the law department and I had to ring up the Principal Secretary Law to remind him. His response took me by surprise as he wanted me to tell him what legal opinion the CM wanted so that the opinion could be given accordingly. It became clear to me that often legal opinions are tailored to fit the thinking of the person in power.

A very revealing incident took place when I was the Principal Secretary Urban Development and the urban local body elections were to take place. They were thirteen posts of mayors and as per the act and rules, there was a clear roster system to determine which seat would be general, which reserved, which would go to women, etc. The CM wanted particular candidates to contest from specific municipal corporations and I was summoned by the CM Office and given the brief to prepare the roster accordingly. I explained that this is not possible as the rules and their interpretation was clear. The stratagem of taking legal opinion was then adopted by the CM Office and the Principal Secretary Law interpreted the rules differently which accommodated eight out of the thirteen proposed mayor candidates. I said that I did not agree with the opinion but if given in writing, I would abide by it. However, the CM was keen that at least three other proposed mayoral candidates should be accommodated in the roster. To my utter disbelief I was called and told by the CM Office in the presence of the Principal Secretary Law that for eight seats, the interpretation given by the law department should be used while for other three, my earlier interpretation should be employed. I had to show my dissent by saying that I could agree with an interpretation I felt was wrong if given in writing, but I had to be consistent and could not possibly choose different interpretations for different mayor seats. At my refusal, the officers present looked at me as they would at a goat about to be sacrificed and I realized that my goose was cooked and mentally began to prepare for my transfer. Imagine my surprise and amazement when the CM saw my point and agreed with it. It just shows that often the officers close to the CM try to be holier than the king. If they put up both sides of the picture to the CM they will invariably get to the right decision.

Secretariat working is all about files which are almost like living organisms having a life and energy of their own. A good Secretariat officer believes in not keeping files pending and he is proud to proclaim that his table is clear. However, this movement of files has little relation to actual decisions being taken and on closer examination, he will find that the files have been sent to law, finance or personnel departments for advice. The files move to and fro with volumes of noting which ensures that no accountability can be fixed on anyone at a later date. A close relative of this strategy is the formation of a committee to examine the matter which takes its own sweet time to give a voluminous report. Even developing a system of tracking files and prescribing maximum time limit for files to stay at a particular desk does not help.

The Principal Secretary of a department is expected to provide leadership to his team. He has to have the skill set to build the team which shares the objectives and goals of the department and work towards its fulfillment. The key task is to prepare the budget of the department, then release the budget to the field officers and monitor physical and financial progress. Above all, he has to assess the problems in his department, resolve them and achieve the required outcomes. Unfortunately, this does not often happen as the officers are more concerned about processes than giving results. Calling or attending a meeting becomes an end in itself and occupies the majority of the time of the secretaries and the heads of the departments. The job of a Principal Secretary is not only to assist in policy formulation but ensure implementation. Often we hear the rather unfair and incorrect statement that policies are good but implementation is poor. The reality is that policies are framed in the rooms of the Secretariat overlooking the harsh realities at the field level and a good policy must take into an account how it can be executed.

Principal Secretaries, HODs and other officers of the Secretariat are averse to visiting the field to see for themselves the ground realities. As Chief Secretary, I had to mandate a certain number of days in a month for the Principal Secretary to be on tour and I personally followed this practice even as Chief Secretary. This is essential to bring about effective public service delivery and the quality of implementation of schemes and projects. It is important to step out of the comfort of your office and see things for yourself.

Communication is vital and often the language used in the Government Order (GO) or instructions is so complex that it becomes difficult for the implementing officers to understand it and they often interpret it in different ways. Once as Secretary Basic Education I tried to ascertain the fate of a detailed GO issued. I found that even the directorate was not clear about it. Worse, as I went further down the line, the District Education Officers were either unaware of the GO or had not understood it. At the school level, I was shocked to find that some principals had interpreted the GO in a manner that was completely opposed to what was intended. It reminded me of a party game called 'Chinese Whispers' in which you sit in a circle and say something in the ear of the person next to you who then does the same to the person next to them. By the time this message reaches the last person, it is totally distorted. The lesson is that communication should be kept simple and field inspections and interactions are necessary to make the officers realize the intent of the orders issued so that compliance is ensured. The engagement with officers should be a two-way communication.

Meeting citizens is an important aspect of the job of a Principal Secretary but unfortunately very few people are actually able to meet the officer; they have to pass through the security system and a complex procedure before they can reach the office of the concerned officer. I used to be amazed as Chief Secretary when people used to meet and request me to speak to a particular officer, asking him to give time to the concerned citizen. This is simply not acceptable. Theoretically, most officers allot half an hour for meeting people but in reality few are able to do so as they have to go through the ordeal of passing through the Secretariat pass office, the PA to the officer and the ubiquitous 'Chaprassi', i.e., the office help. The privileged few and the professional 'netas' are the only ones able to have access to an officer. The system of not being accessible to people is indeed counterproductive as the officers are insulated from relevant feedback which is essential for them to manage their department better. An officer is expected to be open and accessible. Even as Chief Secretary, I had kept one hour to meet people and they could do so without the need of a pass or going through unnecessary security checks. This had a tremendous impact on the perception of responsiveness in the eyes of the people.

In Uttar Pradesh, the unfortunate perception is that it is impossible to meet a senior officer. As an example of the reality of the ease of doing business, I was told by an industrialist that if they want to meet the Principal Secretary Industries, they have to first spend days ringing up the PA to try and get an appointment and then on the appointed day, spend hours in the pass office for an entry pass and then they are made to sit on a bench in front of the office till they are called in only to find that the Principal Secretary is busy with his mobile or files and hardly gives them any attention and advises them to meet the concerned officer. This does not help the industrialist at all, who also told me that, in sharp contrast, in some states you can get an appointment with one phone call and then be assisted into the office of the Secretary without any problems and get a patient hearing and resolution of the problem. This is the difference in the actual doing of business in UP as compared to some other states. Accessibility is very important to give satisfaction to the people.

Linked to the above opaqueness is the curious phenomenon of files or paper not moving on its own. It has to be propelled forward as it does not seem to have any momentum of its own. So many people come to me and request me to talk to some officer so that the officer calls for their file. The curious thing is that when the section officer or dealing assistant tells a person that his file is ready, it will be put forward only if it is asked for by the Principal Secretary. The problem is compounded by the fact that it is almost next to impossible for the person to meet the Principal Secretary and then, which applicant would have the audacity to suggest to the Principal Secretary that he should call for his file. The result is people requesting other officers to put in a word for them or running to politicians or resorting to greasing the palms of the lower-level officers. These efforts are required to make a file or piece of paper move. This can be handled by a system of rigorous monitoring but there is so much paperwork that the top person is not able to keep track of all the papers that are marked down by him. There is no doubt that often there is a shortage of staff which is responsible for this. In the Secretariat, certain departments are considered 'good' and others are 'bad' for obvious reasons and the clerical staff makes all the effort to get them posted in the so-called good departments like engineering or health but rarely would they opt for something like social welfare or administrative reforms. The worst part is that this tendency is not restricted to the lower staff but is also prevalent amongst top officers, including the IAS. In my experience, I have found that IAS officers categorize departments as good, bad or even ugly and use political pressure and other stratagems to get a posting in a 'good' department. Once having obtained such a posting, the officers want to hang on to it and this makes them tow the line for the minister and buckle down to political pressure. He clings on to his seat at the cost of effective working. In fact, this is the main reason that domain specialization in the IAS has not taken place and may not succeed in the future either as most officers would like to specialize in economic ministries with few opting for rural development or social welfare. Glamour, status, power or foreign jaunts are often more alluring than substance and the satisfaction of making a difference. This is unfortunate as IAS officers often do not prefer departments where their presence is most required, and less glamorous ones like elementary education are departments where an officer can make a huge difference.

Important departments like administrative reforms are seen as punishment postings and an officer posted there wants to get out as soon as possible and does not work. I feel the system should incentivize posting in such departments or tag it with a so-called good department. The irony is that perhaps the greatest need today is that of administrative reforms which no officer takes seriously. This is just an illustration and the same story is repeated in case of many vital but 'unattractive' departments. We had an extremely interesting officer at the Mussoorie IAS academy, who was the Deputy Director and narrated how he had been transferred repeatedly in his career to so-called 'bad' departments. His response was to put in a lot of hard work and soon the government had no option to transfer him out of there as wherever he went he enforced the rule book and worked with complete integrity which was unpalatable to the vested interests. The reality is that every cadre post in the IAS affords you tremendous opportunity to touch the lives of the people and bring about a positive change.

If you look through the Secretariat files, you will be surprised to find that a detailed noting has been made by the section officer summarizing the issue under consideration and thereafter, the file travels to different levels till it reaches the Secretary, and often you will find that the officers have merely appended their signature without making any significant contribution. I was pleasantly surprised that as far back as the first decade of the twentieth century, Lord Curzon expressed his dismay at this system of working and commented that a file moves from desk to desk without any value addition. Curiously, more than a hundred years later, the same story is true about the Secretariat's workings, leading to a perception that it is the 'babu' who decides everything. Reforms need to be introduced to see that every file does not travel through all levels and there is accountability for decision-making at each level which would leave the Principal Secretary spare time to think about his job and do something constructive. The job of the Principal Secretary is to continuously keep the outcomes in sight rather than bind himself in miles of red tape. Senior officers must express their views on the file to add value to it and should not be scared to disagree with the viewpoint expressed below. The officers do not commit themselves in order to play safe and escape any charge of corruption, but by doing so, they are actually not doing what they have been selected for.

Sometimes the ministers try to put pressure for some decisions to be made and the file to be prepared accordingly. Upright officers refuse to do so but there are others who buckle down and sacrifice their independence and integrity and collude in the wrong decisions being made. The best policy is always to put down your views with justification and then let the political executive record his disagreement. Of course, things are not so simple and often they take an ugly turn as the minister will not overrule you but is quick to take offence and lament that the bureaucracy is creating hurdles and not allowing him to work and then would make all the effort to get the concerned officer transferred or take out his anger in some other way. When I was Secretary Basic Education in UP, I had a Special Secretary who always wrote what was on his mind. The minister, obviously, did not like him and one day, he was absolutely livid and called me to take action against the concerned officer. I found that his crime was that while submitting a file, he had endorsed it to 'Minister' rather than 'Honourable Minister'. The explanation of the Special Secretary was called for and he was advised to apologize to end the matter but he refused and quoted the rules of the business of Secretariat working which were clear that 'Minister' was the right form of address and nowhere was there any mention of 'Honourable Minister'. I had to agree with him, leaving the minister furious. More often than not, when politicians call bureaucrats obstructionist, it is because the officer puts down his frank views on paper.

The Secretariat working can be done in a routine manner or with a problem-solving approach for which there is a lot of opportunity. A senior officer once taught me something vital. He said that one should view each file from the policy aspect and each individual case that is processed puts up a policy issue and an effective officer is one who then goes ahead and designs policies accordingly. A Secretary has to be creative and should look for constantly improving things in his department.

It never ceases to amaze me that throughout the year the departments are busy issuing sanctions against the budget. The finance department issues detailed guidelines about sanctions after the budget are approved by the legislature and delegates a lot of power to line departments. However, there still a tendency for departments to send all proposals to finance for their concurrence and this leads to unnecessary delays. Even when it is required to send the files to the finance department, the process takes a long time as frequent objections are raised by finance, which take time to be sorted. This leads to an unsavoury situation where most of the funds are released in the last month of the financial year—March— and this is often the reason for an improper utilization of funds, as a result of which the benefit of schemes do not reach the field and the results and outcomes are not achieved. Even when finance approves funds for a project, it releases only a certain percentage asking for utilization certificates and this process takes a lot of time. Ideally if a project is approved then entire funds should be released and then the line department's Principal Secretary and HOD should be responsible for releasing this money after monitoring the stage-wise physical progress. However, the finance department has to monitor the cash flow situation too, otherwise the state may have to face the ignominy of having all payments stopped. One way of handling this, in my opinion, is for finance to sanction the entire funds for the project but give a monthly limit for actual releases and make it mandatory for the line department to release the funds only after obtaining utilization certificates.

Financial prudence is essential because, after all, Civil Servants deal with public money which has to be spent maintaining the highest standards of probity. Moreover, it is the job of the finance department to see that there is no mismatch between revenue and expenditure. However, in government, the meaning of finance is primarily expenditure control which often goes to absurd limits, giving finance departments the label of being negative and the line departments and finance playing a blame game. A very common problem is that sometimes small amounts are sanctioned for projects leading to cost and time overrun which could very well be avoided. Moreover, even departments are fond of coming up with new schemes rather than completing the existing ones as it gives them more political advantage. The result is that a lot of projects remain incomplete and also the maintenance of projects suffers. In my opinion, all departments including finance have to focus on the economic growth of the state and the attitude of finance should also be geared towards this.

Another aspect which has often irked me is the propensity to sanction funds for the hardware and delay funds for software, leading to an asset not being utilized. I would illustrate this with a real-life example of the animal husbandry department which came before me when I was Agriculture Production Commissioner of UP. Ninety-two veterinary hospitals had been constructed but were lying idle as the staff and equipment had not been sanctioned and the files concerning these were shuttling between the department and finance. This happens in most cases as funds for buildings are released but they do not become operational without the required software where the finance department becomes very strict about sanctioning funds. The way out could be to approve the project as a whole, including the building, staff, equipment and other requirements, and funds may be released in such a manner that everything is in place at the same time to make the project operational. The focus has to be on delivering services to the people in a time-bound manner rather than having a penny wise, pound foolish approach. Nowhere is my intent to play down the importance of the finance department and it is their duty to use public funds with the utmost care. A way out which I found to be very useful in my experience as Finance Secretary, was to have regular interactions with the line departments on their important proposals rather than allowing the lower level finance department staff to kill a proposal on technical grounds. I'd like to add that when I adopted this strategy, the line departments were very happy but one day, a delegation of the finance department, Dealing Assistants and section officers, met with me and voiced their concern as they felt my approach was making them useless and no line department was bothering about them! I had to use all my diplomatic skills to placate them and assured them that I would try a positive approach in select cases whereas they could continue with their approach for the rest. An honourable compromise!

It is a very common thing to see in governments that line departments keep complaining that finance is not sanctioning funds while the latter keeps pointing out that the departments are not preparing proper proposals. Even ministers complain regularly about the finance departments to the Chief Minister but the finance department does play a stellar role in proper utilization of funds and I can say that the job of the Finance Secretary is an unenviable and thankless one. He needs the support of the Chief Minister and the Chief Secretary. The situation becomes worse if there is a resource crunch. Finance has to then control the cash flow and adopt stringent economy measures. Naturally, the powerful ministers felt aggrieved about this. I recall when I was Secretary Finance Government of UP, we were implementing a pay commission report of 1996 and there was a genuine shortage of funds which had to be managed every day. Yet, we could see that the line departments were not appreciating this fact and constantly complaining. So much so that the ministers raised the issue in the cabinet too. I must give credit to my Principal Secretary Finance who decided to counter this head-on by educating the cabinet about the realities of financial management and the acuteness of the crisis. He made us prepare a white paper on finances and then we presented this before the entire cabinet. Simple illustrative examples were used to emphasize the point that borrowings cannot be used for consumption expenditure. The effort was worth it and thereafter there was a much better understanding of the financial crisis. The moral of the story is that when confronted with a crisis, an IAS officer should not hide things but be open and transparent and engage the stakeholders so that there is an overall appreciation of the problem.

I enjoyed my tenure as Secretary Finance and I can say without a doubt that the working of the Finance Department is a major determinant of good governance in a state and a posting in the finance department gives excellent exposure to an IAS officer. However, an officer must be careful that the finance approach does not become so much a part of one's working style that one is not able to become a dynamic leader and tends to be overly conservative. When I was in the defence ministry in the Government of India, we heard stories how the then-Defence Minister had sent concerned officers of defense finance to the Siachen glacier to understand the condition in which the soldiers lived so that they stopped putting needless objection on files. The same exercise can be tried out in the states and the finance department officers must be sent to the field to observe the actual working condition and realities. Their interventions, then, would be much more pragmatic.

The Government of India has a wonderful system of internal finance, whereby an officer of the rank of Additional Secretary is posted in the line departments so that he understands the issues facing the departments and he is able to clear files accordingly. In the state of UP, we tried to experiment with the same model but we did not succeed as not many senior officers wanted to be placed on these posts and there were issues in the working of the system.

As Chief Secretary, I found an annoying habit in the Finance Department. They would agree to a proposal in a meeting but then when the cabinet note went to them for comments, they would give their approval but with several riders. This was to shield themselves from any future inquiry. Often I had to hold meetings again to prepare responses to these issues raised by finance. Despite this, a Chief Secretary has to rely on the finance department and should not try to throttle their views. This applies to secretaries of line departments too. However, the leader in the officer has to surface and take control to see that the interventions by the Finance Department do not become roadblocks in the process of development. He has to take decisions to make things happen and accordingly convince finance department to guide him on how to overcome the issues raised by them. If handled correctly, the finance department does respond favourably. The moment an officer is posted to finance, his attitude tends to change.

I must talk about a matter of great satisfaction for me as Finance Secretary UP. I took the initiative to computerize the treasury and completed the project in one year with the help of computer-savvy finance and accounts service officers. It was indeed a revolution and UP was perhaps the pioneer state to do this, even ahead of many advanced southern states which subsequently came to study our model. I had formed a team of officers who were good at computers and encouraged them to study the processes and computerize them. I monitored every week and gave them full support and they did a wonderful job. An immediate fallout of this was that in the districts it was found many departments were drawing salary bills for employees in excess of the actual people working. With computerization, the corruption involved in this process was checked and the salary bills got cut down. It led to antagonizing the vested interests and various unions took up the issue and sat on a *dharna* at Lucknow in front of the Chief Minister's office. The CM summoned my Principal Secretary and looked upset at us having created so much of unrest. He seemed intent on rolling back the entire computerization exercise. However, I explained the entire situation to him and when he realized the revolutionary impact of this exercise, his mood changed and he gave us the go-ahead and also became the biggest supporter of the computerization of treasuries. Innovative ideas always meet with opposition but if an officer is convinced and has the right intentions, he must push ahead, ignoring the initial criticism.

I have already emphasized that the Secretariat officers must be in constant touch with the field officers, especially the District Magistrates in both policy formulation and implementation. There is an interesting story about the ICS days during the colonial regime when a District Officer, on receiving a GO, wrote on the margin 'this GO shall not apply to my district'. This may be an extreme step but points out the necessity of close coordination between the Secretariat and district-level officers. It is important that if a District Officer writes to the Secretary about an issue relating to his department, then the Secretary concerned should look into the matter personally, take action and send a response. This would greatly improve the effectiveness at the district level and make quality delivery of public services possible.

At the top of the Secretariat ladder is the office of the Chief Minister (CM) which speaks on behalf of the CM and as such a lot of weight and power gravitates towards them, naturally. Often there is a conflict between the CM Secretariat and the

Chief Secretary but this is unhealthy and creates two poles of power leading to a divisive administration. It all depends upon the mutual trust and regard between the Chief Minister and the Chief Secretary. The CM Secretariat is definitely a seat of power but should never undermine the authority of the Chief Secretary. It often depends upon the personality of the Chief Minister. A very strong and energetic CM works excessively through his Secretariat, thereby weakening the institution of the Chief Secretary, which is not in the best interest of administration.

I had the fortune to work as Secretary to the Chief Minister for over four years and always made it a point to give full respect and weightage to the Principal Secretary of the departments and the Chief Secretary. It is important that a Secretary to CM does not lose his head and become arrogant and display intemperate behaviour. Sometimes in their eagerness to please the CM, these officers behave very piously and make enemies and also distort the institutional administrative setup.

Close coordination between the CM and the CS is very essential for the functioning of the government and the CM Secretariat can play a very important role in this. For instance, any file put by the Chief Secretary should normally never be turned down by the CM Office, otherwise it will send a very wrong signal to the entire administration and the authority of the CS gets considerably weakened.

The officers of the CM Secretariat have to be aware of the political compulsions of a CM but they should realize that they are not political secretaries but administrative officers whose job it is to brief the CM about the issues in a dispassionate manner and to ensure that the rules and regulations are followed, so that the CM does not have to face any embarrassment later on. The CM Secretariat has to convey the views of the CM to the concerned officers from time to time but this should not be done in an abrasive manner. It was my good fortune to work with three Chief Ministers as Secretary—Kalyan Singh, Ram Prakash Gupta and Rajnath Singh. It was indeed a great learning experience and each one of them had a different style of working but were excellent leaders in their own way. I realized that anybody who climbs up the political ladder and becomes a CM needs to have a lot of positive qualities, talent and leadership traits. I remember Mr Kalyan Singh as a perfect administrator who was fond of going through the files and paperwork. The system was that all the files that came to the CM office from the departments were studied by the CM Secretariat who then a dummy note prepared and put up to the CM along with relevant pages of the concerned file. Kalyan Singh would go through each note in detail and then append his approval or comments on the file. He used to devote at least two hours every night after dinner to dispose files and he did it alone. We would find all the files back on the table, the next morning. He was most comfortable with bureaucratic procedures. He was a strong administrator and always backed his officers. He had a very strong information network and knew all the personality traits of each officer which he used to record in a red diary along with his impressions about the officer. This diary would be produced by him at the time of discussion about postings and transfers, and he would often surprise us all with his acute insight.

He was meticulous and everything had to be organized. The days of the week and time span was fixed for when he would meet ministers, public representatives, media people and officers. He also had a weekly system of 'Janta Darshan' where he would meet citizens. This Janta Darshan was continued by other Chief Ministers too and was a very successful method of maintaining public contact. Mr Kalyan Singh was very strict in matters relating to recommendations regarding transfers and postings made by MPs, MLAs and other party stalwarts. I recall that I was once with him when a very senior member of the party came to meet him and handed him a bunch of applications. Mr Kalyan Singh went through them quietly but I noticed his face tightening with anger as evidently all the applications related to transfers of officers. Suddenly the CM threw the applications at the visitor and told him in clear terms that he had not expected such a senior person to behave like a *dalaal* (tout). The poor visitor shamefacedly gathered the papers and scampered out of the office with as much dignity as he could muster.

He would always patiently hear us when we briefed him on the cabinet notes and liked to discuss a matter in great detail before arriving at a decision. Once he had taken a decision, it was difficult to make him change it. It was during his tenure that we unbundled the leviathan UP Electricity Board into generation, transmission and distribution companies. The power unions went on strike, threatening to cut off the power supply to the state but the CM stood firm and ultimately, the unions had to back out and reforms were implemented.

He was an excellent orator in Hindi and he had a knack of playing with words but he was not so comfortable in English. Once there was a meeting with industry associations and prospective investors in Delhi and we asked him to speak in English as the participants would be able to comprehend better. I wrote his speech. At 7 a.m. on the day of the event, I got a call saying that the CM wanted me to come over. I went to his room and found him attired in a lungi and a vest and poring over the draft speech. He then read out the entire speech before me and asked me for the correct pronunciations of certain words and diligently wrote these words in Hindi on the margin of the speech. He read out the speech several times and waited to hear from me on how it was coming along. I was amazed at this humility and work ethic. Needless to say, he gave a terrific speech at the investment meet.

Mr Kalyan Singh was replaced halfway due to differences with the high command and Mr Ram Prakash Gupta, a septuagenarian, was pulled out of obscurity and appointed CM. It is said he was sitting in a '*dhaba*' (small shop) outside his house when the news was broken to him. He had been out of active politics for more than two decades. Normally, every CM appoints a fresh team for his Secretariat. Accordingly, we were all waiting for our new postings. All of a sudden, I was summoned by the new CM and asked to continue. I became the lone Secretary to be appointed for almost a month.

Jokes began circulating that the new CM was senile and forgetful. I found that this was far from the truth as he had a wonderfully agile brain and was able to grasp whatever we briefed him on. He, of course, was out of touch and did not know many people by name or face. He belonged to an era where politics was value-based. I would like to narrate a small story to establish my point. As soon as he became CM, MLAs started meeting him regularly and most of them gave applications for the transfer of their DM and SSP. Mr Ram Prakash Gupta would write in his beautiful handwriting 'Transfer Kiya Jaata hai' (Transfer has been made). It so happened that he passed this order on so many applications that if all of them were to be implemented, more than half the districts would have new DMs and SPs. I kept these orders in my custody, hoping to speak to the CM at an appropriate time. However, before I could do this, the MLAs came back to him complaining that nothing had been done. The CM summoned me and I had to confess that the papers were with me and I said that I wanted to discuss the issue with him. I explained that this would cause a lot of disturbance in administration and if he would allow me to verify facts before acting. He looked at me quizzically and asked me, 'Do you know who has written these letters?' I told him that they were written by honourable MLAs or MPs. He responded with absolute innocence, 'An MLA or MP never tells lies. If he says something then it has to be right and there is no need to do any verification'. I realized that he was living in the politics of the late sixties, when he was a prominent minister. There has been a sea change since then. It took me some time to convince him and he agreed reluctantly.

Contrary to what people might have thought, Mr Ram Prakash Gupta was very sharp. He was one of the few ministers that I have seen who are comfortable with numbers. In fact, when we presented a file to him he would ask for quantifiable data and would analyze it. I once mentioned this to him and he told me with a smile that he had an MSc in mathematics and had got a first division. His business sense was also acute and he could easily understand issues related to finance and industry.

He spent a lot of time meeting people and as such had less time to attend to files. I was also looking after the crucial home ministry in the CM Secretariat and the files of the home department, which are always urgent, had started piling up. With Mr Kalyan Singh, a relationship of mutual trust had developed and I used to dispose of several matters at my level. However, Mr Gupta, upon taking over, had clearly directed that all matters should be put up to him. One day, I approached him and requested for time to dispose of files. He asked me how many files were pending and I told him that the figure was around 500 and increasing every day. He smiled and said that I should not be worried and gave me time. I presented about twenty files to him and then he asked me to stop and thought deeply for a while. After a few minutes, he told me to clear the files at my level and only put up those matters which I considered to be of utmost importance. I locked myself in the committee room and disposed of all pending matters within two days and continued to do so. I was happy that a relationship of trust had been established.

Mr Rajnath Singh, who succeeded Mr Gupta as Chief Minister, was brilliant and had a great vision. His mind was extremely sharp and it took only a few minutes to brief him on any issue. He implicitly trusted all the members of his Secretariat and encouraged us to speak our minds. His style of disposing files was to allow us to orally present the file to him. He would be very attentive and asked probing questions for which we had to be very well-prepared. His approach was extremely positive and he wanted things to move forward. He was always available to meet officers, public representatives and media, and greet them all with a smile.

Though he was extremely democratic in functioning, he would always take a stand on matters of principle. In UP, he became a legend when he was the Minister of Education and he broke the back of the cheating mafia and conducted 'Cheating-free' board examinations. A performance like that has never been repeated.

Once, a senior minister met him and pressurized him about a matter relating to the industries department. He asked me to look into it and see how it could be done. I discussed the matter with the concerned Principal Secretary and went through the papers, and realized that it was not possible to do this work. I went up to him and explained the situation. He thought for a while and then mentioned that the concerned senior minister was very keen and if I could find a way out. I told him that this was not possible as approving it could create problems for him later on and went to the extent of saying, 'Sir, even if I could, I would not let you sign this file because it does not appear proper to me.' The moment he heard this, his response was clear and he asked me to drop the matter and that he would convince the minister. All through my tenure with him, I found that he never pressurized us on any matter. Besides, he was very forgiving too. Even if he was upset with the conduct of any officer, he never tried to harm their career. Unfortunately, he had a very short tenure, otherwise the state could have done very well under his leadership.

It was a unique opportunity that I got to work with three chief ministers as their Secretary. It was indeed a rewarding experience to be successful at this job as one has to get to know the mind of the CM and act accordingly. It is imperative that one gives free and frank advice but it should be done with due politeness and courtesy. Since the officers of the CM Secretariat spend so much time with the CM, they get an opportunity to sensitize him on various issues of governance and in this way, they can give a direction to the administration of the state. However, this should always be done without being overbearing and a respectful distance must always be kept, no matter how open or magnanimous the CM might be. One should never use the name of the CM to get some work done, unless specifically instructed by the CM directly. Many people meet officers of the CM Secretariat but while speaking to the concerned officer, it is always advisable that an officer of the CM Secretariat never tries to say that he is speaking on the direction of the CM unless he has brought it to his notice. One should be aware of one's limits and it should be clear that the CM is the boss and your role is to assist and advise him.

The state Secretariat is the place where policies are framed and important decisions are made regarding governance across various sectors. At the Principal Secretary/Secretary level, you can make a real impact, provided your approach is positive and 'hands-on'. Any postings below the Secretary level are learning processes about the complexities of government functioning. It is true that in the Secretariat, you tend to be burdened with files but each file has a decision to be taken or throws up issue of importance. Prompt decision-making and rendering unfettered advice to ministers can make a huge difference to the quality of outcomes.

To really play a transformational role, the officer must focus on results and outcomes but unfortunately, the officer is often more concerned about the process than delivering results. I have personally seen many brilliant officers mellow down in the Secretariat to the level of becoming 'inaction wonders'. They disconnect themselves from the field and get mired in the rules and regulations with the results that the files become thicker, with no difference being made to the actual delivery of public services. For instance, if an officer is Secretary in the urban development department and is busy disposing files while cities are full of garbage and filth rotting on the roads, then it implies that his working has no connection with the real issues confronting his department. Similarly, there is no purpose served by the Health Secretary clearing files on a daily basis if the quality of healthcare remains abysmally poor. Teachers remain absent from schools while the Secretary Education is busy issuing detailed guidelines and instructions which have a total disconnect with the realities in the field. This leads to discontentment amongst the people as they are receiving poor quality of public services. It is, thus, mandatory to make better outcomes the focus of each and every department and the performance of all the Secretariat, departments should be measured accordingly.

The Secretary/Principal Secretary has to see themselves as a leader playing a transformational role. She heads a team and it is incumbent upon him to build team spirit, create a culture of prompt decision-making and motivate and inspire his team to achieve the larger goals. It is true that the hierarchical nature of the bureaucracy and the obsession with files, papers, procedures, processes, rules and regulations is ideally suited to maintaining the status quo. It does not have any inbuilt dynamism for change. This makes the task of the Secretary even tougher. She has to be a true leader who can give results in spite of the systems and also have the courage and capacity to be an agent of change. One main requisite is that the officer should have a stable tenure, preferably about three years, to make an impact. Also, the political executive should refrain from interfering in administrative issues and should confine themselves to policy matters.

Arrogance is something the Secretary must shed if she wants to succeed. Just because one is an IAS officer, this does not mean that you know everything. In fact, a major quality of a successful officer has to be humility—the capacity to learn from others, like the specialists and the citizens. The officer has to be transparent and take the views and advice of all stakeholders before a policy is framed.

A department responds to the personality of the Secretary/ Principle Secretary and she has to design the culture of the department and give it direction. True leadership gravitates towards her if the department perceives her as transparent, fair, just and accessible. Compassion and empathy are essential qualities for success at this job.

5

Working in the Government of India

A National and International perspective

A posting in the Government of India is keenly sought after for the national and international exposure it gives and the promise of the career progression that it has. Without a posting in the GOI, you may not be able to get empanelled as Secretary which is a post to which most IAS officers aspire. Not everyone becomes Chief Secretary of his state which is a post equivalent to that of Secretary to Government of India. In fact, often in a particular cadre, not a single officer becomes Chief Secretary but several do become Secretaries to the GOI. This makes a posting in the GOI a very significant step in the career of an IAS officer.

I went to the GOI as Joint Secretary Defence and most officers want to come to the GOI at the JS level as the most important posts in the Union Government are those of the Secretary and JS. In between, there is the Additional or Special Secretary but that post is merely a waiting period before one is promoted to the top post. Most files terminate at the level of the JS and only if a file has to be submitted to the Secretary does it go through the Additional Secretary (AS). The AS has to depend upon whatever work or powers the Secretary is willing to delegate to him. Below the JS there is the Director and Deputy Secretary and these are the officers who process and put up files to the JS.

A dilemma facing the GOI has been the shortage of officers opting for central deputation below that of the JS. In contrast, the post of the JS is oversubscribed. I recall that this issue was raised repeatedly by the Secretary Department of Personnel and the Cabinet Secretary who wondered why officers did not want to join at levels below the JS. Actually, there is no mystery around this as officers prefer to remain in the state because of the lure of a district posting or a head of department level in the state. These posts carry with them much more independent power and authority than that of a Deputy Secretary or Director in the GOI. In addition, the hygiene factors are also very strong at the state level—cars, large offices, personal assistants, staff, comfortable houses and a significant status in society, whereas these perks are often missing in the GOI at this level. This does lead to a strange situation where there is a shortage of officers at one level and surplus at another. Apart from ensuring more facilities, there is very little that one can do to redress this issue. One would have to somehow enrich these jobs. The problem is more severe in cadres like UP and also in the case of insiders to other cadres.

As it is, a posting in the GOI can be a huge culture shock. Coming fresh from the state where she is a person of status and relevance, she finds that she is part of a large crowd with hardly any identity of her own. At the junior level, the officer is left to fend for herself and could at best consider herself a glorified clerk. The office room is not that large and except for the Secretary, no officer has a toilet attached to his room. The Chaprassi is clear about his duties and timings and the personal assistant likes to keep his involvement purely official.

The first shock relates to getting a vehicle. At levels below the JS, there is no question of getting an official car and even at the JS level, most ministries have a car-sharing system. You have a better chance of getting an official vehicle if you are posted in a ministry that has public sector corporations. I was posted in the Ministry of Defence and was lucky to get a vehicle from the Navy. It was a taxi and an Indica, and I felt a little sheepish going anywhere except to the office in that vehicle. Once I had to go to Gurgaon for a meeting and the employee at the toll barrier was insistent that since it was a taxi, the toll would have to be paid.

The second shock relates to the house. You have to keep running to the urban development ministry to plead your case. The state bhawans where you would be staying temporarily start giving you notice about charging the market rate after a weeks' stay. After several months, you are allotted a house which is just about livable. There is no help available for shifting your belongings or settling down.

Domestic help is the next issue. I had taken someone with me from Lucknow but he saw my state of affairs and rightly concluded that 'Sahab has no future!' Within three months, he left. One has to depend on the quarters attached to the house or take the services of part-time help.

Then there is the issue of getting your children admitted in good schools. The principals would not give you time to meet and even the ordinary clerk in the school office would wave you away. The officer has to run from pillar to post in such instances. I was lucky that both the Chairman Central Board of Secondary Education and Controller Examinations had worked with me in the state. Their phone call did the job. The principal of the school I hoped for invited me for tea and granted admission to my son. So much for the glory of the IAS! I was able to achieve this uphill task with relative ease but not many are as lucky.

Medical facilities and contacting the doctor is another issue. I had a harrowing experience just two weeks after I had joined the GOI as JS (Defence). At about 9.30 p.m. one night, my son was having dinner when a chicken bone got stuck in his throat. It was painful and he was having trouble breathing. I was worried that it would block his windpipe and choke him. I was staying at UP Sadan Chanakyapuri and they got me a taxi to take us to Lohia Hospital. The taxi driver asked for a huge sum, refusing to go by the meter and as it was an emergency, I had no time to haggle. I went straight to the emergency wing of the hospital, introduced myself and explained the problem. A couple of junior doctors were in attendance and they gave me a patient hearing and advised me that since this was an ENT issue, I should go to the concerned department. I pleaded that it was an emergency and they should call the ENT specialist but they expressed their inability to do so. I had to walk across the hospital to the ENT wing with my son, where a doctor attended to him but said that he would be unable to do anything until I got an X-ray done. Back again to the emergency I went, and from there, I was directed to the X-ray section after being given a slip of paper. There was a long queue in front of the X-ray room and I requested for priority as this was an emergency but the technician did not agree. I waited patiently for more than half an hour but when our turn came, the technician just walked away saying that he was going to have tea. I rushed back to the doctors in the emergency but they expressed their inability to do anything as the technicians were unionized and would not listen to them. I waited for some more time but my son started complaining of breathlessness. I got desperate and rang up my PA, who lived nearby in Gole Market. He asked me to wait and soon arrived in an autorickshaw and told me 'Sir, you should have gone straight to the RR hospital where as JS Defence, you would have got immediate attention'. All three of us sat in an autorickshaw and rushed to the RR hospital while my PA made some phone calls to the doctors there. As soon as we reached, a surgeon and another doctor were there, who wheeled my son into the operation theatre and came out five minutes later with a large piece of chicken bone. 'It was very close to the wind pipe, sir, you were very lucky,' they told me. How I wished at that moment that I was in my state where the whole issue would have been resolved in no time and with no tension. Needless to say, I slept with great difficulty that night and kept cursing myself for having opted for the GOI.

However, things do settle down. The first two to three months can be unnerving and one requires a strong heart to bear it. Thereafter, the process of adjustment starts and after a year or so, you and your family start liking Delhi which has its own charms. In other words you soon become a 'Delhi-ite' and attune to its style. Soon Delhi and the GOI grow on you and officers start liking it so much that they do not want to come back. I never quite related to Delhi but that is an individual opinion.

Delhi has people specializing in all kinds of things. There are those who can help you in getting school admission and promise to look after your other needs. It is comfortable if you know the right people but then these people are often 'middlemen' and an officer must keep a distance from them, for sooner or later they will ask for a favour. Despite being possibly vulnerable in the initial years, it is advisable to stay away from these smiling 'do-gooders'. However, to my utter amazement, I have found that these people have a lot of access to government officers and have their ears close to the doors to catch every piece of information about officers and official matters. Some of them work in the 'PA Network' and can tell you exactly where a particular file is at any given point of time. I was personally informed by the Defence Secretary that I along with two other officers had been selected for a posting as JS in the defence ministry and that the orders would be issued soon. The Defence Secretary retired and for weeks after that I got no intimation. I had no clue of how I should move forward. One of my batchmates with long experience in the Government of India took pity on me and informed me that there are people who can tell you where exactly your matter is pending and kindly offered to help me out. Lo and behold, three days later, he rang me up to tell me that he had been 'informed' that my file had been approved by the Defence Minister but was lying with a new Defence

Secretary who was reviewing it and wanted to discuss it afresh with the minister. Later events confirmed that the informer had been 'spot on'. So, these middlemen or informers can be useful but sooner rather than later they demand their pound of flesh. You can recognize these people easily as they have a peculiar habit of taking the first name of a senior IAS officer or minister at the drop of a hat and will nonchalantly tell you what 'Ajeet' said when they were having dinner together the other day or playing golf together.

The biggest attraction of a GOI posting is the international exposure. In simple language, it means the prospect of foreign travel and also a chance of a foreign posting. Ministries are categorized according to the avenues of foreign travel that they promise. That is why ministries like commerce are sought after and the competition to get into them is high. When the GOI officers meet each other, the common topic of conversation is the number of countries that an officer has visited. Some claim to have crossed the half-century mark whereas others make tall claims of having scored a century. I happened to go as JS Defence and defence was a ministry which had very few opportunities for foreign travel. If at all they travelled, it was mostly to Russia. Many of my colleagues looked sympathetically at me and said 'could you not manage a better ministry? 'I was told that most officers avoid PHD ministries – personnel, home and defence – as they have the least chances of foreign travel. So, defence, despite being such an important strategic ministry, has few people opting for it. Within the ministries too there is intense competition for the international co-operation desk. A foreign posting or deputation to an international organization is highly coveted.

This is despite the fact that these assignments do not give great opportunities for doing challenging work. Late T.S.R. Subramaniam who retired as Cabinet Secretary and had served in the state, center and in an international organization, had commented in his book that the maximum work is done in the districts, then the state government, then the GOI and finally the international organization where you have a lot of time on your hands. Still, the lure of the international posting is there.

The GOI concerns itself with policy formulation at the national level and is generally not involved in the implementation aspect, which is the responsibility of the state governments. In some departments like defence, external affairs and commerce, all the action is at the GOI level. There are, however, huge GOI bureaucracies dealing with subjects on the concurrent or the state lists. Sometimes, one wonders whether it is necessary at all. For example, the Ministry of Agriculture in the GOI has ten Joint Secretaries whereas agriculture is a state subject. There is a serious case for reduction in the size of certain ministries at the centre and also of clubbing several ministries together as it is strange that the Ministry of Agriculture is not involved with issues related to fertilizer, water or agriculture credit.

The ministries of such size at the GOI exist because of political reasons and also the bureaucratic culture of creating work to perpetuate work and justify itself. The major mechanisms for this are the centrally sponsored schemes where the major financial contribution (60 per cent or 75 per cent) is done by the centre and schemes are formulated at the GOI level with detailed guidelines. The problem arises as no two states are alike. The same schemes will succeed in one state but the conditions in other states will not favor its implementation. Thus, the states constantly argue that funds should be transferred to them and they be left free to design schemes. However, there is no denying that there is greater wisdom available at the GOI due to its knowledge about the best practices in the states, presence of experts and availability of international inputs. The GOI involves stakeholders, specialists and consultants in designing policy and the due diligence done is of a very high order. Yet, there cannot be a universal policy looking at the extreme variations between states. The solution, as usual, has to be in between.

The best model for this has been the Rashtriya Krishi Vikas Yojna (RKVY) implemented by the Ministry of Agriculture. In this, the GOI lays down guidelines and also lists out all the possible projects and allows the states to choose interventions according to their priorities. A committee at the level of Chief Secretary finalizes the lists of projects to be taken up and a senior officer of the GOI is a member of this committee. Thereafter, the GOI approves the schemes at its level, where the main concern is whether the schemes meet the general guidelines. There is a scope for the states to come out with innovative location-specific interventions, provided they meet the overall objective of agricultural development. I feel this model should be replicated in other ministries too because it is a perfect blend of the strengths of both the centre and the states. There was also the problem of there being a plethora of centrally sponsored schemes which has now been attended to by various committees at the union government level, and many schemes have been done away with and others rationalized. Some issues have been raised recently after the Central Finance Commission increased the devolution to the states from central resources to 42 per cent instead of 32 per cent, as the central share in many of the centrally sponsored schemes have been reduced subsequent to this increased devolution, to the disadvantage of state governments. Of course, there are different viewpoints on this.

Seminars and conferences are a major activity in the GOI where there is an involvement at the highest level of Secretary, AS and JS in organizing the stakeholder consultations. These are important because they provide the basic framework for policy formulations. The minutest of details like seating arrangements, refreshments, flower decorations, minute to minute programmes, and even placement of mineral water bottles, are attended to by senior officers. This kind of seriousness is never visible in the conferences at the state level and in GOI, these conferences lead to views being expressed by experts and academicians, along with government officers. Policy formulation at the centre is normally a long-drawn affair which involves detailed stakeholder consultations and examination. I find that many people who are not in government feel that it is just a few IAS officers who, along with their ministers, formulate policy. This is far from the truth. The policy formulation at the GOI level involves consultations with all those concerned and before finalizing, the draft policy is put up on the website for the comments of citizens. The result is an excellent policy formulation process which leads to the designing of very comprehensive policies which are well-formulated, articulated and issued in the form of government policy directives. My only concern has been that these policies have to be implemented at the state and district level and often the challenges faced by the implementing agencies are not considered fully in the policy document. This leads to a general impression that policies are good but implementation is poor which would not be so if policy formulation factors in the implementation issues too. IAS officers have district experience and they should use it in policy formulation to make it easier to understand and implement.

The processes of governance are taken very seriously in the GOI, unlike the states. Take the cabinet note/proposal as an example. In states a very poorly drafted cabinet note is mostly put up which is often difficult to decipher. Normally, the HOD sends a draft cabinet note and the Secretariat reproduces it on its files with very little value addition. But the GOI is different. Here too the HOD will send a draft note but the entire team from the JS and below works on it for days or months, scrutinizing each word and examining all aspects. Commas and full stops are put in order, sentences redrafted and appropriate words used to convey just the right meaning. The GOI has very strict guidelines about the length of a cabinet note, the margins to be left and the number of appendices. My Defence Secretary was very clear that the cabinet note must be dictated by the JS himself. In fact, his style was that he would discuss the cabinet note with the concerned JS only and asked detailed questions about each word, phrase or figure given in the cabinet note. If one was hesitant in answering, he would promptly return the cabinet note with a strong admonishment. The argument that the note has been drafted according to the matter given by HOD was just not acceptable to him. This is in stark contrast with the states where when I used to take a briefing as CS on cabinet notes, I found that the Principle Secretary of the department would bring his HOD and others for the briefing and often would turn to them to explain things in detail. Also, often in states, the cabinet notes are prepared overnight and are poorly drafted but have to be put up because the Chief Minister wants them. In the GOI, cabinet notes are seriously time-consuming affairs and there is rarely any pressure to bring it before the cabinet immediately. In the states often even a few hours before the cabinet meets, instructions come from the top to bring a particular item before the cabinet. Naturally, there are a lot of loose ends in the note which leads to poor policy formulation and difficulties in implementation and often there are frequent changes made subsequently in the policy. I strongly feel that the GOI approach to cabinet proposals should be adopted by the states as policies impact the lives of a large number of people and their sanctity should be preserved. In the GOI it is common to see senior officers writing in the self-appraisal during the annual performance evaluation that they piloted two or three cabinet notes. In states, you will rarely find an officer making a mention of it.

In a similar vein, the business of parliament is taken very seriously at the centre. Very detailed and exhaustive preparation is done to answer the starred questions. For each question, the background and possible supplementaries are all listed out and the minister spends a lot of time getting briefed. I have worked with ministers in the Government of India who were very quick to grasp the issues and handled the questions in an extremely adroit manner. Then there are the various committees of parliament which work rigorously and it is a trial by fire for the Secretary to face a parliamentary committee. Great communication skills, patience and knowledge of his subject are essential for the Secretary to respond to the probing questions of the committee members. Even though other senior officers are in attendance, it is the Secretary who has to face the music.

The officers in the GOI do not spend as much time meeting people as their counterparts in the state government. Maximum time is devoted to clearing files and the ability of an officer to write precise, concise, relevant and logical notes, which is an essential skill. An officer must be prepared to add value especially if the file is going up to the Secretary as it is his contribution to the file which determines the superior's assessment of his performance and abilities. I remember in defence, the Secretary insisted on a detailed note by the JS and would return the file with a sarcastic comment if the JS had just appended his signature to whatever was put up to him from below.

I had an interesting experience when I went to join the defence ministry as JS. The Defence Secretary interviewed me for close to half an hour before he allotted me the work of JS (Navy and Ordinance). Amongst the many things he asked me, he wanted me to comment on a statement: 'An IAS officer's job is 90 per cent clerical'. I pounced on the statement and tore it to shreds contending that an IAS officer has to deliver outcomes and not just prepare summaries, write notes and draft letters. To my utter consternation, I found that the Secretary totally disagreed with me and he was clear that I must know all the rules, regulations, precedents and read the files from page one (in states we often read only the last noting) and then put up everything concisely in one's noting covering all aspects. The Secretary was clear that if you are not solid in your file work then you cannot succeed in the GOI.

There was an interesting case in which I was confronted with the realities of handling file work in the GOI. The Army moved a proposal for some crucial equipment to assist them in anti-terrorist operations in Kashmir. I was immediately convinced of its urgency and instead of marking the proposal downwards for examination, I scheduled a presentation by the Army for the very next day. On the basis of the presentation, I dictated a note immediately for an in-principle approval for the purchase of this equipment. The file returned after more than a month with three to four observations/queries. I felt upset and went to the AS with the file arguing that all aspects had been covered in my note. The AS smiled, offered me a cup of tea and asked me to not become unnecessarily agitated. The AS told me that the Secretary had asked him to speak to me and had evidently said, 'Tell Alok this is not UP but GOI'. On behalf of the Secretary, the AS then gave me an orientation on how the proposal should have been dealt with. It should have been marked downwards from where it would surface after a month or so. At this stage, I was expected to raise four to five queries and send the file back. The file would go back to the Army headquarters and return with the responses after a couple of months. The same drill would have to be followed again and a fresh round of queries raised. This entire process may take close to a year and may be by that time, the army will no longer be interested in the proposal. If they still persisted and the file came back with all clarifications then it should be examined and put up for consideration to a higher level. I was not convinced and objected by arguing that this delay in procurement was not warranted in emergent situations. However, the AS was clear that the Secretary had warned that if I persisted with my style, I would soon run afoul for the CAG, CVC and the CBI. In fact, by initiating the note at my level within a day of having received the proposal, I would be a sitting duck for the insinuations of these agencies with malafide motives being presumed. On the contrary, by repeatedly raising queries and then putting up an equivocal proposal I would be absolutely safe as any agency examining the file would notice that I had exercised considerable due diligence. I felt suitably chastened.

The Defence Secretary was an extremely bright officer who impressed upon me that I should have the ability of segregating those files which required a decision to be taken early from others which needed to be kept pending. He made his point clear by telling me that the files belonging to the latter category should be sent into the orbit so that they may keep circling. He, however, emphasized that I must have the capability of retrieving the file from the orbit if I was required to do so at any time. I realized that a performance of an officer in GOI is determined by the files which tell the story about his application of mind and diligence. Successful piloting of files is both an art as well as a science, and anyone who does not pay heed to this is likely to be chastised.

One thing to be really appreciated about GOI is that systems work here in comparison to the states where the CM or the ministers insist on action to be taken as per their wishes. Rules, regulations and norms are sacred in the GOI and even the ministers do not expect the bureaucracy to bend norms to accommodate their recommendations. In the defence ministry, I observed that numerous applications marked down from the office of the Defence Minister would come back with the observation from the armed forces, clearly stating that no action under rules was possible on the application. The minister would inevitably write 'seen' and return the file. I do not recall the minister ever making it an important issue. In another incident which was narrated to me, I was told that a major intervention in primary education was introduced for the fifty most backward districts of the country and the districts were selected based on a set of parameters approved by the cabinet. It so happened that the Prime Minister at that time was impressed by the project and wanted his district—also backward—to be included in the list of fifty backward districts. Consider his surprise when the file came back to him clearly stating that acceding to his request was not possible as it did not fulfill the requisite criteria. Imagine such a situation with the CM in a state government! The department would have bent over backwards to accommodate the directions of the CM. I recall as Agriculture Production Commissioner (APC), I formulated the Lohia village development schemes and the villages were to be selected as per approved parameters. However, the most influential ministers wanted villages of their choice to be included and there was a lot of debate and argument. Ultimately the criteria had to be modified by saying that 10 per cent of the villages would be selected on the recommendation of the local MLA. There is no doubt that the working of the GOI is far more systematic and professional than the state governments and this is the reason why IAS officers who work in GOI begin to avoid returning to states and want to continue their tenure at GOI. Many officers have told me that they get a great sense of satisfaction while working in GOI as they are subjected to very little undue pressure. I found that even senior members of parliament would always take an appointment to meet an officer and then also put forward their request very politely and would not raise a hue and cry if told that it was not possible to do the work as it was against the rules. In state governments, the MLAs and the ministers expect an officer to change the rules to accommodate their requests.

In GOI an officer tends to get stereotyped depending on the cadre to which she belongs. There are also times when IAS officers from certain cadres get preferred postings depending upon the cadre to which the cabinet Secretary or the principle Secretary to the Prime Minister belongs and also the power equation between the two. Increasingly, the PMO has become much more powerful than the institution of the Cabinet Secretary. Sometimes, UP cadre would dominate and sometimes officers of other cadres would do so. It keeps varying. Cabinet ministers also have a tendency of choosing officers of their cadre, though currently the policy is that the ministers and Secretary should not be from the same state cadre. Similarly, the Secretary has a say in selecting his team and is naturally more comfortable with officers of his cadre. The current position is that the PMO plays a decisive role in selecting the officers and the Secretaries can merely indicate options.

There is a definite perception about officers of different cadres. UP cadre officers are looked at with suspicion as they are perceived as being political, intelligent but not having the desire to go deep into the subject. The officers from southern cadres are supposed to be meticulous, systematic and rule bound whereas officers form Punjab are extroverts and dynamic—so on and so forth. There is no denying that the kind of experience that an officer has in a state moulds his working style and approach. Each cadre does have some distinctive features but overall, these things are dependent upon the personality of the individual and it is not always correct to bunch officers of one cadre together. I recall that as Secretary Basic Education, Government of UP, I made an excellent presentation in a meeting being chaired by a JS from a southern cadre who quipped sarcastically, 'At least UP is making good presentations but let us see whether any real work is done.' I was taken aback and felt most upset. However, it brought a sense of great satisfaction to me when the same JS commented after a few months in a meeting that the best work was being done in UP.

In the GOI, an officer has to reinvent herself. In the state she already has an image but in GOI, she has to start from the beginning and build her image afresh. An officer is not given too much time to make her mark and has to be on her toes from the very beginning. Moreover, in GOI you have to deal with scientists, specialists and experts who often hold the posts equivalent to Secretary and are not willing to accept your authority unless you are able to impress them. Meetings with these people can be a real test for an IAS officer as they can be very sensitive and are confident of their domain knowledge. They have a vast reservoir of specialized experience and the IAS officer has to respect their views. She also has to grasp issues fast enough to be able to lead her team. There is no denying that the intellectual inputs in the GOI are of a much higher level than the states. The experience that one gets from the entire nation can be really enriching. Moreover, the international best practices are made available and one learns how to conduct themselves in international meetings and negotiations.

Performance appraisal of IAS officers is a frequently discussed issue. The GOI Department of Personnel and Training, is responsible for putting in place an appraisal system which would bring out the best in the officers. Frequently, one hears criticism from various corners that an IAS officer is working in an environment of complete security. Once a person gets into the service her career progression is guaranteed on the basis of seniority. Also, it has been found that most officers are graded 'Very good' or 'Outstanding' in a routine manner and there is no mechanism to distinguish performers and non-performers. There is an element of truth in this as even if an officer does not perform well at his job, he does not get an average or poor rating. Actually an adverse entry is quite a serious affair as it blocks the path of promotion and is resorted to only in extreme cases of insubordination, corruption or extremely poor performance. Moreover, an adverse entry is communicated to the officer who then gives his representation and things tend to become messy. In GOI, one often hears a complaint that there is a greater propensity in certain cadres to rate an officer as outstanding as compared to others. Various variants of performance appraisal reports have been designed to make this system more scientific and effective but still it is far from being an objective evaluation system and officers who do not deliver but play safe, comfortably move up the ladder. GOI has recently started a new 360-degree evaluation system for empanelment of officers to the post of JS/AS and Secretary. This module has been taken from the private sector but has raised more questions than it has answered as the feedback is taken from various sources regarding the competence and integrity of an officer but it is possible that the person contacted may have a coloured perception on the basis of his individual experience and hence, his feedback may not be objective. This system has led to a large number of officers not getting selected for the post of Secretary Government of India and this has led to a lot of resentment amongst officers. In any case, it is now no longer easy for an officer to be posted as Secretary to Government of India as there is a system of rigorous evaluation of his performance and integrity. Very recently, the Government of India has announced the Karm Yogi Policy which aims to select the right person for the right job and develop capacity in the officers through training modules besides developing a system of overall human capital management and development. This is a very exciting thought and should lead to considerable improvement in the quality of governance at the GOI level.

The Secretary to Government of India is one of the most powerful and influential posts. The entire department functions according to the priorities and leadership style of the Secretary. It is an immensely satisfying assignment where you can make a big difference in the department that you are heading. It is the Secretary who brings about reforms in his department and also monitors the impact of these reform measures. The AS, JS and other officers are completely dependent upon the Secretary and if they have problems with him, then they are likely to face a nasty time. Room for manoeuvre is less than in the states where an officer can manage his transfer to some other department. A Secretary can really deliver if he gets a decent tenure of at least two years. In the past, officers were becoming Secretary just a few months short of their retirement and hence had no time to leave their imprint upon the department. This has now changed and generally, officers are getting three to four years at the level of Secretary, which is a very healthy trend. Such is the input of knowledge from various sources that a Secretary becomes an expert in his subject. Many non-IAS officers are also becoming Secretaries now as the intention of the government is to choose the best person for such a vital post. This means there is much more competition for IAS officers who have to get to this post with their ability and integrity. There is thus a lot of premium on experience and domain knowledge. Mostly, a person is appointed as a Secretary to a department where he has already worked for several years in GOI and state governments. By and large, the ministers in GOI are also very experienced and have good grasping powers and can give direction to the department.

However, it is still the Secretary who takes the lead in making a department move in a particular direction and brings about a transformation. As an illustration you can imagine the impact the Secretary of Health can have on the quality of healthcare that is made available to citizens all over the country. Similarly, during the current Coronavirus crisis it is the Health Secretary who is leading from the front. At the apex is the Cabinet Secretary who holds the highest post that is possible for an IAS officer to hold. Many batches do not produce even one Cabinet Secretary. His role is coordination amongst the departments, supervision and carrying out the decisions of the Cabinet, and as Secretary to Cabinet, advising the Cabinet on all aspects of policy formulation. In recent years, this post has become one of low profile because of the dominance of the post of the Principal Secretary to the Prime Minister and there are different views regarding this change. Some feel that the office of the Cabinet Secretary has been devalued. I guess a lot depends upon the personality of the Prime Minister and that of his Principal Secretary and the Cabinet Secretary. Despite everything, the post of the Cabinet Secretary is the most powerful post that an IAS officer can aspire to, as has he is the head of the bureaucracy. I recall when I was in Government of India in Ministry of Agriculture, as Managing Director NAFED, I used to attend the meetings of the task force on inflation, chaired by the Cabinet Secretary and I was impressed with the quality of deliberation and decision-making that took place.

In recent years, there have been some allegations of policy paralysis at the GOI level. This has been the result of many Secretaries and senior officers getting into trouble due to some CBI inquiry or the other. The 2G scam and the coal scam are some examples. The tragedy is that some Secretaries who have been known to be extremely honest and efficient became victims of these inquiries and some had to face arrests as well as court cases. This naturally created fear amongst the officers who then began to avoid making decisions which had a negative impact on the economic growth of the nation and quality of governance. If the bureaucratic wheels in GOI come to a halt due to the pressure of several oversight agencies, then the impact is felt by the entire country. From time to time, the Prime Minister and senior ministers have tried to assure the officers of protection if their actions are bonafide. However, despite there being an amendment to the Prevention of Corruption Act, it is still possible for an honest officer to be hounded and once proceedings start against him, there is nobody to protect him. This is a very grave matter and needs much more attention, and also needs the building of systems which would ensure that an officer working with bonafide intentions is not unnecessarily subjected to the four 'C's' – the CAG, CVC, CBI and the Courts.

Working in the GOI can be very satisfying for the tremendous knowledge of a subject that it imparts and the impact you have at the national level. In GOI you are handling policy issues at the national level, taking cross-country experiences into account and you can influence the thinking about a sector at the national level. It is your actions which show the way forward to the entire nation and the role can be that of a major agent of change and reform. The diversity of experience is amazing. To succeed in GOI, one needs to study the department in detail, understand crucial issues, articulate your viewpoint and have the ability to carry officers of other services and specialists along with you. It requires great qualities of leadership to set the goals and milestones for your departments and then lead the entire team towards fulfilling them. A dedicated officer will always find working in the Government of India to be a transformational opportunity.

6

The Chief Secretary: Leader of the State Bureaucracy

From the first day that one joins the IAS, they dream of becoming the Chief Secretary. Of course, the top position is that of the Cabinet Secretary, Government of India, but some batches go without anyone from them becoming Cabinet Secretary. However, not everyone becomes the Chief Secretary. But one can reasonably expect at least one officer from each batch in a cadre to attain the position of Chief Secretary.

The moment one joins the state after finishing the probation period at the Mussoorie Academy, the young officer begins to feel the power and prestige of the post of the Chief Secretary who is the head of the bureaucracy and vast executive powers are vested in him. I recall how in the initial years we used to look at the Chief Secretary with reverence and respect and wonder what qualities of an administrator one would need to have to reach that level. I remember how in the initial years we attended meetings chaired by the

Chief Secretary and observed every action of his. The way he would address the agenda, the excellent summing up of the discussions, the command over the languages, sharpness of mind, the immense grasping power and the uncanny ability of focusing on the exact point or issue where the problem lay. We used to wonder if ever we will be able to imbibe the required traits to hold this august office.

My first meeting with the Chief Secretary came when I was an SDM. I wanted a posting in the hills for which I had an irresistible attraction. Seniors advised me that if I went and put in such a request, they would promptly send me furthest from the hills to a district like Deoria or Ballia. Appointments department is always suspicious of requests and sometimes posts you to exactly the opposite of what you ask for.

I somehow mustered the courage and took an appointment with the Chief Secretary. I almost panicked as I was ushered into a large, beautifully furnished room at one corner of which was an oval table, behind which sat the Chief Secretary. He looked at me questioningly, waiting for me to say something. I blurted out my request to be posted in the hills. He did not cross-examine me. He picked up the phone and spoke with the Appointment Secretary, giving clear instructions. By the evening I had got my orders for district Chamoli nestled in the mountains of Garhwal. Needless to say I was terribly impressed.

How exhilarating it is for an officer to be appointed a Chief Secretary (CS). Officers cherish the moment when the news is broken to them. The very thought of having one's name printed on the wooden panel in the office creates a feeling of euphoria. I was reading an autobiography of an

IAS officer and he mentions this moment as being one of great excitement. He says that he put down the receiver of the phone, looked at his wife who was offering him tea and said, 'Madam, you are now serving tea to the Chief Secretary'. Once the decision is communicated, officers are often in a terrible hurry to join, fearing that orders might be changed. There was this case of a Chief Minister telling an officer that he was going out on tour and on his return, would sign orders for appointing him Chief Secretary. By the evening it was a different story. Another officer was appointed as CS and concerned officer was told that he should not worry as he would be next in line! This is how things can change during the course of a day, regarding the posting of a Chief Secretary.

The strangest case in UP was that of an officer who was recalled from deputation to the central government. The request letter of the state government clearly stated that they want his services as he was to be appointed Chief Secretary. The officer came to take charge and was warmly welcomed at the airport by several officers. But politics played its part and the officer found himself out in the cold being told, 'Pick any other post and we will send you there'. The officer protested and went from pillar to post but he could not succeed and soon found himself deciding revenue cases as a distinguished Member of Board of Revenue. Needless to say that in matters relating to the appointment of a Chief Secretary and his taking charge, things can quickly change.

No wonder there is often an inelegant and un-officer-like haste to take charge amongst those appointed as Chief Secretary. There was an officer who got the office opened at midnight and took charge, fearing the possibility of something adverse happening in the morning.

I recall that as APC, I was having a meeting with farmers in Agra when I was told that Mulayam Singh Yadav Ji and the Chief Minister wanted to talk to me urgently, and wanted me to meet them immediately. I wondered what this sudden message was and started searching my mind to see if I had done something to upset the CM and Mulayam Singh Yadav Ji. With great trepidation, I flew early to Lucknow and drove straight to their residences. 'We have seen your work and feel that you can do a very good job so we have decided to appoint you as Chief Secretary'. This news came as such a surprise to me that I do not think I even thanked them properly. I promised to do my best, reached my house and shared this news with my wife, who was equally thrilled. However, the evening went by and so did the night. There was no news and we began to fear the worst. Nothing happened till lunch, the next day and we were wondering what had happened when the mobile rang at lunchtime. The Appointment Secretary was on the line and he said 'Sorry to disturb you, sir, I have just entered the gate of your house. Please give me a few minutes'.

As soon as I entered the drawing room, the Appointment Secretary got up and gave me a brown envelope saying, 'Congratulations, sir! You are our new Chief Secretary'. It was one of those moments in my career which I will never forget.

Almost immediately, the news was flashed on TV screens. Messages and calls flooded me and as soon I took charge, the TV channels and print media surrounded me and drowned me in questions like, 'What will be your priorities?',

'How will you improve law and order?' I remember saying that my priorities were to build the Lucknow–Agra Expressway, construct the Lucknow Metro improve the power situation to such an extent that 24-hour power supply in urban areas and 16-hour supply in rural areas was ensured. It is a matter of satisfaction to me that during my tenure of a little more than two years I was able to achieve these goals that I had set for myself.

Being appointed as Chief Secretary of a State was a huge honour but it is also a huge responsibility and opportunity. It was a sobering thought. One had reached the pinnacle of one's career but one had to stay there gracefully and avoid hurtling down into obscurity and failure.

The attitude of everyone—officers, employees, media, citizens, public representatives, family and friends—changes the moment one is appointed CS. They all look up to you. The realization sinks in that the buck stops with you. You are expected to take a decision every minute on a diverse range of issues. It is multitasking at its best. If UP was to be a nation it would be the fifth-largest nation in the world in terms of population and is plagued with issues of caste, community, poverty, illiteracy and disease. Above all the CS has to handle the numerous pressures that the political environment of the state puts upon him. When the entire government machinery responds to your style of leadership, it is a great opportunity to bring about transformation in all aspects of governance. It is the ultimate moment in the life of an IAS officer where every movement of his, every action or inaction is observed closely and commented upon. You can justify your chair by making history by shaping events, or you can lie back and let events engulf you. The choice is yours but if you choose the latter then you have missed your opportunity.

This chair is such that I have seen it bring about a sea change in the personality of the incumbent. The sense of authority is so intoxicating that it is difficult to keep it from getting to one's head. I have seen officers who stopped smiling once they became CS while others indulged in a lot of bluster to prove themselves.

I have always believed that the post of the Chief Secretary is one where you should see yourself as a captain of a team whose power and authority is greatly enhanced by the way you connect your energy with that of your entire team.

If I was to theorize, I would list out the following styles of Chief Secretaries and some have a blend of more than one style:

1. The authoritarian
2. The rule- and procedure-bound planner
3. The laid-back one
4. The politically correct
5. The paper-oriented
6. The Democratic
7. The action-oriented and hands-on one

The authoritarian CS is conscious of his power and likes to impose his authority on everyone. He does so by acting very busy and keeping a huge distance between himself and other officers. He himself works hard but is quick to point out that others are not doing anything. Such a CS creates a dysfunctional atmosphere where there is fear of rules and team spirit is conspicuous in its absence. The authoritarian culture flows downwards in the government with each officer putting all the blame on his subordinate. The CS is like a strict disciplinarian but not able to bring any real achievements to the table.

Then there is the quintessential bureaucratic CS – the rules and procedure man. There is nothing wrong with rules and procedure being followed. The concept of accountability demands that you abide by rules and regulations and processes. Violations will land you in trouble. However, too much obsession with processes leads to ignoring the real purpose. The outcome becomes secondary. Such a CS is satisfied if the file is complete in all aspects, irrespective of the time taken or actual result achieved. He visualizes and plans but does not break the vision down to actionable points and leaves the issue hanging in the middle. For lack of performance, he blames other officers without realizing that it is his approach that is inhibiting results.

The laid-back CS is comfortable and ensconced in his chair and will not venture into anything new. He avoids innovation and initiative. His logic is that he had reached the top and he must enjoy his position. His approach to the job is quite simple – he will attend to any file or paper that comes to him but he will not initiate anything new or ask for any papers or review anything in detail. Such a CS allows the status quo to continue and in fact encourages things to remain as they are.

The politically correct CS knows which side of his toast is buttered. He knows to survive he has to earn the goodwill of the Chief Minister and other important political leaders. He knows the clout of each and every political figure and tailors his responses accordingly. Political acceptability is his main focus. Whenever an administrative issue comes up for discussion, he does not examine it professionally but switches on his political antenna and tries to read the signals. He will avoid any immediate decision-making and prefer to brief the Chief Minister or other leaders and get a feedback on the political ramifications. He sees his role more as a political advisor than as a professional head of the bureaucracy. Needless to say that decision-making is hampered and the bureaucracy ends up giving only the advice that is politically palatable.

There are Chief Secretaries who are great planners. They are extremely intelligent and go into elaborate details when anything is referred to them. However, their approach is paper-oriented and the ponderous examination of each issue leads to slow decision-making. Such an officer is fond of meetings, calling for self-contained notes, past precedents and wants a lot of data to be put up before him. He is also fond of taking the advice of consultants, and organizing workshops and seminars to discuss issues. He is more intent on drafting perfect cabinet notes and does a detailed scrutiny of the government orders being issued. The result is that he is a very busy man who keeps his team of officers even busier. Yet nothing much happens or moves off the ground. He is brilliant on paper but is disconnected from the field realities.

The democratic CS is popular as he listens. He allows officers to speak and incorporates different views in his decision-making. He is accessible. But sometimes when a tough decision is to be taken, he does not override or overrule others and gets his thinking muddled. Too much democracy without the intent to lead the team in a particular direction often leads to confusion and a lack of clear directive to the field officers. Once again, public service suffers. Participative administration is essential for good governance but it should not degenerate into a free-rein style of leadership.

Lastly, there is the hands-on, action-oriented CS. He combines the strengths of all the above styles but does away with the pitfalls. He has enough experience to know what is required of him. He is aware that rigorous monitoring, field visits, a motivated team and a positive working environment are required to translate policies into actions. Delivery of public service of projects or development works are his priorities. He does not centralize things. In fact, he encourages decentralization and result-orientation at all levels. He prioritizes and monitors the top priority items at his level. He knows the qualities of his team and uses each officer according to his ability. It is not that he is careless about policy-making or does not do due diligence, but there is a clarity of thought regarding the purpose of this exercise. He is able to build team spirit. He has to be democratic and accessible but avoid getting into a status quo situation. He should be able to influence his team towards the goals that are in the interest of the people and the government. He has to avoid the pitfalls of a democratic leadership by the very force of his ideas and intent. He should be not to be taken for granted and his demeanour should show that he means business.

He has to be proactive and his team members should be given freedom to act but be held accountable for results. He does not scold but persuades. He is not sarcastic or critical but motivational. His team has confidence that he will stand by them, support them and not sacrifice them if a mistake occurs.

Such a CS is also aware of how the political executive thinks. However, he examines the issues professionally and arrives at an administratively correct course of action. Then he also considers the political ramifications and uses his intelligence to present his decision in a politically acceptable manner. Often, he has to spend time convincing the political executive about the proposed plan of action.

The entire bureaucracy looks up to the CS and mimics his style of functioning. The kind of leadership he provides is of utmost importance because that sets the tone for the entire administration. The success or failure of a government is judged by its ability to implement schemes, projects and policies. Implementation requires a hands-on proactive approach. It is true that the CS is an extremely busy man yet he can find time to monitor, inspect and provide the requisite execution leadership. Dealing with files and cabinet notes should not become all-consuming.

One of the most significant tasks of the CS relates to the posting and transfer of officers. A CS must know his team well. He may take feedback from other officers and even members of the public. A good idea about the competence and integrity of an officer can be gauged by taking detailed feedback. Then the CS can easily make his own assessment. Just a couple of meetings, interactions would give him an idea about the strengths and weaknesses of an officer. My experience has been that most senior officers and especially the IAS officers, are extremely intelligent, hardworking and competent.

However, all of them do not have the same abilities. Some officers are very proficient in regulatory departments while others are development-oriented. You need to be tough, a stickler for rules, enforcer and hard task master for one, while the other requires much more flexibility, creativity, innovation and even subjectivity. The regulatory officer may do brilliantly in home, tax-related departments, environment but feel out of place in agriculture, rural development or education. In fact, social sector departments like education and health require a totally different mindset. If you do not match the special competence of an officer with the mindset and attitude required for particular job then he will not be able to deliver to the extent you want him to. The CS has to choose the right kind of officer for a district posting. Not all officers have the aptitude to perform in a district. I recall the case of an officer who was brilliant and committed yet was reduced to tears during his posting as Director of Information. This post requires one to be constantly available to the media on mobile and also physically. This particular officer felt that this was a waste of time as most of the time the media had some recommendations to make or some work to be done. The Director of Information needs to be open, accessible, communicative, patient and responsive. Similarly, different jobs require different skill sets and it is the primary duty of a CS to post the right man at the right place to ensure effective governance.

But the CS will not always have his way in postings. The Chief Minister has to approve and he can have his preferences. However, with the proposal explained well, the Chief Minister will approve. The problem comes when there is a tremendous pressure on the CM to remove an officer or post a particular officer. Then even worse is the fact that officers actively lobby for certain posts. All posts in the IAS cadre are such that you can make a tremendous impact if you do your job well. The disabilities welfare department in UP is one where the government sends officers it does not like. However, there was one officer who took his work so seriously that this department came to the forefront and did outstanding work. I also vividly remember that once I was posted as Secretary Basic Education, almost everyone sympathized with me—'You are going to look after primary schools at this seniority!'—and offered me oodles of advice on how I should try and get my posting changed. I thoroughly enjoyed this post and I was able to use all my creativity and innovativeness and found the experience to be extremely satisfying. The department gained and I was surprised to find at the time of my transfer (after three and a half years) that there were several claimants for this post.

But reality is that officers rate certain postings as desirable and others as punishments. It relates to the kind of power you can wield in a particular department or general perception about a post. Such officers use political clout to have their way even though the CS may feel that this officer is not the best choice for a department. The result is that often the performance suffers. So the CS does not always have their way in postings and transfers. Yet he is successful at least 75 per cent of the time and that is good enough to enable him to build a team of his choice and try to post the right man at the right place.

The primary responsibility of the CS is coordination. He has to ensure that the entire government works as one. He has to make every member of his team share the same vision and work towards it. To achieve this he has to lead by example. He cannot say one thing but do another. For instance, a CS may ask his officers to be prompt in their decision-making but avoid taking decisions himself. He has to lead by example if he has to create a working environment where officers are accessible, polite, responsive and result-oriented. A CS does not have to interfere in every issue related to a department but at the same time, he cannot keep a distance from the working of the departments or issues raised by them. Often the Principle Secretary of a department will like to discuss a file or seek advice from the CS on some important issue. The CS should encourage the officer, and after a patient listening, offer his advice. Some CS evade the responsibility by saying, 'It's your problem, you resolve it'. This response, I feel, is not correct. The CS has to mentor, advise and guide his team. Also when a matter is referred to him, he may take the view of all those concerned but arrive at a definite decision. The CS needs to have broad shoulders to take responsibility for his decisions and actions. This quality of any leader always results in his team supporting him fully.

As Chief Secretary I made it a point to review every department every month. I reviewed the financial sanctions issued against the budget, expenditure, the funds that they have obtained from the Government of India, physical progress of all majors schemes, their development agenda and performance vis-à-vis the points related to the particular department in this agenda. I feel every government must have a development agenda which should focus on priority programmes and schemes of the departments. For instance, the health department may have a development agenda specifying targets of infant mortality rate, maternal mortality, complete immunization, etc. The department then knows the issues it should lay emphasis on. The impact of this is that the Principal Secretary of the department will review his department every month and make a presentation to the CS. In this manner, the entire team will know what is expected of it and will consciously work in the required direction. The CS also gets firsthand feedback on the working of each department as well the performance of officers concerned.

Monitoring is an activity often ignored in the government. Imprecise feedback is taken and reviewed but this is not proper monitoring. Proper formats need to be developed which ask all the relevant questions and give a clear and accurate picture of the performance. But reporting systems on paper are not enough. Nowadays, technology is a great enabler. Videos and photographs uploaded on mobiles, GPS systems, Interactive Voice Recording System (IVRS), biometrics, mobile apps and video conferencing are all being used to monitor projects better. It is also possible to monitor projects in real time. The irrigation department control room in UP shows the real-time position of each and every tube well and canal in the state. Similarly when we went ahead with an ambitious plan of planting ten crore trees in a day in the state, the obvious questions asked were about the reliability of the data and survival rate. GPS technology helped us resolve this. The forest department had each and every sapling planted on its computer screen and could monitor its survival rate in real time. The result was an almost 98 per cent survival rate of plants. Similarly, IVRS technology was used to monitor the number of school children having mid-day meals on a particular day. Biometrics was of great use in an attempt to check teacher absenteeism.

But, despite all the miracles of technology, there is no substitute for the old-fashioned, time-tested method of monitoring and inspections. Officers must go to the field to review the actual situation on the ground and assess how their officers at that level are responding, behaving or performing. It also enables you to get direct feedback from the public which is the most vital part of any monitoring. Public perception depends upon the outcome and that is the sole indicator of real progress or development.

I had prescribed three days in a month for Principle Secretaries to leave their offices and inspect schemes at the ground level. For instance, there is no better feedback that the Principle Secretary of the health department can get about the functioning of his department than by visiting the district hospitals, community health centres and primary health centres. In turn I had asked the Principle Secretaries to prescribe the number of days their head of department should visit the schemes at the field level. This exercise should be repeated down the line to the district and subdivisional levels. In my monthly meetings I would monitor the number of inspections done and reports uploaded. This made a big difference to perceptions about the functioning of the government.

As Chief Secretary, I made it a point to undertake at least one, if not two, inspections within a month. I would start early by the state plane, reach a district headquarter, inspect the hospital, a police station, a Tahsil and some other projects and often visit a village, too. Thereafter I would have a meeting with all the public representatives of that division/district and attend to their grievances. This would be followed by taking applications from members of the general public and I would follow this up with a meeting with the members of industry, business and trade. It is only after this that I would start the review meetings on law and order and development. The day would be rounded off with a press conference. In this way I got a very true and complete picture of the working of a district/division and its problems and issues. Needless to say the entire government machinery in the district was toned up and a great stimulus was given to development programmes.

We often forget that our officers and employees are the people who deliver schemes to the citizens and it is important to keep them motivated and satisfied. I had issued a circular to all Principle Secretaries to have a monthly meeting with their employee associations and redress their grievances. I feel very often we tend to take the grievances of our employees lightly and the result is that the problems spill over to the streets in the form of demonstrations and threats of strikes. A regular dialogue can avert this kind of a situation. Moreover, it reflects on the workings of a department if it cannot redress the grievances of its employees and allows them to escalate the issues to higher levels.

The relationship between the Chief Minister and CS is an extremely close one. The CS cannot survive or deliver if he does not have the confidence of the CM. I had the good fortune of having Mr Akhilesh Yadav as the Chief Minister who trusted me completely and gave me space to work. He would articulate his vision and ideas and leave it to me to carry them forward. It was my job to work out detailed schemes, policies, projects, and translate his vision into reality. Mr Akhilesh Yadav was a young and dynamic Chief Minister committed to the development of the state. He always desired excellence in execution from the bureaucracy. He was impatient to put the state forward on the path of development and he is rightly called the 'Vikas Purush'. Governance works best when the CM and the CS work in tandem. However, there is a word of caution. No matter how much freedom the CM gives the CS, the latter should never take it for granted and never commit the mistake of taking the CM lightly. The CM may give total freedom of action, but the CS must keep him briefed on every issue of importance and take his views. A close working relationship of mutual trust, faith and confidence is the idea.

The CS is also Secretary to the cabinet and this is also another important task that he has to fulfill. Cabinet meetings are normally held on a fixed day or on the date indicated by the CM. The agenda is finalized by the CS. Departments take the approval of their minister and send cabinet notes to confidential sections which put them up before the CS. The CS then examines if all the required formalities of a cabinet note have been fulfilled and accordingly approves it to be put up before the cabinet. There could be agenda items which have wider ramifications and the CS should brief the CM before the cabinet meetings on such items. Normally, the practice followed is there at least one day before a cabinet meeting, the CS holds a detailed briefing session in which the Principle Secretaries of departments present their agendas. Finance and law departments are present to facilitate any discussion. The CM Office normally briefs him on the agenda but I followed the practice of taking time and briefing the CM on important cabinet proposals. The CS sits next to the CM or to his right, just behind him. Principal Secretaries of law and finance are also present. The concerned Principal Secretary is called to present his item. I normally followed the practice of leading the agenda note myself as CS. Most items would go through without a query. In the event some issues were raised, I would respond to them and allow the Principal Secretary to supplement. The CM expects the CS to have the ability to pilot the agenda and skillfully handle the interjections of ministers, specially the senior ones. A very close relationship develops between the CS and the cabinet members. I recall that prior to my retirement, when I thanked the cabinet in my last meeting for all their support and confidence, they stood up and gave me a standing ovation. It is one of the memories of my service that shall always remain fresh and fill me with immense satisfaction. The minutes of the cabinet meeting are prepared by the CS and this has to be done with a lot of caution and deliberation. Approval of the CM is taken before issuing the minutes. Immediately after the cabinet meet, there is a press briefing which I used to hold as the CS properly and correctly informing the media.

Following up on cabinet decisions is a very vital task. Normally I would insist that GO be issued within three days of a cabinet decision. I had tasked my principal staff officer to rigorously monitor action taken on cabinet decisions. If this is not done then often the cabinet decision is not acted upon for months, leading to poor governance.

All the ministers and public representatives have great respect for CS. On his part, the CS should be polite, courteous and responsive to them. The situation can sometimes get a little tricky. For instance, the CM may not like a particular minister and would not want his proposal to be approved. However, politically the CM would not like to annoy the minister. It is then left to the CS to resort to bureaucratic methods to scuttle the proposals without stepping on anyone's toes. Subtlety and diplomacy is of the essence. This is required all the more when there are senior ministers who are themselves aspiring for the post of the CM and like to convert every issue into a matter of prestige. The role played by the CS becomes all the more important to maintain a delicate balance.

The Chief Secretary is supposed to be responsible for the workings of all departments in the government but I often found that they give less time to law and order and focus entirely on development works. An ex-Chief Secretary told me specifically to avoid getting into law and order and crime-related issues and leave them to the Director General of Police and Principal Secretary Home. I somehow do not share this viewpoint. Law and order and instilling a sense of security in citizens is the prime responsibility of the government and should get the maximum attention of the CS. In fact when I took over as the CS and the media quizzed me about my priorities, I listed law and order and energy as my two areas of emphasis.

Nothing damages the image of a government more than incidents of sensational crime or disturbances in law and order. As Chief Secretary, I used to start my day with a fifteen-minute meeting with the DGP, PS Home and Additional Director Intelligence. This proved to be most effective. A lot of information was exchanged and areas of concern and action debated upon. It also led to a unified presentation to the media.

I also made it a point talk to the district Superintendents of Police (SP) and District Magistrate (DM) to know if there were any major incidents in their districts. This worked wonders. The District Administration would be alert to answer the queries raised by the CS and also try their best to control the situation or make arrests at the earliest. Since the CS was directly talking to the District Administration, the DGP and PS Home would also do the same as they knew that the CS would have got direct feedback from the districts.

Law and order used to be the foremost agenda in the quarterly meetings of the DMs and SPs which I regularly took as CS. The first half of the meeting was devoted to law and order and second half to development works. I found these meetings most useful. The CM would come for about one hour and address the officers, thereafter the CS would continue the meeting till late evening. Every month on various issues, I found that conducting video conferencing with DMs would improve the performance. These sessions are useful in monitoring specific programmes or projects in detail. However, there is no substitute for a face-to-face meeting every quarter.

There are certain Chief Secretaries who hold far too many meetings. Not only are they in the meeting hall for the better part of the day, they keep a lot of senior officers busy with them, too. This tendency to hold a meeting at the drop of a hat should be avoided. Also, meetings must be short, to the point and result-oriented. Decisions should be taken and perfect coordination ensured to make the officers work as a team. I would always make my staff officer go through the agenda and brief me on decision points in advance. This made it easy for me to guide the discussion towards the crucial issues and make decisions. I also made it a point to indicate the time when a meeting would start and when it would end. Generally I did not allow any meeting to go beyond one hour. Proper minutes would need to be prepared and action on decisions taken earlier had be reviewed to make the meetings effective. The CS has to pilot the meeting and he should be aware of the direction he wants to give it. Participants should feel free to voice their views but the CS needs to moderate the discussions. Often as CS, I found that there were certain senior officers who were cynical and if allowed to speak unchecked would contribute to the derailing of the agenda. The skill required here is to move ahead without snubbing the officer concerned. One CS whom I have admired a lot did this beautifully. He would respond by saying, 'That is a very good point and we should bear it in mind'. He would then move forward.

A particularly sensitive issue involves the attitude of the finance department. It is common to have meetings where finance and department concerned hold different views. It is also natural because it is the duty of finance to maintain financial prudence, and to see that every rupee is spent well and correctly. The departments on the other hand requires sufficient resources to achieve results. It is never advisable to reject the advice of finance but the objectives of the scheme concerned also need to be met. As CS I tried to handle this by creating a positive atmosphere and encouraging both finance and the concerned department to work out a solution. More often than not when the finance department realizes the CS wants a particular decision to be taken, they tone down their objections and often suggest a way out.

Often finance writes a negative note on a cabinet proposal. Such proposals should be considered for presentation before the cabinet only if the department concerned has adequately responded to the objections raised. It is a call which the CS has to take and he needs to exercise a great degree of caution. This situation becomes all the more sensitive when the CM or a senior minister wants to have the agenda placed before the cabinet and consequently there is a lot of pressure on the CS. However, the CS must not forget that ultimately it is his responsibility to ensure that the finance and law departments have given their concurrence to a proposal before it is placed before the cabinet.

Court orders on a variety of issues occupy a significant portion of the CS's time. There are many PILs or other petitions in which the court directs the CS to form a committee at his level and review the progress and periodically inform the court. A track of such orders needs to be kept in the CS office. Not only must meetings be held but court orders should be read very carefully and compliance on all points ensured. The CS is the highest level of the executive and if the court finds that even at this level things are not moving, then they can pass adverse comments on the working of the government or often summon the CS too.

There has been an increase in the tendency of the courts to call the CS in person. This is not a healthy situation because it is the department concerned which has to ensure that action is taken as per the directives of the court. For instance, if encroachments have to be removed then the urban development department has to act. If the issue is that of Ganga cleaning then it is the urban development and environment department who must respond. However, often the court is left with no option but to call the CS as the department concerned has not been taking adequate action despite repeated orders of the court or the concerned officers or state counsel have not been able to explain the issues to the court.

Sometimes one gets the feeling that a summoning order is unreasonable. The state law department and the advocate general are quick to advise that we must approach the Supreme Court against any order of the High Court. I have seen this happening in a couple of cases and more often than not, no relief is given by the Supreme Court making it all the more embarrassing for the CS. My response used to be to comply with these court orders and appear before them. Later on one could raise this issue when one called upon the Honourable Chief Justice (CJ). I found that the Chief Justice was always very responsive and took appropriate steps to resolve the issue. It always helps the CS to keep his communication channels with the CJ open. This is the best method to avoid a Judiciary–Executive showdown or a feeling of bitterness between the two.

Some very small issues can create a distance. Often the budget allotted to the courts is the bone of contention. The judiciary feels that the executive is deliberatively not giving them the required funds whereas the finance department has its own logic. I recall that as CS I had to appear before a seven-member bench headed by the CJ and respond to the security and modernization needs of the court. It was a little difficult to explain to them the objections raised by the finance department. However, I genuinely felt that the requirement was legitimate and we cannot talk of a thriving democracy without strengthening the judiciary. I assured the court that funds could be provided and then sat across the table from the Registrar General and the finance department to iron out the differences and provide funds in a phased manner. We built the new High Court building in Lucknow during this period and it is one of the most imposing and stately buildings you will see. I reviewed the progress every week to see that quality work was done and the project implemented on time.

The Advocate General (AG) is the bridge between the government and judiciary. It is important that the AG is chosen with great care and not merely by political considerations. He should be a person whom the courts respect and who has an excellent rapport with the CJ. The AG can communicate with both sides and see that no conflict is created.

There has been a phenomenal increase in the number of PILs filed in the Courts. Many of them are mischievous and are filed to malign an officer or create a roadblock for the development project or to satisfy the egoistic needs of an individual. Many lawyers have made filing of PILs their only business and some of them resort to PILs as a means of blackmailing. Generally the courts are able to discern the difference between a genuine and a malicious PIL. Scores of PILs are dismissed on the first hearing itself and often with costs to deter habitual PIL litigants. I had observed during my tenure as CS that the CJ of the High Court had clearly directed how a PIL should be treated and during his tenure, the frivolous PILs failed to see the light of the day.

However there are other PILs which have a genuine bearing on public interest. The courts are well within their rights to go beyond the relief sought and broadly base this discussion to push the executive into resolving a matter of public interest. Often the executive invites such PILs by not doing its duty or being callous towards a public grievance. More often than not the executive does not act because of political reasons. It is here that bureaucracy actually gets a lot of help from the courts in carrying out their legitimate function. In fact the bureaucracy often welcomes such directions from the courts because they can use it as a shield to withstand political pressure. For example, everyone is aware that encroachments have made the city roads narrow, leading to traffic congestion and unsanitary conditions. However, the moment an encroachment drive is started, vested interest groups build political pressure to make the authorities buckle down. I found the orders of the court very useful in this regard. They had directed that the CS chair a committee and review removal of any encroachments in the city of Lucknow. Needless to say, we were able to bypass political pressure and carry out successful encroachment drives. Sometimes the executive tends to view court directives as an unnecessary imposition. Whereas some directives of the court may not be very realistic, I feel that the executive can often vastly improve the level of governance in politically sensitive issues through court orders.

The worst that a government can do is to take up a confrontation with the judiciary. It never helps. So many sensitive issues are before the court in which an anti-establishment view can be taken if the attitude of the executive is non-cooperative. Democracy works best when both the wings work independently and seek to serve public interest. An attitude of mutual respect and faith is essential for good governance.

A significant aspect of governance is a relationship with the office of the Chief Minister and the CS. The CS is senior to the officers posted in the CM office. Yet the CM Office is the voice of the CM. Once again, it is important for both to work together. Over the years the CM Office has acquired a lot of powers. During my time as District Magistrate, I recall that we only knew the CS and rarely approached the CM office. But things have changed now and the District Officer approaches the CM office on most issues. This is a stark reality and the CS may as well accept it. However, if the CM office and the CS become rival centers of power, then it is detrimental to overall governance. I have had the fortune of working for four years as Secretary to CM and two years as CS. I always followed a style whereby the prestige of the CS and the other senior officers was maintained. Even if it was my job to communicate the views of the CM, I always did so politely, though making it clear what the CM desired. Sometimes one notices that officers of the CM Secretariat develop a lot of arrogance and speak rudely to officers senior to them. However, once again, I found that as CS, the solution lay in keeping the channels of communication open with the CM office, and to see that the two work in sync. It also helps if the CS maintains a direct line of communication with the CM.

You cannot be an effective CS today and shy away from the media. It is true that the bureaucracy is expected to be anonymous and do their job quietly. The political figures are the ones who face the media. However, the office of the CS is one from where the media expects news bytes, briefings and responses. The CS must develop a healthy relationship with them to see that the media gives adequate coverage to the work done by the government and also gives a balanced portrayal of any incident or issue. After almost every important meeting or in the aftermath of any incident in the state, the media expects a briefing from the CS. I always responded because it is important to put forward the government view. Even late at night, print media journalists would ring me up for some reaction or information. I was always accessible and responsive. This helped build an excellent rapport with the media and we got their support on many contentious issues.

It is also very helpful to keep a close relationship with the editors of print and electronic media. They often give very bold and correct feedback on the workings of the government and also provide valuable suggestions. Media responses enable you to look at yourself in the mirror. If you take it positively then both your image and that of the government shall improve. The media reactions represent the voice of the people which must be heard.

Most government projects suffer from time and cost overrun due to the obsession with procedures and file orientation. Processes are necessary to ensure accountability since public funds are being spent. I found that officers avoid decision-making or take the shelter of procedures, queries and asking for more information in an effort to protect themselves. There is a tendency now to keep looking over the shoulder to see how CAG, CBI or CVC will view a decision. Corruption is not only to be condemned but acted upon strongly. However, systems need to be evolved which will protect an honest officer who takes decisions in public interest. Such an institutional mechanism does not exist at the moment, leading to a feeling of huge insecurity amongst officers. The political executive does make statements about protecting honest officers but appears helpless or indifferent when an honest officer is harassed or made to suffer. In fact, the worst happens when governments change. It has become an unfortunate tendency of the government to try and find fault with the decision of the earlier government and start a spate of enquiries. These enquiries are often motivated and results decided beforehand. Unfortunately, it is not the political executive who suffers but the officers who have signed the files. Opinion needs to be built across the spectrum to see that such incidents of witch-hunting are avoided.

The current institutional arrangements of protecting honest officers are not encouraging prompt decision-making. The IAS officers are paid to take decisions in public interest. This becomes all the more relevant in large projects where huge amount of government funds are involved. The quality also suffers and the benefit does not reach the citizen on time. In such situations the officer has to take a decision and it is not correct to make him suffer for such a decision taken in public interest just because some minor procedure has been overlooked. The intention of the officer is the criteria which should be used to evaluate his decision.

The CS has to take the lead to build the culture of decision-making. He has to lead by example. The rest of bureaucracy has its antenna tuned to the signals emanating from the office of the CS or his personality. If the CS tries to evade his responsibility by taking shelter in formation of committees, taking opinion of other departments unnecessarily or refers the matter to the CM office then the rest of the bureaucracy falls in line. They also resort to similar stratagems and a culture of shirking responsibility pervades the entire governance structure. The ultimate sufferer is the public for whom the entire government should be working. However, if the CS is decisive, he is seen as the one who always takes responsibility and then this culture travels through the length and breadth of the entire bureaucracy energizing the entire governance structure. The common man also begins to perceive the government as one which is delivering results. 'Work is visible in the field' is the comment of the public in such a situation. A spirit of general positivism pervades the state. It is also important for the officers to feel that the CS would support them if any decision of theirs goes wrong. This support at the top creates a feeling of security in the entire team of officers and then they work to fully realize their potential.

The government is often criticized for its slow functioning and inefficiency. Particularly in the case of implementing large projects, the record of the government has been poor. Most government projects suffer from time and cost overrun and also poor quality of implementation. The question to be asked is whether the government system is inherently incapable of delivering in the project mode. However, this is not true. I will explain this by describing two projects during my tenure as CS which were implemented in record time and showcased what the government can achieve.

The first was the construction of the Lucknow–Agra Expressway, a six-lane expressway expandable to eight lanes and covering a total distance of 328 Kilometers. It was the biggest expressway in Asia and it connected with the Yamuna Expressway which links Delhi to Agra. The construction of this expressway, in a record time of twenty-four months, made it possible to cover the distance between Delhi and Lucknow in five hours. The significance of the expressway would only be fully realized in the years to come. All of central UP would be thrown open to economic activity. One can visualize agriculture mandis, warehouses, logistic hubs, entertainment complexes, hotels and restaurants, and industries coming up on both sides of the expressway in the next ten years. Substantial improvement in the per capita income and quality of life of people living in the districts of Firozabad, Etawah, Mainpuri, Unnao, Kannauj and Auraiya would become visible. The economic benefits of this expressway would be transformational.

After the Detailed Project Report (DPR) of this was prepared, it was found that the cost would be around 15,000 crores and Public Private Partnership (PPP) would be the best method to build this road. An effort was made but it became clear that no private party was willing to make such a huge investment as they were not sure of the returns. We discussed the annuity approach to PPP with several prospective infrastructure companies but none were willing to come forth. In fact, the entire environment was not conducive to PPP in highways/expressways. The National Highway Authority also gave up the PPP route in several projects and adopted the EPC method (Engineering Procurement and Construction). The Government of India had issued detailed guidelines about EPC. We decided to take this up. This would involve substantial commitment of funds but the Chief Minister accorded the highest priority to this and we all started working on ensuring that timely funds would be available for these projects. The Principal Secretary Finance worked out various permutations and combinations to make funds available.

The first activity was to acquire land which is often the most troublesome part of any project. We had to acquire land from about 30,000 farmers. The CM personally talked to the concerned people and made this possible. We gave the responsibility to District Collectors. A committee under the District Collector was constituted and empowered to negotiate with the farmers and arrive at an acceptable compensation figure. As per the recent amendment to Land Acquisition Act we prescribed an upper ceiling of compensation at four times the circle rate. Rigorous monitoring of this was done through video conferencing with collectors. All activities till registry of land in favour of UP Expressways Industrial Development Authority (UPEIDA) were monitored using a time frame. UPEIDA was a body created specifically to handle such projects and it reported directly to the Chief Minister and not to the PWD Minister. The Collectors took great initiatives once they realized the importance of the project. The performance of each Collector was discussed in great detail and a spirit of competition generated between them.

Through this process we succeeded in acquiring required land without any dispute or court case or conflict. So many large projects do not see the light of the day for years after they get caught up in protests and litigation regarding the land to be acquired but this was an administrative miracle. The Collectors acted promptly only because they were convinced of the support from the top. The rates finalized by them were approved by UPEIDA to give the Collectors the required security cover.

The bid document was prepared by a consultant selected through a transparent bidding process and RFQ (technical bid) and RFP (financial bid) documents were then prepared by this consultant and approved by the bid evaluation committee and the cabinet. All the valuable suggestions received during pre-bid were discussed and a decision was taken. The bids were floated and we got an encouraging response. The bid evaluation committee approved the bids after comparing them with the estimate prepared by Public Works Department which was the body authorized for this. The entire project was split into five sections and separate developers were selected. To get the best contractors, we had launched a massive awareness drive which created a lot of interest amongst the reputed construction firms and this brought them to the bidding table.

A major function as a media event was organized to launch this project. The developers were talking of minimum period of thirty-six months to complete this project. It was made clear that no more than twenty-four months would be allowed and this was further reduced to twenty-two months by the Chief Minister at the time of launching. 'Government projects may talk of completion within two years but end up taking seven to eight years to complete' was the talk going around.

We selected the most dynamic officers to handle the project. I was clear that we needed officers who can take risks and prompt decisions and are effective field officers. Having the right man at the right place is a basic principle of leadership and in my experience, I found that not all officers are suitable for all kinds of jobs. While posting officers, the CS should have the capacity to know their strengths and weaknesses and utilize them accordingly. A square peg cannot fit in to a round hole.

The essence of completing large projects on time lies in monitoring. I decided to monitor this project every Monday at a fixed time. These weekly meetings were not merely review meetings but were forums of interdepartmental coordination and decision-making. We used the reverse clock method. We fixed the date of completion twenty-two months from the start of the project. Then we worked backwards and fixed the timeline for each and every activity. Crucial decisions were taken across the table which in normal government functioning would take months. These Monday meetings removed the need to go into procedural wrangles and considerably enhanced the pace of implementation of the project. Of course, the CS had to take responsibility for the decision.

Monitoring of progress was done through charts, tables, photographs, videos and also inspection at the site. Challenges came on the way like the unexpected crises of availability of stone grit and other construction material as a side effect of an enforcement drive against overloading of trucks.

However, we were together able to find a way out of this since the intent was clear, the goal was shared by everybody and the CS was willing to take decisions on the spot rather than take refuge in files.

The approach, attitude and team spirit succeeded and we were able to deliver this expressway in a record time of twenty-two months. The quality of the work was outstanding as testified by an Indian Air Force plane landing on this expressway. This project succeeded because the CM gave us a lot of freedom of action and his total support. The government machinery achieved an almost impossible task and it just shows that with political will and strong leadership anything is possible.

In a similar vein was the implementation of the 9 km-long first phase of the Lucknow Metro. Once again this was done in a record time of twenty-four months. The Doyen of Metros in India, Mr Sreedharan, who was also an advisor to the Lucknow Metro, was candid enough to remark that this was the fastest construction of a metro that he had seen. The decision to go ahead with a metro against a rapid bus corridor was taken by the Chief Minister as he felt that this would have a much greater impact on the life of the people. An initial DPR was prepared and submitted to government of India who gave their in-principle approval.

The next decision was to appoint a technical person as Managing Director. Applications were called for and an extremely fair and transparent interview process conducted. I chaired as CS and Mr Sreedharan was on the selection committee. We selected the most competent applicants. There was no interference by the political executive in the selection process at any time. The Chief Minister personally ensured that the entire selection was done on merit. This freedom to select the best team purely on merit was a very important step in making this project a huge success. Along with the MD, we did a purely merit-based selection of the entire top management team. This team then prepared a detailed DPR after consulting all the stakeholders. Tendering process for the construction agency was done in record time and the developers selected. And work started. It must be borne in mind that we had not received PIB clearance from Government of India till then. The clearance was delayed due to technical and political reasons but we went ahead with the project by providing funds from the state government budgets. We negotiated and finalized the external funding agency but their fund flow was also dependent on Government of India PIB clearance.

Once again we used the reverse clock approach to complete the project on time. A tight schedule of twenty-four months was finalized and the date of trial run of the first train was decided. We worked backwards from that date fixing timelines for each activity and identified the officer responsible for the same. These timelines were broken into targets and as CS I started reviewing the project every Monday. In fact the Lucknow–Agra Metro review was held immediately after the Lucknow–Agra Expressway review, every week. These meetings brought about close interdepartmental coordination and resolution of problems.

In between, with great effort, the PIB clearance was obtained. As CS, I had to personally go and present the case before the PIB and only then was the approval granted.

The fact that the Finance Secretary was my batchmate was a great help. This eased the way for foreign agency funding to flow and the project got the funds required without disrupting the implementation schedule.

A major crisis erupted over the tender for the train. The financial bids for those who qualified the technical bids were opened. However, it came to light that the firm which had the lowest tender also violated a crucial clause of the bid document—non-disclosure of the fact that it had been blacklisted by DMRC and World Bank. Much lobbying and political pressures were made to bear on us to award the tender to the party. We felt that it would not be proper to award the contract to this party as the bid condition had been violated. I convened a meeting of the board of LMRC where Principal Secretary Finance was also present to discuss the way out of this situation. The view of finance was clear that we should go for a re-tender as the second lowest bidder had quoted 70 crores more than the lowest bid. Indeed, this was the safest course of action but it would have pushed the project back by at least six months if not more. I took the call and awarded the tender to the second lowest after briefing the CM who supported me. Before doing so I persuaded the managing director of LMRC to convince the second lowest bidder to reduce his price by 70 crores. The party reluctantly agreed and we were now on safe ground as no additional expenditure was being incurred by LMRC. Soon after, the interested groups came into play and the matter went to court. We presented our case before the court through an accomplished lawyer and the verdict was in our favour. The project had been salvaged.

Needless to say on the appointed day, the first train arrived and trial run started amidst great fanfare. It was once again a celebration of what dedicated team effort backed by political will can achieve. It once again demonstrated that if the attitude is right, intention clear, decisions taken promptly, strong and firm leadership provided, the goal shared by all members of an inspired and motivated team, then even in government and in UP, major projects can be completed on time.

In a similar manner, we implemented the Dial 100 system for law and order which ensured that within twenty minutes of making a call, police assistance would reach a citizen. More than 3000 vehicles were deployed and a state-of-the-art command center was built in Lucknow to make this possible. Special training was given to police personnel deployed on duty and statement of procedure (SOP) worked out in great detail. Despite the surprising resistance from certain sections of the police force to this path-breaking initiative, we were able to successfully implement it within two years.

In addition, it gave me great satisfaction that during my tenure, we could create Janeshwar Mishra Park, which is amongst the largest parks in Asia, an international cricket stadium which was rated by many ex-cricketers as the best stadium in the country. Development of the Gomti River Front was another excellent project we took up and built the Jai Prakash Narayan Convention Center on the model of the India Habitat Center in Delhi. Sadly, the last two projects have suffered due to change of government.

It is not possible for the CS to go into the detailed working of each and every department. In fact it is not even advisable. However, there should be a clear mandate to each department and the priority issues monitored at the CS level. Development agenda of the state was formalized and at least three to four items of each department figured in this development agenda which as CS, I monitored regularly. This process gave an impetus to the work culture in the state and made it positive, efficient, result and outcome-oriented.

Prompt decision-making and leadership qualities are required in a big way to handle natural calamities and disasters. The Bundelkhand region was plagued by three years of successive drought leading to chronic food shortage and misery for the people of the area. The CM Mr Akhilesh Yadav directed that we should leave no stone unturned to provide relief. He wanted distribution of food items to be done with an open heart. Relief packets were prepared. The DMs were authorized to procure items at their level through tendering process. At some places, the CM went to distribute relief packets himself. At others, the officers arranged for distribution at the village level. In addition, a special drive for preparation of job cards under MNREGA was started and major works of water conservation taken up to provide employment to the people of the area. There were 107 major tanks for water supply in Bundelkhand and all of them were silted. We desilted all these tanks and dug them up to make them ready to store water when the rains came. As a result MGNREGA's target of providing employment was more than exceeded. Detailed route charts and action plans were prepared to provide drinking water to areas of water scarcity, crops which survive on less water were sown. Electricity supply of more than twenty hours was ensured. All this action was taken in time to avert a major crisis.

Similarly, when UP farmers were faced with the badly damaged crops due to persistent heavy unseasonal rains and hailstorm in the months of February and March, we responded by conducting a very prompt damage survey and began to distribute relief as per the natural calamity guidelines and the extra amount of compensation that the state government decided to bear. The quick response and relief distribution helped in alleviating farmer distress and showcased the sensitivity of the government to the travails of the farming community. At the top level, natural calamities demand a sensitive and compassionate understanding of the situation and a prompt and effective response.

Despite the preponderance of official duties, the CS along with their spouse have a leadership role to play in the social and cultural activities around them. In UP, we have a Civil Services Institute—a club for the Civil Services which was the hub of activity. It all depends upon the interest taken by the CS and his wife. I strongly believe that these activities lead to a feeling of camaraderie and team spirit amongst the officers which are vital for effective governance. My wife and I made it a point to have social evenings with music and dinner every month, where officers and their spouses came. These activities are often as instrumental in developing team spirit as the formal official ones. The wife of the CS can also play a meaningful role. UP has a wonderful Akanksha Society where officer's wives and those from civil societies take up activities for empowerment of women and poor children. Akanksha prepares masalas, sweets, snacks, by using the help of poor women who are trained to do this work in a most hygienic manner. So much so that Akanksha has become a brand name for purity and gives employment to over a hundred women. During my period as CS, my wife was able to lift this organization to another level by having workshops for girls and women on women's security, free self-defence classes for women, making them aware of the laws relating to women and distributing aids and implements to persons with disabilities. They ran an excellent school for poor children where free text books, uniforms and mid-day meals were provided. Free computer education courses were run for poor girls. All this gives the message to society that officers and their families are not isolated from them but actively want to give back to society. It goes a long way in building the image of the service also, which is otherwise perceived as being arrogant and distant. My wife was also the Brand Ambassador for Road Safety. Such measures help in spreading public awareness on vital issues. The close relationship amongst the officers' wives does create a very positive environment in the state.

The post of the CS gives you a lot of power. It is important not to get carried away. I have seen so many officers change dramatically once they became CS. They start believing that the world is to do their bidding. Arrogant and obnoxious behaviour becomes the norm and they start treating even senior officers poorly. This leads to isolation of the CS from his team. It creates a negative environment where sycophancy rather than merit rules the roost. It leads to a dysfunctional work culture and is reflected in an average performance in the field. In fact one can gauge the performance of a CS by the way he handles power. If ego triumphs, then output can be a disaster. To be level-headed and balanced is important. The CS has to know themselves to be able to handle the situation with maturity.

The job of the CS is transformational. He can make a lot of difference. It is the pinnacle of a career in the IAS. One should work so that people remember him long after he has retired.

7

Myths and Realities about the IAS

The IAS, as a service, is at a crossroads today. It has to determine its own future. In public perception, though individual officers have won great acclaim, the service as a whole is much maligned. The negative perception has reached a stage where people are even questioning the relevance of continuing the IAS as a service. The IAS officer is being viewed as a vestige of the colonial era; haughty, distant, unresponsive, arrogant, vain, ill-mannered and ineffective. He is increasingly being viewed as out of step with the fast-changing, dynamic, technological and economic environment. The common refrain is that the bureaucracy is an obstacle to the progress of India and the bureaucracy is synonymous with the IAS in the minds of most, conveniently ignoring the 99 per cent bureaucracy which is non-IAS. Rigidity, process orientation, no accountability for results are some of the prominent criticisms of the IAS. Increasingly, the service is losing its halo of integrity, neutrality and anonymity.

The future of the IAS is in a fluid state. It can continue in the same vein and allow the negative perception to increase to such an extent that it leads to the extinction of the service. On the other hand, it can wake up, introspect, do a lot of soul-searching and reinvent itself to be relevant to the demands of a fast-changing and modernizing society.

The IAS cannot watch in isolation, oblivious of the fact that the public services are not being delivered to the satisfaction of the citizen and the pace and momentum of economic development in India is not enough to pull the country out of the morass of poverty and backwardness. It is time that the service realized that it is their responsibility to take India to the next level.

Whereas it is imperative for the IAS to look within, I must add in all humility that the IAS is also a victim of a lot of unfair and uninformed criticism. The impression is that the IAS has unbridled power and is in a position to do anything. If things are not happening or development is slow, then people are of the opinion that the blame lies squarely at the door of the IAS. Critics find the IAS unaccountable and blame them for not guiding the political executive correctly. As I have said earlier, the evils of the bureaucratic systems are laid before the IAS. Any talk of civil service reform focuses on the IAS as if only the IAS needs to be reformed. There are certain myths being propagated like lateral entry into the IAS being the panacea of all evils. Little thought is given to the glaring fact that the bureaucratic structure and system is the problem, and not the IAS alone. The reform therefore has to be structural and systemic. Tinkering with the problem with half-bit solutions and incorrect diagnosis would only add to the chaos rather than provide a solution.

One comment often heard is that the IAS does not have domain specialization and, hence is not suitable to handle the complexities of modern-day administration. I was chairing a seminar one day and I found the chief guest saying, 'How can an IAS officer who has studied history or anthropology tackle different departments?' According to him, this was the main reason for ineffective governance. Then people are also critical of the fact that an IAS officer may be handling agriculture one day and industry the next. Also, the tenures are very short and do not allow the officer to gain domain knowledge. This argument is extended further and taken to its logical conclusion by arguing for the lateral entry of specialists into the IAS. Just recently, the Government of India has made a start in this direction by recruiting ten JS-level officers through lateral entry. If this argument is extended further it would imply that the Secretary of every department should be a specialist. For example, an agriculture expert should be the Agriculture Secretary rather than a generalist officer of the IAS. This, if accepted, would mean that the IAS has no relevance and should be phased out to be replaced by the specialists.

To most people, the above sounds very logical and rational. However, we are dealing with public policy and public governance, and the Secretary is the head of the administration. The skill set required is very different from that of a technical job. Even otherwise, there is no limit to specialization. A specialist goes into the details of fields which get narrower and narrower. Let us try and take the example of the health ministry. If we want to argue that a specialist should head the health ministry instead of an IAS, then we should have a doctor at the helm of affairs. Now which doctor? Nephrologist, neurologist, physician, surgeon or liver transplant expert? There are so many narrow specializations that it becomes difficult to choose. Hence, this idea of domain specialization is sometimes carried too far. There is no limit to specialization and a specialist is often a person who knows more and more about less and less. Is that the quality we want in the Secretary to the health department? Let us talk of education. A professor or director of a higher education institute or university understands higher education but has very little idea of the problems of primary schools in remote areas. What kind of a specialist should then be Secretary Education?

Moreover, there already exists a system where a Secretary takes the assistance of technical experts in policy formulation and other issues. For example, if you take the Agriculture Ministry in the Government of India, you find that at the Additional Secretary/Special Secretary level, there are posts of Horticulture Commissioner and Agriculture Commissioner to advise the Secretary and his team. Now both these officers are technical experts. Further, there is a separate Secretary for Indian Council for Agriculture Research (ICAR) who looks after agriculture research and development, and agriculture education. Thus, in the existing system itself, there are experts and specialists working closely with the IAS Secretary. This is largely true of other departments in the Government of India and now increasingly in the state governments too.

The job of the Secretary is to coordinate. He takes the views of all those concerned before finalizing policy.

For instance, before finalizing the industrial policy, the views of all the industrial associations are taken onboard. Policy making is not done by some Secretary of the IAS sitting by himself, assisted only by a couple of Additional Secretary/ JS-level IAS officers. It is a consultative process where those who have domain knowledge are not only consulted but their views given due weightage.

In addition to this, a system of having consultants to guide you has evolved over the years. For instance, if a project has to be taken on Public Private Partnership (PPP) you hire a consultant who prepares the bid documents, conducts the entire process of selecting a concessionaire and often even monitors the implementation. These consultants provide specialized inputs to the administration. A recent example is how Ernst & Young worked hand-in-hand with the administration in UP to organize the massive Kumbh Mela. So it is not as if the IAS officer is deciding policy and major issues on the basis of his own gut feelings and there is no domain-specific input being taken by him.

Besides, let us understand the work that the Secretary to the Government does, assisted by his team of Additional Secretaries, Joint Secretaries and others. He attends to parliament matters. One of his main jobs is to ensure the accountability of the executive to legislature. He prepares answers to parliament questions and briefs the minister. The heads of departments who are technical officers give their inputs in drafting the replies. Then he also prepares briefs for any issue concerning his department taken up for discussion or reply in the parliament. He also attends the meetings of the committees of parliament and faces the questioning by Honourable Members of Parliament who grill him continuously and relentlessly on various issues relating to his department. Communication and parliamentary skills of a high order are required to handle this responsibility.

Then there are legal matters and court cases where again you need a different kind of experience to draft written statements or prepare statements of a case and appreciate its legal aspects. The IAS officer does this for the most part of his career and, hence, is well equipped to handle it.

The Secretary needs to be a leader. He has to coordinate, plan, execute and develop a team which is motivated and committed. These qualities do not need domain specialization. Further, the Secretary has to master the art of working with the political executive, the minister. He also has to be well-versed with how to prepare and pilot a cabinet proposal. He needs to have knowledge of financial rules and processes, and apply them to any decision that he takes. He has to be adept at noting and drafting. Now due to the nature of their duties, these qualities are present in the IAS officer since the early phases of their careers. Not being a subject-matter specialist is nowhere a handicap for an IAS officer to discharge the functions mentioned in this paragraph.

The most important aspect of the job of a Secretary or a JS is to coordinate. He has to bring different departments or wings of his domain together to work in a coordinated fashion to fulfill the overall objectives of the organization. Now coordination is an administrative quality and does not require specialized knowledge of a subject. It is leadership that, through years of experience, an IAS officer is able to inculcate. The same holds true for the ability to motivate people, inspire them, monitor and measure their performance and make them have the right attitude so that they are enabled and energized to work as a team. In essence, at the level of Secretary to Government of India or State Government, it is the leadership qualities of an officer that matter far more than being a domain specialist. I am not saying that all IAS officers have these leadership qualities but many do and it is these officers who reach the top.

The important thing for a Secretary is to grasp the crucial issues and challenges confronting her department. This does not require any great specialized knowledge but a high level of general awareness, intelligence and logical skills. All it requires for a Secretary is to listen to his team comprising of specialists and IAS officers to arrive at a blueprint for action. Success or failure after that depends upon the decision-making skills of an officer and his ability to plan and execute in a manner that the outcomes are achieved.

We talk about the performance of various ministers and grade some of them as being dynamic and getting results, while others do not perform as well. Now rarely is a minister in India a specialist. He is a pure generalist who brings to the table his immense knowledge of the people, the pulse of the common man and a huge dose of common sense. He provides the political will and leadership, whereas the Secretary supplements it with his administrative ability to make things happen. The specialist is essential. He has to be a part of the system to render advice. In the Government of India and State Government, the system of taking advice from specialists already exists. Whenever a particular project has to be completed on time or a policy delivered, there are mechanisms like having special-purpose vehicles, missions or other executive agencies which are headed by specialists, and who go about the business of delivering results. My argument is that this tendency of blaming everything on the IAS officer being a generalist is a myth. Moreover, in the Government of India, normally the Secretary to a department has been an officer who has served as JS in same department for about five years. Naturally, he will be having a lot of domain knowledge also. Slowly the state governments are also following a similar path. For instance, in UP, whenever we choose a Finance Secretary, we try to ascertain whether he has had previous experience in the finance department.

One of the criticisms of the functioning of the government is that departments function singularly and do not work along with other departments. A specialist heading a department would have the propensity to look at issues from her standpoint. An IAS officer having worked in various departments has the mental training to take a more holistic view. To get results and outcomes we have to avoid working in silos and coordinate the efforts of various agencies. For example, if you want to reduce infant mortality, you have to coordinate the efforts of health, nutrition, hygiene, sanitation and education departments. Hence, the need for a broad, general and synthesizing approach rather than a narrow domain-specific and exclusive approach.

I read an article in *India Today* written by a reputed TIE entrepreneur based in the US. He is a brilliant man and was strongly of the view that the IAS does not have subject-matter specialization and as such is not suitable to handle twenty-first century challenges. As an example, he said that there is tremendous scope for the semiconductor industry in India and no IAS officer can be expected to draw a road map for this industry; he is right. However, if you choose a technocrat as Secretary Industries, he may not be from the semiconductor industry. He may be from heavy machinery, fertilizer or any other such industry. Would he be able to draw the road map for the semiconductor industry? And if you have a person from the semiconductor industry as the Secretary, would he appreciate the nuances of other industries? Or would you want to have a separate Secretary Semiconductor to the Government of India? Then we would end up having a different Secretary for different products—quite a messy arrangement! None of these Secretaries would be able to work with each other to bring about the industrial development of India. The solution lies in creating a semiconductor cell in the ministry headed by a technical person who will formulate policies for this sector. Overall, the coordination would still have to be left in the hands of an IAS officer. Needless to add, some of the most outstanding work in departments like information technology has been done at the center and the states by IAS officers. Just to give some examples, I would like to quote the case of Ram Sewak Sharma of the IAS who had a PhD in computer sciences and implemented the Aadhaar Project as the CEO under the Chairmanship of Nandan Nilekani. Similarly, the Ayushman Bharat Scheme is being successfully handled by Indu Bhushan an IAS officer. There are many such cases which show how IAS officers are competent enough to handle specialized projects. You only have to select the right person.

Most people have welcomed recent recruitment by lateral entry at senior levels in the Government of India. There is a cry for opening more such posts. First of all, there is always the issue of selecting the right person and often in this highly politicized environment of ours, it is always possible for officers with the right political connections to get selected. I have personally seen glaring examples of this in the state government (UP). There is, in the rules, a provision to select officers from other services (Technical) into the IAS. For the last several years, no such recruitment has been done because in the past most of the officers selected have been closely linked to political leaders or senior bureaucrats. It is almost impossible to have a merit-based system in this. True, the officers selected are chosen by the UPSC so it can be assumed that the selection has been fair. But then the selection has been from among those who applied. Not all the best people have applied. I do not think the best talent from the private sector would ever opt for lateral entry into the government. After twenty years of work experience, a performer in the private sector would be earning approximately a crore, annually. In fact, it would be much more. Why would he join the government at a salary of about twenty-five lakhs per annum? It is borne out by the recent selection too. Most of the people selected are from public sector organizations.

There is a mechanism for doing this too. Mr Nandan Nilekani was made head of the crucial UIDAI project. In a similar vein, technical projects can be put under well-known technical leaders who can bring about transformational change. Still, the ministry-level coordination would have to be done by an IAS officer. I would go a step further. I feel putting specialists in administrative posts held by the IAS or other Civil Services today would amount to a waste of their time and talent. Instead of contributing on the basis of his technical knowledge, the specialist will get buried under a mountain of papers and labyrinthine processes. In trying to find his way out of this, he will lose touch with his area of specialization.

If you look at the Government of India, you will find that it is not only the IAS officers who are posted in a department. There are officers of all Civil Services working in various ministries. You will find officers from Indian Forest Service, Audit and Accounts Service, Indian Revenue Service amongst others. These officers bring with them their experience and specialization, which adds to the diversity of knowledge in government. Many brilliant officers from these services have contributed significantly to governance at the centre.

Further to the votaries of domain specialization, I would advise them to take a look at the level of the minister. Rarely is a minister a specialist in his subject. There was Dr Manmohan Singh in finance and today we have Mr Jai Shanker in external affairs. But these are exceptions. Even a ministry like finance has a minister who is a lawyer, teacher or full-time politician. In our system of parliamentary democracy, it is not the specialist who becomes a minister. I read that a leading economist of India once commented on this situation by saying that it amounted to the blind leading the blind—meaning the political executive and IAS officer. I am not sure I appreciate this view. If you really want to have a system headed by a specialist then he must start with the minister who takes all policy and important decisions. There is an example of UP, where as Principal Secretary Technical Education, I had a minister who had barely cleared Class 10. However, here again it is the leadership quality of a minister that makes a difference. People from humble origins and with no claim to academic excellence have been great leaders. The politician brings to the table ground realities and the pulse of the people without which any development policy is not possible. In fact, the system works because there is a people-oriented vision, broad knowledge and high level of awareness and execution skills which are reflected in the system which has stood the test of time. A domain specialist will find it difficult to understand the genuine concerns of people better than a politician who spends all his time with people and has been elected to the post. He represents the will of the people and that is the most important thing in a democracy.

Even in the private sector, we do not have domain specialists always becoming CEOs. It is his leadership quality that has taken him there. Recently, I read that the top executive of Indigo had joined OYO as a CEO. Now one industry deals with civil aviation and the other with hospitality. They are as different as chalk and cheese. In most private sector organizations, the sales and marketing people reach the CEO level. At the top, the qualities required are those of handling people, communicating, coordinating, team building, grasping the essence of the business, motivating the team, inspiring people, making decisions, monitoring and evaluating the processes. These are all leadership qualities which do not necessarily require domain specialization. I just read a book titled *Range*, written by David Epstein which has been considered an outstanding business book. The argument he makes in it is that it is not the narrow specialist who succeeds but a person who has a range of interests and abilities, and has the ability to take an overall approach to problems. Such a person in the view of the author is better suited to multitasking and in responding to a changing environment. The governance environment of today is dynamic and disruptive. It is only a person who can respond to different points of view, continuous change and is flexible and open in his opinions, who can respond properly to such an environment.

My experience has been that often even the departmental officers are happier with an IAS officer than with their own departmental heads. I found that there is always a lot of politics in each department and most officers are aligned to one group or another. There are allegations of favouritism and lack of impartiality. The IAS officer brings in a culture where he treats all members of a department equally and fairly. Moreover, I found that those who had worked for several years in a department are quite rigid in their views and not willing to entertain new ideas. For example, I became Secretary Basic Education in UP. The Director Education and his team were convinced that teachers were not interested in teaching and that the union was always bent on creating disturbances and problems for the administration. Along with UNICEF, I prepared a plan of introducing 'Joyful Learning' in primary schools. The idea was to use storytelling, song, dance and role-play to make the children learn with joy. The Director Education and his team opposed the idea by saying that the teachers would never change their style and the teachers' union would vehemently oppose it. However,

I went ahead with the idea and called a meeting of the teachers, union to fully involve them in this. I motivated them to take the lead on this and they responded. To the utter surprise of my education department officers, the teacher union office bearers were the first to take part in the training, and introduced joyful learning in their schools. This is just an example to show how an IAS officer can bring fresh approach to resolving problems in a department as he does not have a baggage of legacy issues and opinions to hold him down.

When people talk of domain specialization they seem to refer only to the IAS officer. What about the officers of the Secretariat service who control the actions in a department and most of the Under secretaries and Deputy Secretaries are from these cadres? They are all generalists but with a specialization in secretarial work. Where all would you want to bring in technical experts? Would a domain specialist want to do the work of a section officer or Under Secretary which primarily involves putting up a paper under consideration, listing pros and cons of a proposal, pointing out precedents and past orders and also examining the legality of the proposal? However, there are aspects of technical departments where the Secretariat system is not able to properly analyze a proposal. A colleague who was an electrical engineer before joining the IAS was posted as Special Secretary Energy, Government of UP. He told me that he had to initiate the file to examine any technical proposal because his section officers and Secretariat officers below were just not able to understand the proposals. In such cases, special cells are created and manned by technical people who do the processing of such proposals.

However, I am not completely rejecting the idea of domain knowledge. After the first fifteen years of service, the IAS officers can be made to specialize in domains but this should be in broad areas rather than narrow disciplines. For instance, an IAS officer can specialize in social sector comprising of health, education, nutrition and social welfare. He can then be given special training in these areas and posted accordingly. Other suggested domains can be finance, infrastructure, agriculture and rural development and others. My idea is that even if one feels that domain knowledge is required, the IAS officers should be slotted and developed in particular areas of specialization. This would bring in the best of both worlds. It would perhaps be a much-needed reform in the IAS. Recently, a colleague of mind gave me a revolutionary idea. He was of the view that reverse lateral entry should be allowed. This implies that IAS officers should have a window through which they can work in private sector, public sector or educational institutions and acquire domain-specific knowledge. The idea is challenging though fraught with difficulties. The point I am trying to make is that rather than only thinking of bringing people from outside through lateral entry, conscious effort needs to be made to develop specialization within the IAS.

I have talked about the leadership qualities being the basic attribute of a top-level government officer. Nowhere am I implying that the IAS has exclusive right to this quality. Many domain specialists are also brilliant leaders. Conversely, many IAS officers are not good leaders. There are a vast majority who simply uphold the status quo and do not propel their organization or departments towards a greater future.

However, there are better chances of finding leaders in the IAS or Civil Services because of the field experience they get. The years spent in the districts as SDM, Chief Development Officer and eventually District Officer are great learning experiences. It confronts the officer with the realities of India and the extent of its backwardness. This exposure at the field level equips a civil service officer with practical knowledge which helps him/her in framing the right policies and getting them implemented properly. A lateral entrant does not have this exposure. In fact I read an article by D.V. Subbarao (ex-RBI Governor) who, while accepting the idea of lateral entry, called for a system whereby the new entrants should first be sent to the district for a reasonable period to acquire field knowledge and then involve themselves in policy formulation. I support this idea.

Curiously, most people think that just by allowing lateral entry into the IAS, the entire problem of public service delivery will be solved. They have to understand that an IAS officer has to function within the limits prescribed by a bureaucratic system. If lateral entrants have to function within the confines of the same system then they would also not be able to achieve much irrespective of their domain knowledge. The IAS officer does not function alone. He is supported by a large lower-level bureaucracy which stays put. If there is no change at that level then nothing will make a difference.

Besides, bureaucratic culture is one where processes rather than outputs or outcomes dominate. The reasons for this are historical as well as contemporary. The government has created for itself a network of processes based on the premise of disbelief and lack of trust. British-administered

India used native officers at most lower-level posts and did not trust them at all. They, thus, created a maze of rules and procedures to ensure that the native officer was left with little or no power. Unfortunately, even after Independence we have carried the same system forward.

Processes should be the means but they become ends in themselves. Actually, an officer is safe if he follows the rules and procedures. It does not matter whether he achieves the results or not. I have seen so many dashing and dynamic IAS officers mellowing down and becoming procedure-oriented after a couple of shocks and setbacks. An IAS officer shall face a departmental enquiry or even a CBI case if some minor procedure has not been followed, even if he has achieved excellent results. However, if he does not achieve results he will see no grief. This is the reason many officers lose their idealism on the way and adopt the 'safety first' dictum.

The four C's make the work of the IAS officer more difficult. The Courts, CVC, CBI and CAG emasculate the creative and positive approach of an officer. Any intelligent officer knows to stay on the right side of the four C's and the best strategy for this is to do nothing. Handle files and paper properly, refer every possible issue to committees, write good notes on files and take approval of the higher authorities on almost everything and this makes one a successful officer. Decisions are best avoided in this approach and problems are allowed to linger.

In essence, the entire internal and external environment is one which discourages dynamism and result-orientation. Those who do not follow the system are punished whereas those who still maintain their zeal and produce results are never rewarded. The signal is clear: perform and perish or maintain status quo and succeed. No wonder the majority start working according to the system.

I am not trying to paint a negative picture or be unnecessarily pessimistic. There are still a lot of officers who are doing outstanding work and maintaining their idealism. These are remarkably self-motivated officers for whom inaction is an anathema and who gain satisfaction by making a difference. But sadly, the majority is not like this. We have to change the bureaucratic culture and systems to see that most IAS officers are concerned about outcomes and not red tape. This is the cause for civil service reforms. Merely introducing lateral entry and not changing anything else will result in these lateral entrants not being able to contribute. In fact, if they try to be too innovative and dynamic, then they can possibly regret their decision for ever having opted for the government.

An issue closely linked to domain knowledge is that of stability of tenure. IAS officers face frequent transfers, particularly in states. This does act as a deterrent for the officer to acquire knowledge of his department and try to get results or outcomes. The Government of India is better in this respect. Normally an officer spends five years in a department as Deputy Secretary/Director or JS. However, states like UP are notorious in this regard. An officer can get transferred three to four times in a year. There is no doubt that this seriously affects the performance of the officer. The reason behind these transfers is largely political. There is no doubt that officers also try and get themselves posted to more powerful assignments. However, it is the political executive and political reasons which, more often than not, are behind the frequent transfer of officers. It varies from state to state with some states having a very good tradition where an officer is generally not shifted before three years. But in a state like UP, the average tenure may often come to one year. It is worse for the District Magistrate. The UP average for the DM would be around six months.

There is no denying that there should be a conscious policy and institutional setup which allows a minimum tenure in a posting, if not for three years. Various administrative reform committees have sat on this problem and the Courts have also stepped in. As a result, there is a Civil Service Board (CSB) which recommends transfers. In UP, the Chief Secretary chairs the CSB with the senior-most IAS officer and Principal Secretary Appointments being members. However, this is just to satisfy court orders. In reality, the decision is taken at the highest level or level of CS and the minutes of CSB drawn up accordingly. The CSB does not question frequent transfers of officers nor does it record any reasons. Every transfer is always in 'public interest'.

The above system suits the political executive as he has the power to shift officers and thereby control them. In fact, the political executive has very reluctantly agreed to have a CSB and makes sure that it is only of ornamental value. I recall that UP government, in fact, filed an affidavit before the Honourable Court, opposing the CSB system and argued that in a democracy the power to transfer officers must be at the discretion of the political executive to ensure accountability.

Those who are outside the system would never understand the sinister way in which this power of transfer breaks the back of the bureaucracy. In a bid to hang on to their posts, the vulnerable officer gives up the idea of giving fearless, independent advice and tries his best to please the Chief Minister or minister concerned. The boldness to work as per the constitution and insisting on the rule of law is badly compromised as an insecure officer tries his level best to accommodate the wishes of his political executive.

The minister often takes refuge in the allegation that an officer is not allowing him to work or is becoming an obstacle. The minister will allege that the officer is not taking decisions and slowing down the work. This argument is lapped up by the media, intellectuals and members of the public. You often hear the lament that IAS officers are too rigid and averse to decision-making, as a result of which public service delivery is suffering. It could be true in some cases but generally it is the officer who insists on rules, fairness and transparency and refuses to do illegal work, who becomes inconvenient and is branded as being an obstructionist. This is why the CSB system has to be made effective to protect officers who are genuinely trying to do well.

If the Chief Secretary is bold and is not afraid to speak up for his officers, then he can bring a certain degree of sanity into the system. The CM Secretariat can also play a positive role in this. I recall that when I was Secretary to CM, the Sarva Shiksha Abhiyan (SSA, a Government of India initiative in primary education) had been launched. We had an officer who had worked for several years in education and was doing a wonderful job. The minister wanted her transferred out. The reasons being the huge budget that SSA had and its governance structure being such that the minister had no role in it. The Principle Secretary of the department, the Project Director and the Chief Secretary were involved in the entire process of planning, decision-making and fund allocation and monitoring. The minister tried to interfere but the project director did not allow him to do so. The minister was wild and complained against her to the CM, and wanted her to be transferred and replaced by an officer of his choice. The CM was willing and called me to inform the Appointment Secretary. I realized that this change would damage the SSA programme where the state was doing well. I took a stand and explained my viewpoint to the CM. He also understood the implications and the transfer did not take place.

Similarly, when I was Chief Secretary, we were implementing the Samajwadi Pension Scheme where Rs 500 had to be given as pension per month to targeted beneficiaries. The amount had to go to the woman of the family. The scheme was costing the exchequer around Rs 3000 crores and there were more than 50 lakh beneficiaries. The Principle Secretary Social Welfare was an extremely meticulous and conscientious officer who went about implementing the scheme with a lot of zeal. He used the PFMS evolved by the Government of India to transfer the amount directly to the bank account of the beneficiaries on the first of each month. He undertook a rigorous exercise for identifying the beneficiaries in a fair and transparent manner. The Social Welfare Minister was upset. He argued that the scheme implemented in this manner would not help the government as they would not be able to benefit their supporters. The Principle Secretary Social Welfare refused to accommodate the wishes of the minister. The minister requested the CM for the transfer of his Secretary. The CM agreed. However, I took a stand and briefed the CM about the excellent way in which this scheme was being implemented and how if the minister had his way, then the scheme would get a bad name. The CM agreed. The minister, of course, was very upset and told me so. This is another example of how, if the CS or CM Secretariat takes a stand in the interest of governance, such transfers and postings can be avoided. Needless to say that in both these cases, the concerned schemes were implemented very well which would not have been the case if the officers had been transferred.

Another interesting case came up when I was Secretary to the CM. There was a young and dynamic officer whose batch was due for district posting. The CM, however, saw the caste of the officer and was of the view that because of this, the officer would favour the opposition party and should not be posted as District Magistrate (DM). I was aghast and spoke up that I knew this officer and that he would make a very good DM. His caste had nothing to do with his abilities as an officer. The CM reluctantly agreed and he was posted as DM and he did a very good job too. However, I was deeply pained to find a decade later, that the political people had managed to identify this officer with his caste identity and in self-defence the officer had also started acting accordingly. He got excellent postings in one government and was shunted out in another. He was, ultimately, identified with the political party. Many transfers are done on the basis of caste, especially in UP, and also there is this tendency to identify officers with political parties on the basis of their caste or having good postings under a particular government. Sooner or later, the officers concerned also start responding in a similar manner. The loser, of course, is good governance.

The politician alone is not to be blamed for this. In UP, at least, many officers have willingly got themselves aligned with a political party and then extracted maximum advantage when that party is in power. They suffer when the government changes. It is also true that the political executive often commits the mistake of identifying an officer holding an important posting in a government with the ruling party. Often the officer concerned suffers for no reason with change in government. However, there is no denying the politicization of officers and the exploitation of this vulnerability of the officers by the political executive.

I have seen many Chief Secretaries accepting the instructions of the CM in having an officer shifted but it is the CS who will decide where he is posted and who will succeed him. Even this approach will maintain the sanctity of good governance and uplift the morale of the officers.

The disease of transfers is much more widespread in other state services. Normally, a Class-II officer and below should be transferred and posted by his head of department. But in reality, you find that his power has been usurped by a minister. The transfer lists are prepared in the office of the minister with little regard for performance. The IAS Principle Secretaries, I have noticed, often adopt the strategy of letting things be and not interfere. Actually, any intervention will lead to a direct conflict with the minister and the officer will not be able to concentrate on the more worthwhile schemes and projects.

Just a few days ago, there was a glaring example of how a transfer can derail governance. An Indian Forest Service

officer was posted as Field Director Dudhwa National
Park for just about a year. He had done brilliant work
against jungle mafias, controlling poaching and illegal
tree felling. He was introducing technology to manage
the park better. He had really made an impact. All of a
sudden, he was transferred. Nobody knows why except
that everybody had a sinking feeling that the wildlife and
forest mafia is behind this. Imagine the impact this would
have on Dudhwa National Park, and also on the morale
of the officer. I am sure nobody has brought this to the
notice of the Chief Minister, otherwise this would not have
happened. It is a duty of the senior officers to bring such
issues to the knowledge of the chief minister. Recently, the
UP Chief Minister stayed the transfers done by the health
and irrigation departments after receiving complaints.
The Principle Secretary Rural Development has worked
out a system of performance-based transfers after taking
the options of the officers concerned. This is an excellent
example of good governance and shows that the transfer
industry can be regulated. I am told that the Haryana
Government has done a wonderful job regarding transfers
of teachers, eliminating the political pulls and pressures.

Nothing breaks the back of good governance more
than these frequent, motivated transfers because of which
performance suffers. There is no question of getting results or
achieving outcomes if you cannot fit the right officer in the
right place. The basic concept of good governance is that
the right man should be chosen for a job and then given
sufficient tenure or time to give results. That is why the system
of CSB and similar institutional arrangements are important.

Transfers and postings have to be handled in a professional manner if public service delivery is to improve.

People blame the IAS officer occupying the top post in a department for not giving results. They do not realize that often he is saddled with a team which is not selected on merit. I often hear people say that IAS officers should take a principled stand on all issues irrespective of what the minister says. They say that the worst that could happen to you is that you get transferred. But believe me, frequent transfers can truly demotivate an officer. He finds that he has not been able to do much in short tenures. He does not feel a sense of achievement. Moreover, transfers can adversely affect your family life; for example, the education of your children. It can be really be unsettling. An officer has a family to look after and has to move around in society. The political executive has realized that by using the single instrument of transfer, they can bring the bureaucracy down on its knees. The power game is clear and the astute politician plays it very well. But it is the citizen who suffers because the public services do not reach him.

The solution lies in having tenure of at least two to three years for all senior posts and if the officer has to be shifted before that, there should be strong reasons for the same recorded by the CSB or other similar institutional arrangements. This sounds like a simple solution but is extremely difficult to implement in the current political scenario. Some NGOs in UP have gone to court on these issues. I guess only intervention by the Courts will resolve the problem. Transferring officers is a lucrative job and politicians would not like to lose control over it.

It is not as if officers are not to be blamed for this state of affairs. As I had pointed out earlier, officers have categorized certain postings as good and others as not so good. They make all the effort to get the former postings and often use political pressure to achieve this. Once again, having an institutional arrangement would check on such officers and even identify them. I found as CS that many officers approach the CM or CM Office to get good postings. Often they behave in such an obsequious and undignified manner that it is downright embarrassing. In the states, officers are keen to become DMs and exert a lot of pressure for this. Often an officer takes the help of a powerful politician of a district to get himself posted there. Needless to say, this officer has to work as the pawn for the powerful politician as long as he stays and loses the image of neutrality and fairness which is essential for him to do justice to his job.

Things have reached to such a level that young IAS officers, fresh out of the academy, start exerting pressure to get postings of their choice. In UP, I found as CS that these officers were using political influence for their postings. I was genuinely surprised as this was something we could not even think of in our time. Besides, we did not even know any politicians. To my surprise, the officers were asking for districts like Noida, Ghaziabad, Lucknow and Agra—all urban districts and big cities. I made it a point not to allow this and post fresh officers to backward districts of eastern UP and Bundelkhand. Actually, the learning value is much higher in such districts, especially about revenue and development matters. In districts like Noida and Ghaziabad, the young officer runs the risk of learning all the wrong things at the very beginning which can influence his thought process for the rest of his career.

Whenever I have addressed young IAS officers or aspirants, I found that the foremost query in their mind is related to the issue of political interference and how to deal with it. In our democratic setup, the elected political representative is the boss and he is in a superior position as compared to the civil servant. This is not to be resented because this is the constitutional scheme of things and the civil servant must realize that the elected MLA/MP/minister is the representative of the people and it is the people whose will is paramount in the functioning of a democracy. Therefore, Civil Servants have to do away with this attitude of feeling superior to all and give due respect to the elected representative. It is a given that political functionaries will be involved in the process of governance and as such any intervention by them shall not be viewed negatively. However, the guiding principle is the rule of law. A civil servant has to abide by the Constitution, law, rules and processes. Irrespective of the level and intensity of political pressure, he has to govern in a straight line. It is not up to him to please the politician in power. It must be kept in mind that in the event of an enquiry, it is the civil servant who is held accountable for any violation as it is he who signs the papers.

Political intervention is acceptable in a democracy but interference is not. The civil servant has his powers clearly defined and laid out, and he has to function within these parameters. Intervention is in public interest whereas interference is only in the interest of the politician concerned. The former strengthens democratic governance whereas the latter leads to corruption, nepotism and is the very antithesis of good governance. Unfortunately, in our political system today, the politician is more often than not in the negative interference mode.

Believe me, not all politicians are bad, of course. Just like in any other section of society, Civil Services included, they have their share of the good, the bad and the ugly. It is thus important for an officer to understand the politician they are dealing with and tailor his responses accordingly. Good governance is the goal an IAS officer has to strive for and not bow down to unjust political pressure. Sometimes, he will have to pay the price for this and the politicians may not hesitate to use the weapon of transfer to try and subjugate the officer.

A politician may not be as highly educated as the IAS officer but there is no denying that he has certain qualities the IAS officer does not. For one, he has a far better idea of ground realities than any officer because he spends his time in the field, mingling with one and all and gets instant and real-time feedback on everything. He has a first-person account of how the development schemes are getting rolled out, the corruption at the ground level and the less than satisfactory quality of work. I always found that you can rely on the feedback given to you by a political figure and as an officer, I made it a point to ask the politicians to give me a true picture of the situation at the ground level. Officers go by reports and information systems, whereas the politicians have the pulse of the people and their ears close to the ground. He is able to catch all formal and informal vibrations whereas the officer has to often go by what is reported to him. An officer, especially in a district, can govern far better if he has a system of listening to the political representative of his district; whether they are from the ruling party or opposition.

These days, District Officers listen more to the political representatives from the ruling parties and ignore the opposition leaders. This is not a healthy practice as by doing this, the officer is cutting himself away from a lot of useful information and critical feedback that can be used in a constructive manner. I remember keeping my door open to all public representatives and listening to them without fear or favour. Unfortunately, state-level ministers and sometimes CMs also have a very narrow way of looking at things. They want the officer to meet, listen and act according to the ruling party members, even if they are small-time party workers, and ignore the opposition leaders. Consequently, many officers today are scared of listening to the opposition representatives.

To be successful and effective, an officer must keep his doors open to all and be equally responsive. If he behaves in this manner, he will escape the tag of being linked to any political party. An unfortunate trend these days is the linking of officers with a political party if they have held good postings during that regime. This is a favourite game that narrow-minded politicians play. The result of this is mass transfers or even enquiries against certain officers considered to be close to the earlier government. It is true that some officers are genuinely aligned to a political party and reap rewards and punishment accordingly. They deserve it. No IAS officer or civil servant has any business to be aligned with any political party. This will erode his credibility as an officer. Such officers have lowered the prestige of the service and have certainly not been true to themselves. In UP, this trend has been on an alarming rise for the last two decades or so. The worst part of this is that these alignments are often on caste lines—the Dalit bureaucracy is linked to BSP, the Yadav with SP and the upper caste with BJP. The caste alignment of the bureaucracy is like a termite eating away at the very base of the governance system. I am told the story is similar in many other states, notably Tamil Nadu and Bihar. The foundation of the IAS has been on the dictum of neutrality and impartiality. These are the very attributes that are severely compromised if the officers get linked to political parties. This trend needs the strongest possible condemnation but it is very much there and not likely to be wished away in a hurry.

Not all officers holding good posts in a particular government are linked politically with the party in power. Many officers do their work honestly and in a neutral fashion. They get good assignments because they are hardworking and efficient. It is professional excellence which gets them the good postings. However, the current trend is for the new political dispensation to view all such officers with a coloured vision.

I was Secretary to Chief Minister for over four years in the BJP government from 1998–2002. The succeeding government viewed me as being close to the BJP. Then after returning from the Government of India, I was given excellent postings by the BSP government, who even made me Agriculture Production Commissioner (APC) a post which is second to Chief Secretary in UP. The SP government in 2012 initially put me in the list of blue-eyed boys of the previous government. Subsequently, when they observed my work and saw my neutral and impartial behaviour, they revised their opinion about me. Initially, they made me Infrastructure and Industrial Development Commissioner (IIDC) along with APC. Then the SP government made me Chief Secretary and I continued in this post for over two years. On my retirement, the SP government made me Chief Advisor to the Chief Minister. The BJP government which came to power in 2017 branded me as being pro-SP. There should be some mechanism to protect officers with integrity against such politically motivated hounding. Once again, the Chief Secretary and the Chief Minister's Office can play a major role in this.

In any case, political vendetta has become the norm rather than exception these days. Every new government wants to setup enquiries against work done or projects executed by the earlier government. Often development projects started by earlier governments suffer gross neglect and public money is wasted. There should be a law against this. Projects where public money has been spent should be completed by the successor government. The real problem comes when these inquiries are directed against the political leadership of earlier governments but it is the officers concerned who have to face the music. It is an officer who signs the papers or takes decisions and can easily be held accountable. It is a fact that if you are on a fault-finding spree, then you can do so in any development scheme or project implemented. Such stories keep coming in from almost all the states and the central government is also not immune to this malady. All political parties are falling into this trap which ultimately leads to slow and ineffective governance during their tenure.

The reaction of the IAS and other officers is typical. They realize that the future governments may hold them accountable for work done or decisions taken now. So the simple remedy is not to take a decision, persist with the status quo and always cover your tracks. A negative mindset is created in the entire governance hierarchy and this negativity is so pervasive that it kills all initiative and creativity. The worst part of this political witch-hunt is that straightforward, honest officers often find themselves facing an investigation. Nothing can be more demoralizing for the bureaucracy!

Most ministers are balanced and sensible people who will accept if an officer tells them that some action is against the rules and cannot be done. The tragedy is that there are quite a few who feel that an officer is posted to do their bidding and has no business to talk about right or wrong. Their rationale is that since they have been elected by the people, they know what is best and that the rules should be bent to accommodate their wishes. Only the other day, a very senior IAS officer was telling me how he objected to a draft government order on the grounds that it was unconstitutional. The minister was livid as the issuing of this government order was likely to benefit his political constituency in a big way. He had the temerity to call the officer and upbraid him by saying that it was for the minister to handle the issue of legality or otherwise, and that the officer just had to sign. The officer refused and was promptly shifted.

It did not end here. When the post of the Chief Secretary fell vacant, this officer lost out because the minister concerned complained in writing against him to the Chief Minister. This is the fate that can befall IAS officers. I found that the

State Civil Service Officers and other officers are subjected to much more serious political onslaught. I was Secretary Basic Education in UP, when I got a written order from the minister suspending a senior officer of the education department. This officer was outstanding in his work so I protested. The minister was very annoyed. Evidently this officer had not carried out an illegal order of the minister. I did not issue the suspension order and antagonized the minister who started working towards my removal.

If all IAS officers and departmental officers take a stand, then there is very little that the political executive can do. However, the reality is very different. For each officer taking a stand, there are half a dozen willing to compromise. A politician is very good at reading people and he reads the officers very well too. He knows whom he can pressurize to do his bidding and whom he should leave alone. If an officer is upright and honest, a politician will not ask him to do anything wrong.

Many critics of the IAS point out that once an IAS officer is selected, she automatically rises to the top without there being any test of her proficiency. This is largely true as seniority, subject to merit, is the criterion used for time-bound promotions. Merit is gauged from annual confidential reports which are normally written without much seriousness and generally tend to give a positive assessment to almost all officers. To some extent, this system has been improved upon now by the Government of India through the introduction of 360-degree evaluation. Not more than 30 per cent of a batch now gets promoted to the level of Secretary. Recently, the Government of India introduced the concept of Karm Yogi which aims to develop human capital in the Civil Services and is a laudable move. Also, I found that if an officer acquires a bad reputation, then he generally does not get a good posting even though he might be promoted to the next scale. The performance evaluation system needs to be radically changed to see that for each level of promotion, only the performing officers get promoted. Also, it is important to develop the skill set of an officer through regular mid-career training programmes. Several committees have deliberated on this issue and now every IAS officer goes through a well-designed mid-career Phase-II to Phase-V training programme at various points in his career. I had earlier talked of a broad domain specialization and these training programmes can be suitably modified to meet the needs of each domain. Performance in these training programmes should count towards promotions.

Designing a scientific and objective performance-evaluation system which separates the wheat from the chaff is essential. Of course, there is no such thing as a completely objective performance evaluation system. The element of subjectivity and personal bias is to be found in the best of systems. Yet an effort can be made at making the system more rational, based on tasks assigned, and performance and grading on the required attributes. The system should be such that not all IAS officers automatically reach the top and only those who performed well and acquire the right leadership skills climb up the bureaucratic ladder.

The service is at a crossroads. It is being pilloried from all sides and certain decisions are being taken which may soon end the service. One of my batchmates describes the state of affairs by tweeting 'RIP IAS'. Yes, the IAS could allow itself to be buried and rest in peace or it could emerge stronger, vibrant and much more relevant. Just like we tell human beings to look inside themselves to discover their real self, the IAS too has to take a candid look within and then reinvent itself to become a tool for bringing about positive transformation in society.

IAS officers must change. The service must re-discover the ethos of its halcyon days. If it does not do this, then the external forces shall push it into irrelevance. The IAS officer, to be appreciated, applauded and to maintain his status in society, has to undergo a vital transformation. The service must reform itself to be able to make a difference to society. Each individual officer has to introspect, analyze and reorient himself so that the entire service gains and contributes to society.

If the IAS wants to be the premier service, then it should behave like one. Its members should display the highest standards of integrity—both financial and moral. If the service cannot stand out on the basis of its integrity, then there is no difference between the IAS and others and no reason for it to exist. The officers of the ICS were known for their integrity, as have the IAS officers over the decades. However, there is a discernible decline and today the service is being confronted with an increasing amount of corruption in its ranks. There was a time when only a handful of IAS officers could be called corrupt. Today, that percentage has gone up. The result is the loss of respect and prestige in the eyes of the general public who now think nearly all IAS officers are busy minting money. This is not true. There are still a vast majority of officers with impeccable standards. The service has to weed out the bad and present before society a sparkling example of integrity. An incorruptible IAS is the best medicine for survival.

The desire for increased material benefits and a life of comfort and glamour have led to increased corruption in the service. In addition to this, the process of development has placed a lot of discretionary funds in the hands of the IAS officers. Coupled with this is the scenario where businessmen and other private players are only too willing to bribe their way into getting decisions in their favour. Somewhere along the lines, the shame associated with an unclean reputation has also evaporated and today you find officers justifying their conduct. I have been taken aback to find how many competent officers lack integrity. Their intelligence and capability works in both directions.

I was reading a book written by the extremely honest and dedicated officer of the IAS, M.N. Buch. He has analyzed this subject of corruption and divided it into three parts: 'Jabrana', 'Nazrana' and 'Shukranama'. Jabrana implies extortion and is the worst kind of corruption. I have seen IAS officers withholding files so that the concerned person approaches them and they strike a deal. I was once approached as Chief Secretary by an old friend whose matter was pending at the level of one of my Principle Secretaries. He told me that he was willing to strike a deal with the officer but the amount asked was in the region of 5 crores which was a bit too much. He wanted my help to get the amount reduced. I was aghast and told him that it was not my job to broker deals and confidently told him that I would not allow corruption. I rang up the concerned officer, mentioned the case to him and asked him to clear it within three days and inform me. Three days later, the file came with a legal opinion and clear recommendation of the officer that we should seek a clarification from the court as a large amount of government money was involved. There was no option but to agree with the recommendation even though I knew it was deliberate. To this date, my friend has not got relief. I have retired and so has the concerned officer. The other day, my friend ruefully told me that he regretted the day he came to me. He could have begged, borrowed and bribed the officer. It would have saved him so much of time, stress and even money! Such are the ways of officers who indulge in the Jabrana mode of corruption. If you comply, your case is cleared; if you do not, then your file is sent into the orbit and is never to return. Mercifully, there are not too many who belong to this category.

Nazrana is the most common form of corruption. In this, there is no force or pressure applied by the officer but he does not say no if someone offers him money or any other consideration in kind. Expensive Diwali gifts are a common medium of such corruption. Then there is the system of 'traditional amount' which comes to officers even if they do not do anything specific in return. In UP, it is shocking to see some SSPs taking a fixed amount from the police stations every month and some DMs taking a percentage cut in all development works sanctioned by them. There was this young DM who got his Project Director District Rural Development Agency arrested because he wanted a larger cut than the traditional amount. He moved from Nazrana to Jabrana. When this was denied, the hapless Project Director had an FIR registered against him and landed behind bars.

The worst part is that corruption has become a way of life in society and people are willing to offer benefits to officers to maintain good relations and reap the rewards on any particular day. One IAS officer justified his Nazrana approach by saying that, 'After all, I do his work and if he does give me something, why should I deny it? I am not forcing him to give me any consideration.'

Many years ago, I was DM Ghaziabad. The district was undivided Ghaziabad and had the highest target for the annual excise (liquor shops) auction. Some of my predecessors, I was told, had been compromised by the contractor who was an exceedingly influential character. I, along with SSP and the District Excise Officer, decided to break his monopoly and generate larger revenue for the state. We decided to take action against the mafias. The strategy was to ensure that the auction was a truly open one, done transparently. Preventive action against the mafias was taken. Strong police arrangements made and the message spread across the state that anyone is welcome to participate in the auction. This had never happened before. The same person had been succeeding in the auction every year and nobody else participated out of fear. Through the District Excise Officer, the existing contractor suggested a 'win-win situation' to me. The target set by the government was 10 per cent increase in revenue. He offered to bid for 12 per cent higher than last year, thereby ensuring that I exceeded my target and his interest was also served. I refused as I was fully aware that the potential of the district was much more. Then he finally sought an appointment with me and when he came, he bowed before me and placed a bag full of jewellery in front of me. I told him that I did not take anything from anybody and he should take it back. He looked at me pleadingly and said, 'Sir, this is just Nazar. It is a tradition to give this Nazrana to the Hakim (Ruler)'. I forced him to take it away. Needless to say, the auction was done transparently and honestly and the revenue went up by 100 per cent. It was a different matter that eventually the highest bid was of this very contractor. He did not want anybody else to come in at any cost. So, Nazrana is often couched in terms of 'paying respects' with no relief being immediately sought but it is a deceptive mechanism whereby the officer is influenced to take a decision that suits the Nazrana giver.

'Shukranama' is the third variety. It is a way of saying thanks after the work has been done. Nothing has been demanded and the work done is on merit. But this innocuous way of saying thanks also has a hidden agenda—to influence future decisions. Taking any kind of favour from anyone at any stage, compromises the integrity of the officer and is corruption whichever way you look at it.

Unfortunately, the age of materialism has affected the civil servant too and they crave the good things in life. So many officers send their children abroad for studies and others keep piling up property. They justify to themselves that they are doing their work efficiently and with commitment and as such are allowed to take 'fringe benefits'. Actually, there is no justification for such an approach. Besides, I don't think you can really deliver if you do not maintain your integrity.

Every generation of Civil Servants has their share of the honest, the ambivalent and the downright corrupt. However, without attempting to cast any aspersions, there has been a gradual decline in the standard of integrity and this has had its impact on the credibility of the service and the image of the officer in the eye of the common man. I believe it might be the extension of age limit for writing the IAS exam and the increase in number of attempts allowed has played a role in contributing to this decline. Candidates are joining the civil service at an age by when their attitudes and value systems have already been crystallized and it is difficult to mould them.

If the IAS has to maintain its 'Numero Uno' position, then it has to set an example with its commitment to integrity. Civil Servants have to do a lot of soul-searching. They must realize that any breach of integrity leads to the erosion in the halo surrounding IAS officers and lays them open to exploitation by self-seeking politicians and power brokers.

Financial integrity plays a very big part. Integrity however is a very comprehensive and pervasive concept. The ICS and even the IAS was known for its unflinching commitment to it. Today we cannot say the same for the current 'avatar' of the IAS as rarely do officers stand up for their views or for what they think is right. They are more concerned about what the political masters want from them. They do not put up inconvenient comments on files and more often than not, use their ability to prepare a file in a manner that the design of the political boss is achieved. As the adage goes, 'For one officer who is not prepared to bend, there are several who are willing to crawl'.

Once again, there is hope as there are a lot of officers who stick to their principles and give their views frankly and boldly. The only cause for worry is that the number of such officers is going down over the years. This is not to say that the ICS officers or early batches of the IAS were averse to towing the political line. Only that they were fewer and also the politicians were less aware of their powers. Today, the political executive will instantly brand an upright officer as obstructionist and lament the bureaucratic hurdles in getting things done. The journalists and self-declared experts will join in the chorus.

The IAS officer has to go by the rules but it is also true that he makes the rules. Creating miles and miles of red tape is his specialization under the garb of developing systems and ensuring probity. It is not the IAS officer who is a problem but the bureaucratic system and processes which are the source of all negativity in the administration. Therefore, process engineering has to be a continuous process. It is the responsibility of the IAS to simplify the rules and processes so that administration becomes dynamic. However, the IAS often shirks this responsibility. Actually the miles and miles of red tape is great protective armour for the IAS officer and he willingly accepts being a part of it. This is the reason that the label of being change-resistant is frequently laid at the door of the IAS and there is a justification for this. I have seen that as an IAS officer grows in seniority, his capacity or willingness to take decisions and modernize systems goes down in direct proportion. This is the peculiarity of the IAS and other Civil Services. The higher one goes in the hierarchy, the more insecure he becomes.

If the IAS has to maintain its status as a service with a difference, then its commitment to integrity has to be total. Integrity means bringing to the fore all your inner qualities in the service of the people and the nation. If the objective becomes merely self-serving and concerned with one's own survival, then one is neither being true to themselves or to the service. To my mind this falls under the larger and wider scope of the term integrity and is perhaps its more relevant aspect.

The biggest threat to the system of governance has been the unholy nexus that often develops between a corrupt politician and a corrupt bureaucrat. Nothing is impossible for such a team and they get along perfectly. They are fully synchronized and together get their hands on public money, at the expense of the poor citizens. The IAS, as a service, has to look within itself and weed out such elements or else there will be stories of scam after scam which will be a result of this unhealthy partnership.

Humility is a great virtue in a leader. It is a rare quality to have in the corridors of power. IAS officers are often immune to this trait. Arrogance is a quality which has become synonymous with the IAS, leading to its members distancing themselves from the people they are meant to serve. Accessibility and responsiveness are the hallmarks of a good governance system but arrogance acts as a hindrance. Such an officer is concerned only with himself and is always conscious of his status and sense of power. He expects even ordinary citizens to bend and bow before him and reserves the right to be curt and rude. It is often impossible to meet a senior IAS officer. I found it to be strange that the UP government had to issue orders that the District Magistrate shall be in his office from 10 a.m. to 12 noon to meet people. Does this need orders from the government? I recall that as a District Magistrate, I used to spend much more than two hours to meet the people and would keep my doors open to them at all times. Gradually, the District Magistrates started spending more time cloistered in their camp offices. UP officers are particularly guilty of being inaccessible. Even if they do meet people, their attitude is so dismissive and abrupt or even callous that the citizen feels he has not been heard. Arrogance is self-perpetuating and ultimately harms the officer. It removes him from reality, leading to an administration confined to paperwork and plans. If the IAS has to fulfill its role and obligation to society, it has to shun arrogance and embrace humility. A genial smile, a courteous and polite response, a patient hearing does not cost much but leads to a far more humane and sensitive administration which is the sine qua non of good governance.

I have seen tremendous arrogance in people holding top managements posts in the private sector or in wealthy businesses. I have seen that the moment anyone is given even a little bit of power, he begins to flaunt it. This is the very nature of power. To keep a level head after getting that power requires tremendous strength of character. Yet, if one is able to get over its trappings and relates without ego to people, then the rewards in terms of credibility and acceptability are great. There are so many stories of District Magistrates getting unlimited adulation in their districts, provided they have come down from their high tables of power and shown understanding and compassion for the common people.

Humility, empathy and compassion are the essence of a caring and responsive governance system and the officers of the IAS should actively cultivate these traits. So many issues come up before them every day. If he does not have the emotional intelligence to genuinely understand the sentiments of the people coming to him, then he will not be able to deliver. Effective public service delivery is linked to this.

A quality which flows from this is the quality of listening. You hear with your ears but you listen with your entire being. You hear the words, the tone, the mood and concern, and the extent to which the problem is affecting him. You also see the non-verbal signals: the body language, the gestures, and then understand the man and his problem in totality. This quality of listening is all the more important in the IAS because an officer moves from one job to another and the best way to make a success of his job is to listen to those who have been in the organization for a long time. It does not pay to try and impose your views from the first day by trying to show you know everything. Unfortunately, IAS officers are guilty of this which alienates them from the organization right from the beginning. So listen deeply and intently before you speak. Also an administrator must listen more and speak less and should have a penchant for action rather than words.

A question that often crops up before officers is whether they should be strict or lenient. I feel this is like choosing between black and white, and ignoring the several grades of gray in between. It depends upon the situation and the context where an officer has to be strict or lenient. There are officers who are sticklers for punctuality. There are others who are always finding fault with the subordinates. Such officers create an atmosphere of awe and fear. People will work because they are afraid and not out of a genuine sense of team spirit. Strictness should not be equated with rigidity, obstinacy or an attitude that ignores the human nature. Strictness should denote a commitment to values and uncompromising integrity.

Some officers have a pathological desire to take action against subordinates in the name of integrity. This is often counterproductive. I have seen officers who project themselves as crusaders of honesty, believing that everyone else in the organization is dishonest and ruthlessly takes actions against all. An officer is supposed to be honest and he is not doing a favour to society or the government by being so. It does not give him the license to be rude to others and irrational in his actions. The best thing to do is be firm in your actions without being uncivil and rash. I was DM of Ghaziabad in the early nineties when it was known as the Wild West and was overrun with the mafia. My SSP and I took the strongest possible action against the mafia and led to them leaving the districts. The property prices went up in the district as peace and calm returned. Yet all this was done firmly without a show of too much anger. Action was taken within the confines of law. One day, as I was sitting in my collectorate office and my ADM was with me, all of a sudden, the noises in the collectorate fell. My office door opened and the peon bent to greet a person in kurta pyjama accompanied by two of his henchmen. My ADM also rose from his seat to greet the intruder. I knew he was the biggest don of the district. Yet the dialogue between us was extremely civil. He introduced himself and I looked at him and asked him to take a seat, which he declined with the wave of his hand and spoke in a gruff voice, 'You and your SSP have done everything possible to ruin me. I will not discuss that but tomorrow in your court is my case regarding the suspension of my arms licenses and their confiscation are coming up. I request you to release my weapons as they are necessary for my security.' I told him that I will look into the matter in an unbiased manner and decide as per law. He walked away and soon the collectorate breathed again with my ADM wiping the sweat off his forehead. Needless to say I cancelled his licenses the next day and confiscated his weapons. The point I want to make is that tough action can be taken without behaving arrogantly, rashly or being in a perpetual state of flared tempers. Honesty does not give you the license to denigrate others.

I recall when I was Secretary to the Chief Minister, there was a very young and vivacious officer who went about eliminating corruption with the zeal of a crusader. The net result was that he did not last in any posting for more than a couple of months. He was appointed Managing Director of Uttar Pradesh Electronic Corporation (UPTRON). True to his habit, he found everyone there to be involved in corruption and wielded the stick. More than 80 per cent of the officers of UPTRON were suspended or were served a charge sheet. There was a strike and demand for immediate removal of the MD. The CM called me and told me that the transfer orders of this officer were to be issued immediately. I resisted and put my point before the CM that this officer has the right intention. Frequent transfers would break him. We need to encourage zeal in young officers, but I assured the CM that I would counsel him. The CM relented and I called the officer. I told him it was important to get work done and make the organization move forward rather than break everything with a hammer. I pointed out that there were other means to achieve his objectives. I narrated to him the example of another officer with a similar bent of mind who followed the strategy of identifying a few of the most notorious officers in an organization and took action against them immediately. He called this strategy the hanging of a 'scarecrow' which would put the others in check. The idea was to create fear in the minds of the dishonest so that they mend their ways. Branding everyone as corrupt and initiating action against them would effectively derail governance.

One of the Chief Ministers, Mr Ram Prakash Gupta, decided against sane advice to launch a frontal attack on corruption. It was decided that all pending cases of vigilance would be disposed of at the earliest. Files were called for and inquiries were completed. One of the first files I pored over related to a case of disproportionate assets, where filing an FIR against the officer was recommended. I was drawn toward a table presented by the anti-corruption department which showed the officer's known sources of income and the expenditure he had incurred. To my amazement I found that he was being found guilty of having assets worth Rs 136.50 in excess of his income! Mercifully, the CM agreed with me in dropping the matter. I found several such files which cause undue harassment and lead to a lot of wastage of governance time. Action against corruption has to be taken in a manner so that the big fish are caught. Often the investigating agency does not have the skill set to do a detailed inquiry and just goes by the signatures on the file. It is a relief that the Prevention of Corruption Act has been amended to safeguard decisions taken in a bonafide manner by honest Civil Servants.

Corruption can be controlled by the officer at the top if he himself is honest and believes in accessibility and transparency. People below him are then scared because they know that every information can reach him. Further, governance systems can be designed to make the process open, transparent, reducing discretion and thereby reducing corruption. Above all technology now offers real-time solutions by eliminating the direct interface between the officer and the citizen. This has been seen by designing a system where all clearances are given online and within a prescribed time period. Corruption has been greatly reduced by such measures. Many states have passed the Public Service Guarantee Act which has timelines for clearances to be given by the departments and this has certainly helped in controlling things.

Corruption ultimately should not be a low cost, high reward activity. The system should be such that it automatically points a finger at the corrupt and there should be a fast-track process of punishing the officer.

One of the main traits that an IAS officer is supposed to have is that of neutrality. However, I am in slight disagreement here. The IAS officer should exhibit a bias in favour of the poor, marginalized and under privileged sections of society who are expected to be the main beneficiaries of a welfare state. The IAS officer has to be sensitized to issues relating to women. He has to rise above caste prejudice and communal thinking and always focus on the weaker sections of society. I recall that a case came before my court when I was a Subdivisional Magistrate (SDM) where a rich landlord was laying claim to the land of an evidently poor person. The former was assisted by a battery of top lawyers, while the latter was being represented by a lawyer who was not even able to open his mouth. I realized which side the truth lay and passed judgment in favour of the poor person. The opposite party went in appeal and the case was remanded back to me with strictures—I had not evaluated the evidence on record. This time I was most careful. I again give a judgment in favour of the poor person but was careful to write a detailed judgment evaluating all evidence and proving my point. It gave me an immense sense of satisfaction.

The great pleasure of being in the IAS is to be able to solve the real problems faced by society. The service gives you the power and authority to change things and make life better for people. No other job gives you this much of an opportunity. There can never be a boring moment in the service. Each day will throw up fresh challenges and test your ability and commitment. People talk about roads, the power supply, education system, quality of healthcare and debate about what should be done. The IAS gives you the position to actually do something about the issues confronting the people and the nation. It is a service which gives you the opportunity of being a transformational leader. The list of things you can do is endless. All it requires is a lot of dedication and commitment and integrity.

The IAS must take the blame for the poor quality of delivery of public services to some extent. But it is not entirely the fault of the IAS officer. I hear many people blaming the IAS for all that is wrong with development. They feel that the IAS is all-powerful. But this is not so as I have stated earlier. The politician is the decider and the IAS has to work in the given system. The officer's career and posting depends so much on the political executive and representatives that he is forced to play a subservient role. Further, he has no control over the team he commands, and he has no liberty in hiring his team or changing it. A leader can't deliver results if he has the wrong type of officers in his team.

Having stated the above genuine limitations, I must add that there is no reason to be pessimistic. Despite all the occupational hazards, the officer still has a lot of authority. His job is to make things happen. It is not for him to revel in status quo or master the art of spinning yards of red tape. He has to rise above the processes, attain a level above the ordinary and deliver results. The thrill of the IAS is in the ability to change the environment around you for the better. It can be done, provided the officer has the right attitude at all times and his focus has to be on the goals. He should strive to mold his team together and achieve results. Countless IAS officers are doing a great job. *The Indian Express* just awarded District Collectors for their outstanding work. I also found so many officers to be creative, innovative and performance driven. The work done by such officers needs to be documented as the best practices to inspire and guide others.

The service has to raise its level of consciousness. The IAS officer has to realize his true status and be confident of his ability and authority. His very thought process has to change and way he looks at his job and role has to undergo a major change. In short, the IAS has to reinvent itself and focus its energies on the development of the nation and in resolving the problems of the marginalized and the poor. Such a service shall never lose relevance. The IAS has to continuously prove itself to survive. The IAS officer has to realize that it is his job to make a difference by delivering outcomes. The service has the talent and inner strength to make it happen. The IAS has a glorious future if it realizes its inner potential.

Epilogue

Retirement from government service is inevitable. Every IAS officer has to one day retire and join the ranks of the ordinary citizens. The only memory that remains with him is the difference he has made to the life of the common man, the poor and the underprivileged. When in service, the years go by at a terrific pace and soon you come face to face with the retirement day. I retired after having received a three-month extension as Chief Secretary UP and I remember that I was as absorbed in my work as any other day, till late evening. There were urgent meetings, files to be disposed of, visitors, appointments and important policy decisions to be made. Soon, the day was over and I handed charge to my successor and left the office. I became emotional as officers and employees lined up on both sides to wish me all the best and accompanied me to my car. It took quite some time for the feeling to sink in that I was now a retired IAS officer and the daily routine of thirty-eight years had come to an end.

Retirement can be painful if you do not take it with the right attitude. If you continue to be attached to the power of your office, then you are bound to feel depressed. But if you approach retirement as the beginning of another chapter of life, then you have much to look forward to. Often IAS officers become flexible and weak during the last years because they want to continue holding onto a job post-retirement and with this objective that they approach the political executive and try to get favours. There is nothing wrong in a post-retirement assignment as an IAS officer has gained a lot of experience which can be useful to the government in any capacity and also that the age of sixty is not old. In fact, he is still full of energy and enterprise which should be utilized. The problem comes when an officer is so keen to get a job after retirement that he begins to adjust to every demand of the political executive and forgets that his primary duty is towards the citizens. The unfortunate thing is that post-retirement jobs are given to officers who are close to the government in power and have little relation to merit or competence, and it is this that brings about the change in the behaviour of the IAS officer. The worst-case scenario is when some IAS officers deviate from the path of integrity in the last years of their service as they are mentally confronted by the thought of financial hardship. It is true that all the perks of office go away with retirement and you get 50 per cent of your last pay as pension but this is how it is and one should not allow this factor to weaken their value system and sense of ethics.

Retired IAS officers then look for jobs outside the government, and private sector corporations are only too keen to engage them. They offer a huge salary but the job profile is to liaison with existing officers and get the work of the private sector organization done. I recall being offered a job with emoluments of Rs 5 crores per annum but as I probed deeper, I found that my main job was to meet with senior IAS officers, call them for drinks and dinner and thereby influence them to make decisions in favour of the corporation concerned. I soon realized that this basically is the job of middlemen and brings down the image and status of an officer, and refused the offer even though I had never seen such amounts of money in my life. More often than not, this is the kind of job which is offered to most retired IAS officers and they should stay as far away from such assignments as possible. Of course, it is a different matter if a retired IAS officer is taken on the board of directors of a reputed company or his services are used for strategic advising.

An IAS officer has such valuable experience that he can give back to society. One of the best ways of doing this is to teach students of administration and management, and also avail of opportunities to address in-service officers. Besides, one can contribute articles to newspapers and even write books to document their experiences so that new entrants to the service gain from it. Many IAS officers do a lot of voluntary work and many set up NGOs to work closely with society. There is, thus, a lot of significant work that an IAS officer can continue to do after retirement to give himself a feeling of still being relevant.

Retirement gives you the opportunity of doing things which you always wanted to do but never had the time. I have always been fond of reading and found that I could devote a lot of time to it and this has given me immense joy. In a similar way, many IAS officers have pursued their hobbies after retirement. Some have taken to painting, others to photography and so on. It also gives you a wonderful opportunity to travel around the country and abroad and enjoy vacations and see new places with your family which you could never do while in the service. It also gives you time to look inside yourself, develop yourself spiritually and be at peace with yourself and view life with equanimity. I find that retirement affords you the opportunity to live a much fuller and more satisfying life than while in service. You should lower your expectations from serving officers and members of the public to maintain your sense of happiness and contentment. I have seen many IAS officers getting upset after retirement when the serving officers do not answer their calls or respond, or members of the public who used to fawn over them now ignore them. These things should not be taken to heart as this is the way the world works.

The greatest sense of satisfaction comes from memories of the work you have done to make a difference to society and the lives you have touched. A colleague of mine has called these moments the 'Bharat Ratna' moments. Because nothing can give you more joy than the realization that through your actions, you have changed the life of somebody for the better or brought about a transformation in society which has greatly improved the quality of life for the people. Even after retirement I found that many people keep coming to meet me and remind me of some action of mine which had helped them a great deal. Their sense of gratitude makes you feel that you have done something worthwhile in your career.

You get a sense of elation as you see the changes around you that you have been instrumental in bringing about. It is not the memories of the powers that you exercised or the comforts that you got or your status in society that gives you a feeling of inner satisfaction. It is the realization that you have used your power to make a significant contribution to society and that gives you inner joy and contentment.

People in different careers than the IAS also find time to do work for society and this gives them a lot of satisfaction. The IAS gives you the opportunity to serve the society in various ways as part of your job. There is no other job which can give you this contentment and diversity of experience. It is a truly enriching experience, depending on what you make of it. If you use the opportunity merely for personal gain or advancement, then you have wasted your time but if you have genuinely worked for the people with a sense of public service and total commitment and integrity, then you have utilized the opportunity to the fullest and can look back upon your career with a sense of pride and satisfaction. The IAS as a career should be treated as a platform to make a huge difference to society.